THE WORLD-PRIEST.

AUTHOR'S MOTTO.

"To fill the eye with visions of God's nearness;
Open the mind with visions of God's greatness;
To fill the soul with all the Spirit's fulness,
Inward and outward man's whole life to live,
Breathing God's peace and joy and blessedness."

THE

WORLD-PRIEST.

Translated from the German

OF

LEOPOLD SCHEFER,

AUTHOR OF "THE LAYMAN'S BREVIARY."

By CHARLES T. BROOKS.

BOSTON:
ROBERTS BROTHERS.
1873.

CAMBRIDGE:
PRESS OF JOHN WILSON AND SON.

TRANSLATOR'S PREFACE.

FIVE years ago, the present translator sent forth to the American public a version of the "Layman's Breviary." He would not have counted that *love's labor* as *lost*, even had the book fallen dead on its way from the press. It had, indeed, no such fate. It cannot be said, perhaps, to have quite reached the *public* yet; it has, however, found its way to a wide and still widening circle of appreciative souls.

The "World-Priest" followed the Breviary, in Germany, at a distance of ten years: it was published there in 1846, when the author was sixty-two years old. It was one of the many love messages sent forth to the world from time to time out of that peaceful and pleasant country home, which had been made his by the kindness of the Muskau family, a distinguished member of which (Prince

Pükler Muskau) had been his early friend, and had taken him as a companion on his Oriental tour.

The writer of a Life of Schefer, prefixed to the late editions of the Breviary, says the "World-Priest" was its author's "favorite book." It came out the year following the death of the author's wife; of whom he speaks in these touching words: "But, out of doors there, as much grass may grow above her head, as in the long, desolate days and nights ever can grow; *within*, — no grass grows over a life-crushing, real sorrow."

A sympathetic reader will have no difficulty in conceiving how deep a hold this affliction took upon him, and what an elevating effect it had upon his soul, who recurs to the piece in this volume, entitled "To the Widower," as well as to many others on bereavement and kindred subjects. He will notice, indeed, how large a proportion of these poems turn upon the trials and sorrows of life, its disappointments and compensations, upon the yearnings and aspirations of the human heart, the immortality and divinity of the spirit in man.

The biographer before quoted speaks of Schefer as "the Germanest of the Germans;" and compares him to Angelus Silesius, Jacob Böhme,

Rückert, Göthe, and Jean Paul. The name of this last writer will be especially recalled to readers of the extraordinary dream contained in one of the pieces of this collection, entitled "The Eagle."

A translator need not be supposed to agree with every thought or sentiment of his author. There are many things in Schefer's poems, which, literally interpreted, may well seem wild enough. The charge which would most naturally be brought against him is that of Pantheism. Now, a poet's creed must be interpreted, not by the letter, but by the spirit. There is one sense in which Pantheism is opposed to Atheism, and means that no person or thing exists but God in the universe; but there is also another sense, in which Pantheism stands opposed to that bald and blank *Mono*theism, which gives us only a secluded and solitary God; and, in this sense, Pantheism, as the doctrine that God is in all things and beings and events, is certainly a Christian one. Such a spiritual Pantheism as Schefer's may be more than pardoned by one who remembers Paul's words: "Of Him and to Him and through Him are all things."

The title of this book might have been translated, not infelicitously, the "Priest of Nature," or "of the Universe," or "of Humanity;" but, inasmuch as the word "Welt" has the same indeterminateness of meaning as "World" in English, it seemed best to render the phrase in this bald and literal manner.

May this "World-Priest" find a good acceptance, and do a good work, in our Western world also!

CONTENTS.

	Page
The German People	1
Consecration	3
Development	5
The Two Powers	6
The Light of the World	10
The Teaching of the Stars	12
Thousand Pearls for a Tear	17
The Pure Stars (Zoroaster)	21
Claim thy Birthright	24
The Past Eternity	26
This is Life Eternal	31
Self-condemnation	33
A Life Within and Above	35
The World Above	36
God's Child — no Heathen	39
A Greater Evil than Death	42
It takes All to save One	45
Conquest of the World	47
The Historical Sunrise	50
The Reward of Knowledge	51
The Soul's Keeper	54
The Universal Temple	56
Anthropodicy	60

	Page
The Couples	61
Holy Wrath	63
The Highest Paternal Joy	65
Openness	67
The Bird of Wisdom	70
Solon and Sesostris	73
The End of all Things	75
The Duty of the Open Ear	79
Who ever put back the Sun?	82
Compulsion	84
The Saviour: Impossibility	86
Divine Sense in Child's Play	91
Providence arraigned	94
Man's Grief and Mother's Love	98
Coming home from the Burial	101
Man can do his Part	105
To the Widower	107
The Dead Son	109
Job: or, Man	112
The Good God	114
Goodness	117
To the Widow	119
The Beggar-man	121
The Cause of Death	123
Live as an Immortal	127
Perfection	129
Sorrow	132
Be Content with thy Lot	135
The Long Night	139
The Sun-sick (A Peguan Easter Song)	141
The Complaint cleared up	142
Our God	143
Redemption from Living Death	147
Love to All, Faith in all Things	151

	PAGE
The Desperate and Reprobate	152
Put away the Sword	154
Antiquity	157
To-day: the Keystone of the World	159
The Wonder-workers	162
Life — A Battle	168
The Deaf and Dumb Mother	170
Hope	173
Memory	176
Violet's Breath and Heaven's Spirit	179
The Highest Spirit	182
Let None offend Thee!	184
To the Meek Man	185
The Might of Love	186
The Worm and the Sun	188
The Wealth of Wisdom	191
The Inner Want	192
Children's Joy	194
The Three Treasures of Life	196
Follow the Lord upon His Ways	198
Quiet Greatness of the Good	200
To whom thou doest Good	203
The Goddess near at Hand	205
Home, the Sacristy of Heaven	207
The True Life	208
The Hall of Spirits	210
Perfection	213
Our Own	214
The Refuge of the Poor	216
The Beggar-man	217
The Saints	218
The Relics	220
Thy Faith	225
Love to God — God's Love	227

PAGE
The Parting 231
The End 234
The Holy Week 238
The Last Parting 241
The Eagle 246
The School 253
Contentment 255
The Pure Soul 258
Mourning for Thyself 260
Marriage 264
Child and Old Man 269
The Human Mother 270
Love for All, no Love at all 273
Shame and Remorse 275
The King of Day 279
The Soul our "Strong Fortress" 281
The Old Beggar-man 283
The Herdsman's Fire 285
Originality 286
God's Human Life 288
God's Patience 290
God's Goodness 294
The Three Heavens 298
The Holy Body and the Holy Life 301
Health 304
The Three Deaths 311
The Three Festivals of Life 315
The Home 319
The House of Life 321
The Credo 323
The Holy Fraternity 325
The Primeval Word 328
The Three Works 331
The Clear Mystery 332

PAGE
The Transitory 334
The Rose for All 339
The Return of all Things 342
Agapé, not "Love" 344
The Sweetness of Life 346
The Past 348
Contempt of the World 352
The Gleaning of Life 356
Love and the World 359
Wisdom 364
Beauty 367
The People 372

THE WORLD-PRIEST.

THE GERMAN PEOPLE.

WHAT image of himself the God shall see
In human eyes and understandings — what
Men recognize to *be* God — that decides
Unerringly: *what way they honor Him!*
And all their temples vanish in the air . . .
The worship stammers . . . prophets one and all
Seek vainly any true validity
Of lasting merit, till the being of God,
Clear and undoubted, free and cloudless, shines
Before the eyes of all men, like the sun
That each man knows and daily sees in heaven.
No faith can save a human soul, while yet
In the remotest land *one* being doubts,
And knows more clearly what all men — believe.
All nations that have lived died of their gods,
And still die of them. First to give them form,
And then, when so shaped forth, to worship them . . .
That nations live for as their holy aim!
And when they have their gods once ready made —
Then do they die, then they themselves are dead . . .
Only the thought on God kept them alive.

So once of Isis and Osiris died
Egyptian people and Egyptian priests:
Their god was made and done and — *they* were done,
Were dead. So when the Hebrews had their God,
Jehovah, made — the nation passed away.
And so with later nations has it fared
Who figured as complete their Holy Ones.
So will it henceforth with all nations fare,
Who quarrel about God and sons of God,
And do not feel the God in their own heart,
In their own speech and in their daily life,
And *as* their life. That race alone shall last —
And all the tribes of earth shall come to it —
The race that owns its God to be the Life
Eternal — life of all and death of all.
The rest were only children all, that dreamed
And scribbled with their fingers on the sky.
But this true God is never pérfected,
Grows ever greater, nearer, lovelier
And blesseder, — He sinks into each heart!
And never dies a heart possessed of God!
And with its God a people lives, with Him
Grows ever greater, fairer, blesseder.

CONSECRATION.

THIS one thing dream not, that thou ever couldst
Enrage a God or make him laugh at thee,
When thou wast set on magnifying man,
To nerve his soul with iron steadfastness
Self-poised and sovereign over death and fate!
For *whom* in truth, then, dost thou magnify?
Whom makest thou self-poised, serene and free?
Sure, first of all, thyself; sure, then, *a man*,
And others then — as surely *only men;*
And as men, unmistakably no less
Than heavenly apparitions of *the God!*
Then deem not that thou art resisting God,
When thou uprisest against death and fate,
And *every terror* that torments His world,
Nay even against this mighty universe,
Which, sure, holds not the spirit captive yet,
That it should not conceive a nobler one,
Should not forever feel its fleetingness:
Yea, even pity — for the spirit itself,
Which lives so on the rack of discontent,
So deeply rent even by the very *love*
Which in its holy conflict almost sinks,
And groans as if on coals: "O were it otherwise!

O were there once a pure, untroubled bliss!"
Then never will the God be wroth with thee;
Nay He will clothe thee as His champion
With adamantine armor; crown thy head,
Call thee *His soul*, and welcome thee at last
Into His soul, when thou one day shalt come
Out from that monstrous turmoil of life's fight,
That endless din . . . himself appeases not!
And bears, against his will, and deeply scorns!

DEVELOPMENT.

THE world, Humanity, man's work and Life,
Unfolds itself and issues forth from naught
But God Himself — the heavenly Cocoon,
That silently contains his power and him.
Reel off the busy, restless, magic star
Forever, — it shall only grow and blow
More full beneath thy hand in sight of all,
And nothing hast thou in thy hands but gold,
And golden has thy every finger grown.
So blooms the violet-colored gillyflower;
The more the Gardener cuts its blossoms off,
The more and ever lovelier ones it bears,
And almost dies in bearing. — Such is all
The *service* even the flower requires! such
The *service God* requires: from Him all take
His blossoms evermore and ever new!
The spirits all are blossoms of the Lord;
So lookest thou in silence when one fades,
That has exhaled and bloomed, its little day,
And now shoots forth in seed. And the new blossoms
'Tis God alone puts forth, new primal wonders;
From naught but Him unfold and issue forth
The world, Humanity, man's work and Life.

THE TWO POWERS.

TWO Powers I name to thee, that rule the world,
And make the fortune and the bliss of all
Who live upon the earth, and overhead
On all the stars delight themselves in life.
These two transcendent faculties are called:
Intelligence and *Conscience!* When the two
Are one, one vision only in two eyes,
Thou mightest call them then the eyes of God.
The two great faculties are equipotent,
For being and well-being matched in power;
Rulers themselves, no ruler do they own;
Free from the violence, the law, of men,
None can constrain and none can fetter them,
Scarce can he stir them to *his* greatest harm.
Man must himself possess them, use them then,
Else none can save him, man or heavenly one!
Thou seest the pious, good and moral man,
As oft as others, wretched — Innocence
Is the soul's health alone, and not the body's.

The stupidest, most ignorant of men
Does wonders oft in greatness by his good heart.
The shrewdest oft does shamefully bad works —

And both live wretchedly and come to naught,
For wanting, each, *one* of the eyes of God.

Naught does it help the bad man to know all things,
To understand their use, appropriate
Their good to himself and turn away their harm —
If he, as man, meanwhile enacts the tiger,
The false and treacherous cat or the wild boar.
What does it help the bear in his honey tree
To know: how great and glorious are ye stars!
How thou dost make the spring, and winter, too,
O sun, and rear aloft the rainbow's arch!
How thou oft puttest on the moon, as mask,
And oftentimes the earth, to scare the moon!
Naught does it help the bad man to know all things —
He sinks to bottom for all that, no light,
No warm and golden kernel in his heart.

Nor does it help the good to will good things, —
Stand at his door all day with open hands,
And make himself a heaven of others' woe —
If he, meanwhile, as man, is like the blind,
Who gropes about on earth as in the dark;
For herbs, eats deadly poison; like the child,
For crabs, lays hold on scorpions; who, to save
His ass from drowning in the fountain, drowns
Himself therein; unskilled to know the signs
Of the storm's coming, goes on board his ship,
And miserably founders in the gale!
Whoso, through error works and suffers harm,

He who is not so happy as a full
Knowledge of holy nature makes a man,
That man has *sinned against intelligence*
No less than he who breaks the moral law,
And who is not so happy as entire
Goodness and truth of heart make any man —
For both of them are swallowed up alike,
And both go in a miserable plight
Down to the pit! for the first requisite —
As is the hand for labor — is a life,
Worthy of God — good and *intelligent.*

Wherefore contemplate *this* with silent joy:
In what degree man strives to know his house,
Each blade of grass, to understand the use
Of every power, in order not to sin
Against the light, but wisely live and well, —
Only God's Spirit puts that into his mind;
And never could humanity forget
Its heart and conscience! For prosperity
Alone it lives and strives! *That* well it knows —
And without soul 'twould live but half a life!
With conscience and intelligence man lives
A whole life! and achieves and wins all things,
Armed with the mind and with the might of God.

Through ignorance and error, poor, betrayed
Good men are brought to such a sorry pass
Of long-lived misery, such bitter pains,
Such irremediably sore remorse,

Such sense of guilt, as ever *guilt* can wreak,
The only proper *guilt* — sin against God's
Inner commands : But nature round about
Is also no less holy a command
Of God, and not the less an iron law,
Nay even more ! *For sooner may the bad*
Be pardoned for his sin, sooner may he
Make good his bad things and restore his soul,
Than ever any man can find a way
To cure an error's evil consequences,
Who knew not, or who heeded not, a law,
Of nature, sinning against God himself !
The wounds which Nature has inflicted naught
Can cure, no penitence and no return
To the firm yoke of her most holy law,
To holy wisdom, to the light of God !
Then honor highly God as what He is,
In all His high and glorious attributes !
Once own them, and He ever is at hand,
To help you, like a servant in all good.

Two Powers I name to thee, that rule the world,
And make the fortune and the bliss of all
Who live upon the earth, and overhead
On all the stars delight themselves in life.
These two transcendent faculties are called :
Intelligence and *Conscience !* When the two
Are one, one vision only in two eyes,
Thou mightest call them then the eyes of God.

THE LIGHT OF THE WORLD.

INTELLIGENCE, thou highest magic power,
Sole wonder-worker of the universe,
Thou Power of Powers over death and life,
Thou Lord of every fate, of every woe,
Tamer of even uttermost despair,
And mitigator of each lighter grief, —
Intelligence! Who art thou, canst thou be,
But God's own insight, God's own wisdom, given
To be the Peacemaker in every breast,
That can feel pain and bear the blows of fate,
And so in that of man, who first of all,
And last and most of all, has need of thee.
Intelligence, thou art the world's sole light,
The sole-sufficing, beaming peace and rest,
As from the sun his silver radiance streams!
Nothing mysterious can give man repose;
Clear vision only brings him happiness,
And brings it to him all unchangeable,
Inalienable; for in all the heavens
Is no one who can change its holy claim,
And make it one word greater, one word less.
To see, to understand, joins one to Truth,
Unites him with the Eternal Source of things.

Man, understanding once his bitterest lot,
Sides henceforth with the Eternal One, becomes
His friend, his champion and his stadtholder,
Having transfigured and refined himself
To his own essence ; being one with Truth,
And one with God, who is the Truth itself.
The Truth — and though it seemed the terriblest, —
Before *that* presence each one bows his head
With silent reverence and speechless awe ;
Full of tranquillity he now beholds
And blesses, what just now had torn his heart,
Had chilled his soul to death, had ground him down
Into the dust and all things round to dust,
Crushed by the rude hand of capricious power ;
For which the ocean had not tears enough,
Eternity itself not time enough,
To spend in lamentation.
No piety, bowed down into the dust, —
No *blind* devotion — no, nor *open-eyed* —
Can do that service to a human soul . . .
Not Love itself can do for thee what thou
Canst, primal Light, Godlike Intelligence !
Upon another's word to rest thy faith,
And were he e'er so honest, is but faith,
Not understanding, *is but ignorance*,
A hollow, unsafe *unintelligence*,
Which makes man wretched with the smallest light.
Intelligence is each man's sole, sure strength.

THE TEACHING OF THE STARS.

SEND forth a sower, who shall sow gold-dust,
And every grain of dust shall be a star ;
Then send a hundred men — a thousand — out —
Hundreds of thousands then — millions of years,
To sow gold-dust that all shall turn to stars ;
Let giants in enormous mortars pound
The hugest suns into clear silver-dust,
To serve for star-seed to those husbandmen,
And every particle swell to a star
In the blue field of Heaven's immensity —
Then sow down all these stars with poppy-seed,
And all the grains out of the poppy-heads
Again sow broadcast, let all these become
Suns, earths and comets up and down through space —
Then hast thou reached, with the enormous sum,
Not yet the smallest part of all the stars
That in the broad and endless halls of heaven
Shine up aloft, bloom, flash out life and live,
Lived *farther back* than thought can wing its flight,
Will live beyond where thought can wing its flight.
(That now is to be only one day's work !)
On wings of lightning thou wouldst seek in vain
To single out thy earth amidst the flare

With falcon eyes long years of Sirius!
Thou wouldst not find thyself, if thou wert not
And sawest thy earth and had thy foothold there
Gazing out thence into the open heaven.
Aye gaze! Look upward, inward through those depths,
Far as the wing of thought will carry thee:
In an enormous aged grotto, *full*
Of ever-rayless night — is the great feast
Of Lanterns celebrated. Round about
Hang the bright lanterns, fair as soap-bubbles,
Illuminated and illuminating,
Seen near at hand, gigantic; afar off
Like glow-worms, twinkling so diminutively;
Therein sit wonderful existences
Who from mere habit fear not one another,
Because they are themselves so singular.
Whate'er is possible, *that* somewhere lives,
Takes form, and is conjoined, made one with One,
Fashioned in beauty, furnished wondrously.
There seest thou giant mothers of the Gods —
(So wouldst thou, in thy human smallness, call them,)
Who carry in their arms children of Gods,
With heads full of intelligence like our gods;
With eyes that pierce far solar distances,
As telescopes for us bring near the stars;
And they, too, also have great telescopes
Whereby they live all through the circling space
As thou within thy little vale of earth.
Each one was born there of a mother, too,
Still young, when, twenty thousand years of age,

Where, in their long protracted life, her race
Have long since known what life is, known themselves,
And by experience made wise and glad,
In heavenly content have spent a life
Unvexed, and satisfied with life have gone
Down to the grave, as saints revered and blest.
O what a train of noble, beauteous forms,
Hundreds of millions of years long, sweeps on
Across each orb in that majestic ring!
For naught are they, as good as naught are all
These golden worlds, compared with all the hosts
That live thereon — that countless multitude
Of fair and holy shapes, incessantly
Descending there to grace and glad the Spring!
And all the shining ones that dwell thereon
Are naught compared with what they *feel* and *do*,
And what through all continually is *wrought*. . .
Compared with all the works they execute,
The fruits of this gigantic tree of Heaven!
And of them all none knows the star called — Earth!
Man and his generations and their works
Have never, even in dream, appeared to them.
Pronounce to all in turn through the vast round
The highest names, name to them all the Gods
And all the saints — not one of them shall fall
Upon his knees before a single name!
Till thou shalt blush for very shame! — But they
Need nothing at our hands — all things are theirs;
Thou seest there, multiplied thousand-fold,
What here below seemed to thee *singular*,

What was exalted by thee high as heaven —
As if, with a poor ring upon thy finger,
Thou shouldst go in to a great diamond mine,
Where even a king himself would be struck dumb
And feel himself a beggar. — Thunderstruck
Thou hurriest to thy home as from a house
Of mourning, aye, as from a charnel-house
Where all lay dead, that thou hadst loved in life —
Thou foldest wife and children to thy breast —
Thou gazest on them, claspest them again,
To warm and win them back to life once more,
To wake thyself *out of the Dream of Truth!*

But when thou kneelest to thy nightly prayer,
Thou mak'st a vow to the great God on high:
"On earth I worship idols nevermore.
The name of God I nevermore pronounce
For awe — I bear it mutely in my breast,
And gladly own His greatness in my heart.
No pride shall tempt me to the thought, that we
Are sole possessors of a single thing,
Even the best, the highest, the only true,
And all the dwellers of the stars must come
Down to the earth — to this our poor hedge school . . .
For our philosophers, forsooth, are Gods
To all the stars in the whole universe. —
The daring dream of man crumbles before
That God who is full of heaven; 'tis buried up
In that heaven full of God — and none henceforth
Obstructs our sight of the great heavens again —

The spirit never will resolve on death
And say: Now, now, I know, I have, all things!
What I may find henceforth — a curse upon't! —
The race of men have risen into God." —

That is the holy teaching of the stars.

THOUSAND PEARLS FOR A TEAR.

"IS nothing left" (the world asks) "to believe,
To edify the heart, ravish, astound,
And by its sacredness subdue the soul!
Is nothing left? nothing? Then let me die!
I *will not* be forlorn, jejune and cold,
The eternal soul shall shine upon my path,
A fiery column! I must reverence
The heavenly! Only then my heart shall feel
Its proper greatness, holiness and love!" —

O world! all, all, is left that ever yet
Has edified a heart, electrified,
And by its sacredness subdued a soul!
He lives — the great, great God — yea infinitely
Greater, more glorious and more near is He
Than ever He appeared to man before,
Behind the thin veil of His firmament;
And lo! His mansion's high and holy lamps
Up there they hang, sparkling like dew in grass!
The miracles, all, all of them remain,
The very doll still counterfeits the child,
And all exists to him that ever was
The lofty being of God: His Avatar!

The coming of all beings to their birth,
All round, a rich and ever-glowing Spring,
The Spirit coming down into the spirits,
Even the tree in blossom fails not! There
Is the young swallow in her nest! There still
Holy maternal Love; the Holy Mother
In her eternal chasteness! and the Child!
The resurrection of the living ones,
The resurrection of the tribes of dead,
The ascension of the dead ones into God,
The still flight up into the ancient God,
The daily, the eternal judgment day
In all the world! the God in every soul!
The *death* of all, who walk not righteously!
The bliss that fills the souls of all the good!
And, added to these lofty things of God:
Beauty, the jewel of the whole wide world,
And Joy! and Love and Truth; the finding still
Of wonders new and without end in God,
The sense of self, the honor to be a *self*,
To carry hence this great self-consciousness,
And not begin to be immortal *there* —
No, to *have lived eternally* with God
In *every one of His old beauteous days*
In the one self-same and eternal moment!
So has humanity all, all the old,
And all the new besides, abundantly,
And all new revelations of the Lord!
And now man can and will have glad success,
Now that he is a spirit within God's Spirit,

And lives with Him the undecaying life,
Wherein what seemed bestowed but once on One,
Now, daily, thousand-fold distributed,
To the blind mole that burrows in the ground
Belongs, and to each worm, as property.

Is not *that* better? And have *we* no more,
Nor longer see, what always was in God!
What He, as His exalted property,
He the disinterested, loving Sire,
Has made the property of every child:
To be arrayed in majesty like Him,
With Him, joint lords with Him in lordliness,
Of all His wonders fellow-wonders, *each*,
Wherein He, as eternal life, appears!
Who blasphemes God, but he who dares deny
His highest, most benignant attribute:
Not from the least and lowliest to withhold
The greatest, the most glorious, most divine
Of all His gifts: His spirit, aye His life
And all the goods his wondrous life contains.
An earthly father does this to his child:
God setting him the pattern, not he God:
Doing in little what He does in great,
Aye in profusion. Then rejoice in God!
God lives not humanly, but men divinely.

So live we now, then, in our day and hour,
Holy are they as old times ever were,
And holy as the starry days o'erhead!

And God is here, as much as anywhere!
Thou canst not take thy way up to the sun . . .
To any star, or temple, in the sky —
The earthly life for thy part must thou live
Down here, and let thy altar be the earth!
I never yet have heard a priest stand up
And preach to men, they should do wickedness,
Nor with the softest whisper counsel it —
Man carries awe for God within his heart;
A child knows what is good, being full of God,
Man errs then only, when he utters names;
And when he names names, think on God alone,
Thou sinnest not then, 'tis he only errs.
So mayst thou live with all men a pure life.
Then where thou hearest any teach and preach
Of God the Lord, thither make haste to go
With gladness and with fervor in thy soul —
Thou hear'st *thy* house — *thy* Father — spoken of!
And earth will be to thee thy altar then,
The sun that shines on all — thy holy lamp!

THE PURE STARS.

Zoroaster.

WHO follows Reason, is a pious man,
God's own Religion that man practises,
And bad and base and graceless is the thing
Done without reason or against it. That —
How moral, pious, wholesome, free soe'er,
It seem, which owns not reason, is *ungodly*.

Here lives a wise old man of sixty years,
A young man, still, you'd say, in beauty's prime ;
And him a maiden loves beyond all else ;
To be his wife she'd call the height of bliss,
Him too would gladden, through the lonely days
And nights of his old age, so sweet a wife,
And yet he looks on her as blind of heart !
Infatuated ! and would hold himself
Stained with the highest crime a human soul
Can work against another, should he yield
To this illusion — nay, this maid's true love ;
Make her his wife and foully . . . ruin her :
The glow of the young heart — the gracious form —
The days and nights of all her coming life —
The holy bosom, which belongs alone
To that true husband's children, whom the *sun*. . .

Whom equal youth marks out for her in heaven . . .
The holy lap, which *they* alone can claim,
Whom he can never nourish — never rear,
Who soon would have in him no father more
To love, and she, a widow, soon would have
No husband, only tears and loneliness,
And grief, with all her true and fervent love.
So he untwines the feeling from his heart,
Even as men loosen from a crumbling stake
The grape-vine it would drag down to the earth.
And yet he would not (as men say) have "sinned,"
If he had taken this poor child for his wife;
And all the pious priests in all the lands
Would piously have blessed the marriage rite!

Who follows Reason, is the pious man,
He only God's pure worship practises.
How great thou art, O Reason! strong, divine!
Thou canst be naught but God's own proper voice,
God's knowledge and belief and love and hope,
The proper meaning of the world, the law
Whereby it shapes itself forevermore,
Which through it shines and o'er it gently rules;
For whosoe'er to reason has attained,
(And by sore pains man comes into her heaven)
He covets not e'en with the faintest wish
The least thing, no nor yet the greatest thing,
Not the most precious gift the heart can crave,
Whereof the voice of this deep oracle,
God's voice, the sacred conscience of His world,

Serenely says to him : Thou dear, good man !
That which thou wishest *is not ! cannot be,*
It is not so, so small : it is far greater,
More glorious than thy fancy fashions it ;
Lift up thy mind and make thee a clean heart !
Then wilt thou see all things that round thee lie
Full of glad life and rich in blessedness —
Lovely and glorious as this universe !
Only think not so meanly of our spirit,
And of His world, that owns and *is* His law,
Simply as thou dost call thy child by name.
Reason is God's own might and majesty ;
It rules and sways thee with a sweet content,
For it is light, and thou its spirit art ;
Which has within itself the peace of God.

CLAIM THY BIRTHRIGHT.

DESPAIR not! Nay, open the door to joy!
Stare not like dead men! Nay, now put on God!
Imagine not, ye have lost any thing,
No not a blessing, not a single dream,
Far less eternal life and blessedness.
The spirit of God, which on the earth ye are,
Can never lose a mote of sun-bright dust;
God lives not to behold by slow degrees —
As an old raven sees his feathers drop —
His treasures, glories, beauties fall from Him. . . .
But, as from some primeval mountain's veins,
More and more lavishly to pour His gold.
Believe this only: *faith* shall turn to *sight*,
On them that walk through night the sun shall rise,
The unsealed eyeballs of the blind shall learn
To measure the remote, the grand to see.
So dreamed, so spake those earlier sons of men:
"Faith shall (in heavenly places) turn to sight."
And thus again an earlier Son of man:
"God's kingdom is within you — is within."
The *you* means *we;* more than Apostles we
Of God, within our hearts we bear God's self.
Within our inner being, that is, heaven,

Already (as revealed and brought to pass)
Already faith is ripened into sight,
To contemplating and possessing God ;
The eye within us has become God's eye ;
Our inner being has become God's being ;
That in us, round us, lives and radiates heaven.
So has the spirit now bethought itself.
Be ye self-thoughtful souls, clear and serene,
Take in the being of God in His clear truth.
The priests are no more the proprietors
And dolers-out of God, to make, transform,
Create Him for the people. . . more than God !
No more they manufacture God and heaven ;
No more thrust out to hell and endless fire !
Their prayers no more absolve men from their sins ;
God *in* us, only, speaks us clean and free :
Himself speaks *to* Himself within our souls.
No more they have and hold the keys of heaven
To every heavenly kingdom in each breast !
No more is man led through stupidity
To blessedness, which means *intelligence*.
No more is man contented to believe . . .
He *looks;* he *knows;* detects and scorns the attempt,
By cunningly denying him a grave
To shut him out from heaven ! By the mere word
Of a priest's scorn, from endless blessedness !
Of God's free Spirit in the mind of man
There is no other Lord than God himself!
And each one is the light, the way to God.
  Despair not! nay, fling wide the door to joy!
Stare not like dead men ! nay, now put on God !

THE PAST ETERNITY.

MAN loves to date his being from his birth;
With this late, late beginning is content,
Rejoicing heartily in this, that he
Did once begin to be, *that he now lives.*
His joy *that now he lives* is the sole thought
That makes him glad he once began to be.
Yet now that he exists, he cares far more,
To know if after death he still shall live,
Than that he now exists, and hangs in fear,
In doubt and dread and terrible suspense!
He has himself embalmed; swathed like a child;
Laid in sarcophagi and mummy-pits;
Buried away in solid pyramids,
That he one day may see the sun again . . .
And then still further see, what is to do,
That he may live on still, while live the stars,
And only with the very last expire:
That he before his death may bury God,
Nail up the coffin, and the golden key
Of the old sunk-in tenement, the world,
Fling down the deepest gulf — to nothingness.
So does he trouble and torment his mind
With thinking of the *next* eternity!

The fairest, proudest, most gigantic plans
The mind of man frames for futurity,
Are all mere child's play, too diminutive
For flower-seed and constellation-dust
To all yon thousand flower-fields of the sky,
To all the stars that there have risen and shine,
And all the hosts of Sons of God that throng
The vista of our great futurity;
And all that Indian sages ever dreamed
Of Paradise; all that Mohammed sang
Of lovely Houris, and the rapturous sweets
Of never-ending bliss; and all that Jews
Have taught of endless Hallelujah-cries
For ecstasy, before the face of God; . . .
Is all mere dream and flower-seed, dim and dark,
To all the glory and felicity,
That every, every spirit shall possess
Through all eternity; that in such clear,
Bright revelation shall encircle us,
As the sun pours to-day, and every morn,
On all the earth, as beams from all the stars —
The golden balls for the fair angel-troops. —

So grasping, so exacting, is the spirit,
And justly, toward the universe and God,
The smallest grain of dust it grudges Him,
Not even an hour will give Him, not one breath!
The fool! The great old purblind, one-eyed fool!
Who like a Cyclops eyes futurity!
He doles out ONE *eternity to God:*

The first, anterior, long eternity,
The ever-blessed and majestical,
The ever-during life of all the days
Down to the day when he himself was born —
This he complacently vouchsafes to God
And never cares to ask for it again!
And never prophet asked for it again!
More than the beggar in the morning asks
For the old straw he *slept upon* last night!
The cunningest, most learned priests themselves,
To whom all elder priests bequeathed their arts,
Who know to still the cravings of all souls —
Care only for the first eternity,
They call it *children's limbo* in the lump!
The fools! The purblind, one-eyed Cyclops they!
Themselves — the dunces — in the children's limbo.

But now what sayst thou to the awful folly
Of priests like these, the highest teachers too,
And of the impious thought of giving God
What is not worthy to be spoken of —
Not worthy of a hope — like that which builds
On the eternity that is to come;
Not worthy of such *silent, inward thought*
As parents give to their poor, *still-born* child!

I, for myself, say naught but one true word:
The living God has lived through all of time,
And through all times he still forever lives,
His life, that only, is eternity;

His life made up the *first* eternity;
That God now is, that also is His life,
And is *thy* life, wilt thou distinguish still
Thyself from God; but His alone, if thou
Art one with God in spirit and in mind.
Then hast thou lived with Him throughout all time;
Then wilt thou still with Him live through all time.
The life of God, however, brings no gain,
It is itself the highest treasure—else
This universe itself might show a fruit,
This universe would one day yield a fruit,
Small fruit enough! For dust and dead men's bones
Are *they* thy fruit, O holy universe!
Nay, 'tis forever they alone who live,
The life of God—that is the fruit of God,
Nor does the death of all bereave the universe.
Yet as men celebrate in the death-hour
A meditation on the future, when
Embarking for the next eternity,
So shall humanity yet celebrate
One day a festival of gratitude
For *that first, by-gone, long eternity.*
And every one who knows the life of God,
Will surely celebrate it in his heart,
Without a priest, a temple or a church.
For whosoe'er has joined himself to God,
As the pure Spirit of the universe,
Has entered even now that holy church,
(Without a consecrating sign, or mark,
Or human name, by which no one above

Would recognize, but only smile and pity him)
And yet is he so still, serene and calm,
In holy fellowship with all God's sons,
Whom everywhere, on all the stars, He owns,
Who live to give God reverence, and themselves,
And walk in free, in native majesty,
And scorning all the cobwebs of the brain,
Subject to no one's pity, no one's smile,
Find welcome entrance, as the sanctified,
Into the great and holy house of God,
And even here as pilgrims walk therein,
Content and blest of God, as His own Spirit.

THIS IS LIFE ETERNAL.

MAN, thou shalt live the eternal life of God.
Eternity of moments is made up,
Of day by day, and night by night, that so
The God who lives thy life, as thou dost His,
May in all moments live a life of bliss.
Learn to distinguish well immortal life
From everlasting, ever-lovely life!
To live immortal were to live a life
Like that of the bright sun and all the stars,
Only, like that of lightning and sea-storm,
Restless and joyless, ruinous to all,
And to itself; 'twere but so much the worse,
Nay, horrible, if this immortal were,
Immortal, never-ceasing, without end!
But life eternal may be human too,
Be transient, mortal, and eternal still!
For hear me now with faithful, pious soul,
With God's great soul now listen as a man:
Eternal life is "life in harmony
With our great laws, which reign unchangeably
Throughout the universe; lead all the stars
And all the clouds; that shape each blade of grass
And every child — true masters of the world,
Working in unison, in essence One."
Even he who lives his fleeting day on earth,

Lives her unending life, and so he lives
The life eternal, if he wills and does
What they within his soul enjoin on him,
As his soul's self; he lives the one true life
Which is to all all of eternity.

So grandly does the universal soul
Escape the shame of mere creatorship
And the reproach of dreadful fleetingness!
For all that lives and moves in heaven and earth
Lives, always lived, to Him eternally:
Each blade of grass and every holy flower,
The cloud that sails away — and the wind's breath
That steers it — and the shadow cast by it
That glides along the ground, all live to Him
Eternally. He the expression is
Of all eternity, and is Himself
Eternal, as its veritable essence.
And man too lives eternally! all men!
The new-born child! The very still-born, too!
Against his will, without his knowledge lives
Each one eternally, as God doth live,
The blessed Spirit of the universe,
Who fills all beings, lives Himself in all;
Else were as transitory, sadly wretched,
Beyond all wretched things imaginable.
Let then each heart of man be full of peace,
Even as God wills, who *is* indwelling peace,
And blessedness, eternal blessedness,
Which gushes up from God in human souls,
For human bosoms are the wells of God.

SELF-CONDEMNATION.

THAT was a false and heartless thing to say:
He is unmercifully damned to hell,
To pain and torment and unending woe,
Who, here on earth, has disobeyed God's law,
And trodden under foot His holy will.—
But were a thousand lives to follow this,
Yet were this life unique, forever so.—

Then for the individual man in vain
The universe has stood, then all in vain
His mother bore him, sun and moon in vain
For him have shone, yea, God himself hath spent
On *him* for naught His labor, force and strength,
Both for all time and all eternity,
Who has not come, as man, to be a man,
Though only simple, and of childish mind.
One human being's loss of happiness,
To him, to his, and the fair universe,
Is greater, sadder, more irreparable,
Than if a blight had come upon the Spring,
Than if a star should, like a blasted bud,
Untimely fall from the great Tree of Life.
Then learn, O man, to fathom all the depth

And weigh the worth of thy momentous life!
Each gleam of sunlight, every drop from heaven,
Each breath of thine, is a peculiar gift;
Far costlier, a thousand times more precious,
Each thought, each fresh emotion of the heart!
Be not astounded, every hour, at this:
Else would astonishment break down thy life!
No: feel it once for all with world-wide sense;
Then be the thought borne in upon thy soul, —
Thy day of life declineth like the sun's!
To lose thyself is the extremest loss:
Then hold thy life to be a sacred thing!
All is to thee as thou art in thyself!
This life thou never shalt hereafter live;
And *sacred* means *secluded*, singular.
To win thyself is highest gain for thee,
Yea, for the Spirit of the Universe.
Hell is no more nor less than nothingness;
Heaven is no more nor less than a right life.

A LIFE WITHIN AND ABOVE.

WHAT dream is this of thine, that all the dead
Know more than any single man that lives,
Having gone in to see the mystery
Within a bright, *interior* heavenly hall
Where all things stand revealed in perfect light?
Dear soul, the dead have only gone away —
Gone to the place from which we all came forth,
Whence they themselves once came upon the earth!
The place, the house, the hall, is but the great,
The universal consciousness, where each
Kindles his little light, that guides his way
Along this earthly road. Long ages since
All living men came thence upon the earth,
Nor knew they one whit more than we who live.
But *that* they knew, and that they uttered forth
Out of their spirit. In like manner we
Have come up also from the self-same deep
And know just that which all the dead folk know!
It is enough then, what all living know:
They know of the One Spirit in the whole,
Know of our Spirit in all; which men call "God,'
And carry in their spirit what He has.
Then envy not the dead, as if they knew
All that which *seems* to thee mysterious;
Nor charge thou blindness upon living men —
Let in upon thy soul the light of truth!

THE WORLD ABOVE.

THE world above I call the realm of men!
Higher than all the heavens themselves it is,
Held up on angels', yea, archangels' hands,
Ay, in the very lap of God himself.
A holy world above is human life,
Far higher than the mountain violet's moss,
Far higher than the clouds have ever swept,
Far higher than where shines the highest star.
This earth is an outblooming from the deep
Bosom of old, eternal elements,
And floats on being's old, eternal sea—
And man is an outblooming from the earth,
Nourished with influence sweet of all the heavens;
The genuine blood of Gods is in his veins,
The truest voice divine fills all his heart.
A holy, inner realm is human life,
Deeper than the world's deepest mystery,
Deep in the bosom of all miracles
And magic; in the very heart of God.
A holy, inner realm is man's own being,
The flower within the agate not so deep,
Far deeper is it than the ruby's glow,
Than the heart's feeling of the universe.
And that the sun lights up the earth for thee—?

The moon for thee beams through the silent night — ?
That slumber falls upon thy waking hours — ?
That in thy nightly slumbers dreams do come — ?
Light — what a wonder-work ! how still and soft,
Yet inexpressibly loud a mystery,
That calls more loudly than with thunder's voice :
" Lo ! God is here ! The earth is here ! The sea !
The day is here — here for your gracious work !
Life's day is here for you ! your only one !
Never will *this* day shine on other men,
Nor more on you ! ye only, chosen ones,
Privy ambassadors to this still realm,
This realm of mystery, — highest upper world :
The Day, the life-day of the busy soul,
To you, you only known, seen clearly through,
Blest, and transparent as your very heart ! "
But sleep is not of waking born to you —
Unborn ye slept through *one* eternity —
But waking — life itself — is born of sleep ;
And out of waking, likewise, dreams do come.
Man's life is the true inner, upper, realm,
Upon the summits of the universe.
Who sleep in matter, live the outside life,
Out on the wild sea of eternity.
Acknowledge this and live as holy spirits,
And holy be to you each human work,
Each thought and every feeling of the heart ;
Eternal once for all, as man, ye hover
Upon this height ! For once, forever, here
In this interior, inmost sanctuary.

And when thou knowest this, then is the din
Of day, and all the noisy work of men,
To thee no more than to the sleeper's ear
The bees'-hum from their blooming linden-house ;
The constant change of seasons then will be
To thee one steadfast time, the time of life !
And life-time, *that* will only be to thee
The period of youth, old age, and death ;
Nay, the impetuous throbbing of thy heart,
And thy heart's love . . . ay, and the tranquil sleep
Of loved ones in the grave, the one serene
And holy rest for thee, in this the true
Blest world above upon the bosom of God,
In this interior of the sanctuary,
Where dust — almost adored — to *beauty* grows,
Where water — grows to sweet and blessed *tears*,
And air — is an ineffably deep *sigh*,
And the whole soul is one dissolving *song;*
And ah ! this common earth — *a holy grave*,
And sweetest life — one day *forgetfulness*, —
To be forgotten — holy rest in God —
A stillness like God's life in ancient time.

GOD'S CHILD—NO HEATHEN.

THOUGH I should die, yet if but God remains,
Then all is left me *that I ever loved!*
Blissful I look into eternal life.
If, though I die, God still remains alive,
That is the one great comforter in death,
The holiest prayer the dying man can breathe,
Yea, the most pious frame, most God-resigned,
A soul, however pious, e'er can reach;
More trustful, beautiful and full of joy,
Than the sad cry: my God! my God! Why hast Thou
Forsaken me!—*This* better prayer of refuge
Acknowledges God's spirit in the soul,
And as the soul itself, and so it sinks
With joy into the life of God, and lets
Its earthly life and mortal frame dissolve,
Filled with God's greatness, yea, and over full.
No priest on all the stars could ever teach
A higher word than this to dying men,
No higher word himself could ever pray,
Than that which makes him the appearing God,
And in the final hour—when he no more
Can see or hear—fills all his consciousness
With the serene, eternal life of God,

With the full foretaste of the eternal bliss
That waits on God, which he shall come to know,
When his pale mortal form shall in the grave
Lie mouldering, yea, when even the grave itself
Shall sink and be effaced, and the old dust
Shall rise and wave in renovated spring,
And the clouds thunder in the upper air,
The sun gleam out aloft, and on the wall
Of the black tempest, every traveller see
A bright peculiar rainbow of his own!

Only let every living man thus pray:
"'Tis not *I* live, but God—if God but lives!
Though I should die—O if but God survives!"
And lo! *one* long eternity is gone,
And God still lives! after so many deaths,
Heaps of dead dust and crumbled pyramids,
Upon this earth and upon all the stars,
God still survives! yea, after the long rule
And proud dominion of all living men,
On this our earth and upon all the stars!
He still lives on, a calm and beauteous life
On this our earth and upon all the stars;
And it is not too childish for a child,
And is the loftiest prayer a saint can frame:
"Though I should die—O if God only lives!"
In that, both child and sage are deified,
The worst who can so pray is deified,
He dreads no image of a judgment day,
He is already risen into God;

He needs no judgment trump, nor burning world,
For him has *hope expired* in blessedness,
For him *death died*, and now God only lives
As spirit, as all men's spirits, he is pure
And innocent as God's own holiest thought.

I heard it from a heathen woman's lips,
One whom no priest had ever taught a word,
Who never read a book;—a living proof:
The human heart is the well-spring of God,
Here on the earth and everywhere above.
And God alone can testify of God,—
The sun alone can witness of the sun—
Who shall hang God upon us as a cross?

Thou with this word of mine canst prove the priests:
If they love God far above all things else.
—"What good is that to me?" replied a Prince;
—"What use is that to God?" said a good mother.

A GREATER EVIL THAN DEATH.

'TWERE idle to deliver men from death,
'Twere a calamity, nay, even a crime,
Than which a greater cannot be conceived.
And now if a wise man propose to do it,
He can mean only *from the fear of death;*
And that is a small fear, and known to none
Of all created things save man alone;
And even of men none knows the fear of death
But he who dreads there vengeance for his deeds.
The child with his pure childlike soul does not,
The poor man knows it not, the sufferer;
The sore-afflicted even hopes for death.
Though he should wholly end his bitter life,
For which the good, who is the modest man,
In God reposing, asks no recompense.
And if one haply could attain to God,
And from his friends could thereby ward off death,
Then would he say: "Man, what shall I concede
To thee alone? What would *they* say to that,
With right, who have already suffered death?
Despair then not for them who gladly died!
And if thou lovest them, then learn from love

To feel with them what they feel about death . . .
The pure and good : nothing and less than naught,
Not what thy true heart feels for dying men ;
For, seeing death, *he* dies a thousand times,
Who sees it not with my eternal Spirit."

Yet should there come to us each year the Prophet
Elias, in his chariot of fire,
And tarry but a moment in each place —
What crowds would press around his chariot wheels,
And lay their sick and dying at his feet,
And beg him on their knees to take them in,
So that they might not watch their loved one die,
Prepare the coffin and the awful shroud,
And see amidst such life the dumb, dead man
Borne silently in the funereal train
On to the narrow, but, to all that live,
So awful pit, the all-devouring maw,
Even by little children called "the grave ; "
And know that the dear form, so often kissed,
So often clasped in love, the heavenly form,
Was now the food of gnawing worms and snakes,
Ghastly corruption's loathsome, awful prey !

How happier far to deem them borne away
In some deliverer's chariot, anywhere,
Or nowhere, feel that they have disappeared,
Been charmed away out of this charnel-house,
And in sweet joy of heart to love them still ;
With every morn to look for their return,

To look in vain, yet still to look, so long
As ruddy dawn awakens them from sleep!

He, then, brings more divine deliverance
Than from mere death, who can deliver men
From *dying*, bitter, sore, untimely dying,
Bemoaned with agony that rends the heart —
And for it gives a gentle and serene
Leave-taking of the world, as if none died. . .
As if men only closed their eyes in sleep,
And sweetly, softly sank to rest and peace.

IT TAKES ALL TO SAVE ONE.

THE fear men felt of old for the old Death,
Who seemed to *live* and still devour the world—
The *fear* 'twas a light task to take away!
To shut one's eyes and not see Death, was child's-play;
But not to taste the pains of death — ah that! . . .
To go forever out from the bright world
Nor feel it bitter, but accept and bless it. . .
To feel the eternal parting as a bliss,
A health to him who went and them who staid—
That is, for wisdom, for intelligence,
The goal that may be reached by long, hard toil,
The travail of the *entire human race!*
The entire human race shall one day save —
The whole alone shall save — one single man —
And with him all henceforth and evermore:
From lamentation o'er the *end* of life —
The end of life — (for that alone were death) —
As dreadful and irreparable loss,
A terrible privation through the long
Eternal age. — Know, then: *a blessed life,*
An unrepining, ever cheerful life,
Even to the latest day of long old age
Redeems the heaven-born child — humanity —

From bitter curses on an end of life, —
A melting of the soul into thin air,
A crumbling of the human form to dust,
And of *all* men, down to the latest day,
Of all the years, many or few, through which
Earth shall endure this child's-play, evermore
Played over by new children, till in turn
Each one grows sick and weary of the game,
And so, at last, the mother, too, herself.

CONQUEST OF THE WORLD.

THE world exists, and its live spirit, too,
Which feels it bodily, as children feel
Their body — hands and feet and eye and ear.
The world exists ; and though amazement thrills
The world's own spirit, that it — that He exists —
No smallest cloud flees for astonishment!
No thunder muffles its tempestuous voice
Because of any other's fright and dread !
No grain of sand flees from a skeptic's glance !
The sun in heaven still stands in all the strength
Of its old immemorial majesty ;
The holy stars hold on their ancient way ;
The great celestial grotto glimmers on,
Roamed through by awe-struck living myriads.
They are themselves, if thou regardest right,
The living spirit of the universe.
Nor does a single mote escape from him,
How oft soe'er astonished at himself ;
No, the star-grotto opens out to him ;
To him, the spirit of the universe,
Each power submits, as its old inborn lord ;
To him all mysteries disclose themselves ;
To him in all his kingdom's mighty range

No miracle remains, no, not the least,
Save: *that he is*, himself, and lives and reigns.
And should a sleeper choose to call a dream
This mighty universe; to think that he
Had only dreamed, or was now dreaming it;
That when his dream should end, it would be gone —
The very *dreamer* proves his dream a truth.
For if there were no dreamer, then no dream.
And should a doubter doubt his very self,
The very doubt proves his reality,
His own, the doubter's, who beholds so fair
This mighty universe — that he would rather
Not see, not own it; nay would be content
That God did not exist, so *he* were not!
For what it *comprehends*, that only can
The soul believe; at home in what is known.
Beauty is greatest of all miracles;
And beauty's self the spirit can spell-bind
And sweetly yoke it to his use by love:
Where beauty is, Love feels no torment more,
But only hope, delight, ecstatic bliss:
To man it comes — as wife! To her — as man!
And they belong henceforth to one another!
They live with one another, for each other;
Each but for each *exists;* and all for them!
And so the word "Religion" comes to us,
A *foreign* and incomprehensible one,
Full of a thousand-fold significance,
Yet never utterly interpreted.
So is there from the one great miracle

A refuge still: none else than Love itself,
Which rescues man even from the Beautiful!
Yet *only Beauty* can enkindle Love,
Goodness wakes only gratitude and praise.
So is the one great miracle subdued
Only in parts, in lesser lovely wonders,
By living souls, and in a living form —
And only through all is there help for all!
The ceaseless hovering in a chill suspense
'Midst dream and doubt and stark astonishment, —
In blest assurance to forget all this,
With full, whole soul soar upward into peace,
Tranquillity, yea, to that rapturous wish:
O that *this* life might be forever ours!

THE HISTORICAL SUNRISE.

ONLY the *possible* history is the true.
Then let not History impose on thee,
Which is but its own view made visible.
A thousand tongues cannot make one thing true ;
For had we from tradition's mouth received,
Unanimously pronounced by thousand tongues,
This word, " *The sun has risen upon our world !* "
All we should know, would be what *they* had seen :
That the horizon of the rolling earth
Sank to the eyes of those old witnesses ;
The Sun himself has never once *arisen*,
'Twas only fancy said, " He is coming up ! "
Then let not history impose on thee,
Only the *possible history*, that is true.
History is history of the mind of man ;
School history, as of what the teachers thought ;
Its touchstone reason is and that alone.
Only unreason has its " *histories.*"

THE REWARD OF KNOWLEDGE.

ONLY what *thou* art, is the world to thee;
Following thy changes it becomes for thee
The thing to which thou dost transform thyself;
To each it is his *snail-shell.* To the child,
When for the very first time in his life
He sees the sun, it is a bright new star,
Just risen out of sleep, — even as the child
Starts up out of his cradle. To the lamb
'Tis mother, mother's milk, and dog and fold
And wood and grass and flowers; to the bee
It is a honey-pasture; to the spider
Only two twigs to hang her nest upon;
A swarm of flies, she needs for nourishment;
A breath of air that shatters all her house.
To the sick soldier, faint with wounds, the sword
Upon his bed is faint and sick with wounds,
Bleeding and suffering with him; to the blind
Noonday is midnight; to the happy man,
The world is one great table crowned with wine,
An echoing gallery to his joyous song;
The old man sees the youngest, loveliest girls
But as night-spectres from his youthful time,
As their white forms by moonlight came to him!

And he would be their murderer, their betrayer,
Would be a breaker of the marriage-vow,
If he should be their husband. To the dead
What is the world? A coffin and a grave;
The worms that gnaw his body in the dark;
The rains that only bleach his naked bones:
The winds that turn his dust to breath of spring.
And so to all the thousand differing creatures
The world is made a thousand different worlds,
To each his own, shaped after what *he* is
And what he needs: even as a glow-worm has
For the reflection of his tiny lamp—
The grass!

And shall not man then learn from this
Aught for his use, his glad enlightenment?
To know is in itself the highest gain:
And *therefore* is he man: to know what is;
And what he knows *around him in the world*
To find all true and beautifully fulfilled,
Working its own fulfilment gloriously,—
To feel all and to feel himself divine.
Then wilt thou own with touched and tranquil soul:
How blessed all, all living creatures are,
Even those who only know themselves, yet *that*
As clearly, warmly, as yon sun on high. . .
As God! since God with *His* clear *Spirit* fills
The little spider, yea divinely lives
With His primeval skill and art her life.
Tranquillity and *joy* are the sweet fruits
Of knowledge and sublimely flow from God.

For see ! most surely God *believes* not ! God,
God *believes* nothing, God has no belief.
God KNOWS ! and sees, and sees *through* every thing,
As clearly as He sees and knows Himself!
And yet is surely blest *without* belief,
As no one ever was of all the fools,
Who make the vain attempt to thrust themselves,
Into another's hollow head and then
To look out on the world with their own eyes
From his eye sockets !
Thou, then, hold to God,
And ever strive to make thyself like God
With all His might, which is naught else than thou.
Thus lightly God translates *His heart in thee*
Into His great pure heart, His knowledge in thee
Into His own clear, holy intellect.

THE SOUL'S KEEPER.

LIFE needs the eternal unction, that alone
Shall make it doubly precious, doubly fair,
The young child resting in its mother's arms:
Her child, so near to her, her very own,
The mortal, that shall sometime fade away,
And yet the eternal, of eternal powers
The priceless work and undecaying life.
Can, now, another being tell the soul
The thing it knew not — did not understand?
What could he do but echo its own words?
The emotion, thrilling, throbbing through itself?
What need, then, has it of that other now?
The pompous stage-expounder of clear things?
The soul of every man is his high priest,
Always at hand and ready at his call,
Early and late, at evening and at morn,
In waking hours by day, in dream by night,
In noisy gladness and in silent grief,
In lingering sickness and in sudden death,
Where none, not one can e'er come near to it,
As, to a new-born child the very *love*
Of its own mother's heart cannot come near —
And yet *his soul* is softly with him there!

And in the soul is all of the Divine!

Then of thy soul be thou, O man, thyself
The keeper! Thou, young man, young woman, thou,
Confide thou all things to thy soul, with it
Converse, advise thyself, instruct thyself,
Out of thine own full store of heavenly wealth!
And as thou needest but to open thine eyes,
Clearly to see the day and all its charms,
So keep thy soul within thee clear and pure,
And all of God shall come and dwell in thee,
And look out from thee and rejoice in thee,
And thou shalt enter into all His bliss,
And He shall give His peace to thee in life
And His tranquillity of bliss in death.

THE UNIVERSAL TEMPLE.

ONE in himself and with himself to be
Is the desirable unity —
The only possible unity for man.
For to be one with others is but sameness;
And nothing that is born, no thing that grows
Is ever like another; less by far
Than face is like to face, or eye to eye,
Is any *soul* like any other soul
In all the world, in its peculiar way
Of looking on the world and feeling it.
Whoever lives is individual,
Without a copy or a precedent,
And holy even to God. Subjection stamps
The brand of slavery on the free-born soul,
To the free universe worse blot than death.
"To show a unity it takes, at least,
Two — if not three" — none ever spake that word;
God does not wait for three or even for two,
That He may come into the midst of them,
But God is in the midst of one alone,
And in *each* being through the universe.
In *one* is there the perfect fellowship
Of God and the profoundest unity —

And if the temple of God is man himself,
And every man the wondrous edifice,
Wherein God celebrates in silentness
His own existence, meditates Himself
In calm devotion, and is to Himself
In all His proper beauty manifest —
Then are there temples, churches, where the rule
Of bishop or of parson never yet
Was known or needed *or can ever* be . . .
For God's is a free Spirit in every soul;
Thought is a *sacred* solitary work,
A work which two can never do together,
For God's is a free Spirit in every soul.
So a *good action* is the work of one,
And each must do it singly by himself,
For God's is a free Spirit in every soul.
Nor are there two religions, can there be,
But one religion, that of God Himself,
And this the God in every man works out
For his own self and by Himself alone.
Religion is God's proving of Himself
To be the eternal and the blessed Spirit,
Who, what He is Himself, that exercises
And that makes happen to Himself alone;
As He in all beholds and feels Himself
Alone, and only His own welfare wills!
The life-creating, life-diffusing, life —
Sustaining soul of beauty and of joy.
Another temple, other house, of stone,
Than this great holy mansion of us all

Is but a dream, a castle in the air;
The heart alone, that is the place where God
Honors Himself by great self-consciousness
And *clear intelligence;* for more than that
God needs not, to maintain a God-like being
Doing and living, either in His own
Spirit, or man's, which is His Spirit too.
The sun once clear, his work is heavenly;
And if a mother only, watch by night
Beside her darlings . . . 'tis *the mother* watches,
The mother with the wealth of her full heart,
And that no stone. . . 'tis the full God-like soul!
And to attach one's self to any less
Enlarged communion than this limitless
And endless immemorial universe
Full of the Holy Spirit and life of God,—
That is to have no hold, no anchorage,
Stupidly to reject the church of God;
As children creep away out of the sun
Into a hut of leaves and keep stock-still
And wait until their father finds them there!
The true man, full of the clear Spirit of God,
He — God's own Spirit in a human form,
Needs not to seek another sanctuary
Than where he is in this broad universe,
Nor any other church for fellowship
(Not even two, no, not so much as one)
Save all the living beings everywhere
In every form; nor can he ever give
To other men more than his very self;

Nor dares he give them less than his *whole self,*
Much as he needs them for his joy and life.
To do God's kindness is no martyrdom !
And if it gave itself and others pain,
Then of all evils virtue were the worst.
No — God-like action is but joy of life,
And all its work is only life and joy,
The happiest and the fairest soul is God.

ANTHROPODICY.*

THEY say: "If thou reposest on thyself,
And dost revere thyself as thy most rare
And costliest possession — then hast thou
Cut thyself loose from God and all mankind."

When thou art subject to thyself — thy soul —
Then only dost thou yield obedience
To the great, common soul that lives and moves
In all around thee — and to every child
That needs thy service and thy helping hand;
But art thou not yet master of thyself,
Oh then thou surely art none other's yet!
The spirit that makes thee subject to thyself,
That is none other than the freeborn master,
Who to serve others fain would live, as thou.

* Corresponding to "*Theo*dicy," — meaning *vindication of man.* — T.

THE COUPLES.

THAT which must needs form unions, commonwealths
Is weak, and owns its weakness to the world.
What cannot hold together of itself,
Even as the sun's compact and solid ball,
Or like the body of a man or beast,
Or even a blade of grass, a single body, —
A puff of wind shall presently dissolve.
More than whole nations is the single man,
Nobler in energy and quality,
In sentiment and high, divine descent.
Then, wilt thou be a whole and genuine man —
Shut thyself *out* from nothing that is good,
Shut thyself *up* to nothing, no one less
Than the whole universe and all it holds
Of true and beautiful! No human church
And no community of choicest heads
And hearts, is yet the whole, free universe!
Whoso cuts off, who shuts off other men
From his own fellowship, by this same act,
Cuts off, shuts out himself from all the world —
That man has nailed himself to his own cross.
The true man stands erect on his own feet.
In his own mind all things are bright and clear!

In his own heart all blissful and serene !
His happy life is a free pilgrimage : —
With *this good man* forth now to do this work,
With *that* one to that other ; *ever free*,
Constrained by nothing and by nothing taught,
Save by his own heaven-lighted consciousness.
Thus only is there genuine godliness !
Thus only virtue, moral dignity
And worth, and last of all *obedience*,
The greatest, for even God obedience yields
To His own love and His own gracious Spirit.
Thus now the unions all dissolve themselves,
As all communions do and nations *all*.
In turn, by reason and the highest love,
All imperceptibly dissolve themselves,
And each becomes the firm and solid sun,
The couples are transformed to sister suns,
To wedded suns, free with their several lights,
Their several forces circling in the heavens.
And so there comes on earth a starry heaven,
Wherein the stars are human minds and souls
Full each one of its own divinity ;
For without freedom God would not be God,
And without freedom no one were divine,
But even the worm with freedom is divine,
And he is free who with a God-like mind
Executes as a sovereign his own law.

HOLY WRATH.

OF all annoying and afflicting things,
Grumbling about them is the very worst!
They're nothing till they grow to gloom in man.
Glumness is life's first real poison then
And vessel for it is there none—*but man:*
But say: *what* men, now, chiefly fall a prey
To life's afflictions and annoyances?
And who then reap therefrom a grumbling mind?
Ignorance and inexperience sow the seed
Of the disease with their own hands, and then
They in their turn from others reap the crop.
On *patient* men too, even on *souls resigned,*
The misery falls, who are not well forearmed.
And "saints" are not the saintliest, in sooth,
Seldom the wisest; so they come to grief.
No shield against all sorrows is a heart
Full of good-will and truth and patient trust.
Even sheep are slaughtered; they too freeze, being shorn;
And even patience has its anguish too.
The spirited, nay even the angry soul,
Can best repel the shafts of misery:
It stands upon its guard defiantly,
Wards off, and feels, enheartened, its own strength,

Whom sickness, death and graves stir up to wrath,
Who mourns not o'er the friend that lies there slain,
Mourns not, nor quails, but burns with holy *wrath*,
Wrath only, — that man feels not grief nor death,
He is in strength like to the mighty gods.
Above them and their groaning world has he
Set himself up on high, and now he stands
Confronting it with pure and clear-eyed spirit.
And so we find in all the great, in all
Heroes and prophets, all who ever have
Wrought great things: *wrath! the bearer of all woe*
As child's play! witness of all weighty acts:
As of the flood, and the redemption, once,
Nay, an "indignant" prophet raised the dead. —
And that is the thrice holy might of wrath.
The godly wrath that looks with scorn on pain;
That looks with scorn on misery and on tears,
Strong in the simple child-like might of God —
For which there is no death, no destiny,
But only fiery glow in purest heart.
The might of anger is the highest might;
It burns out all that e'er afflicted thee.
O man! stir up that fire within thy breast! —
Meanwhile the silly sheep are only shorn;
The patient ones are *going to be* redeemed;
The dead shall be *one day* roused from the grave —
Anger *awakes* the dead, creates the world.
Indifference sees the world to ashes sink,
Contentment finds in life a snare and foe.

THE HIGHEST PATERNAL JOY.

TO be a king — oh noblest state of man!
A father of so many thousand fathers,
Of mothers, daughters, sons and darling babes;
Of mountains full of herds and forests full
Of game; of field, vale, meadow, fount and stream;
To be a king and a good father too,
Of the young roe and of the trembling hare
And of the smallest tree beside the road:
By wisely-ordering and protecting power,
A faithful hand — extended graciously
O'er all the land — that softly leads o'er night
Lost ones to hospitable homes; awakes
From slumber; guides the darling little ones
Early to school: flings wide the temple doors,
A grateful refuge to the burdened soul;
Lends helpers to the sick: to poor folk bread;
Even to the dead secures a holy grave,
And o'er the grave mound plants the linden tree:
That gives to all each highest gift, nor needs
To take from any, what it gives to one,
So that no single child may have to weep!
That life may be to each a joyous thing,
For joy the highest treasure is of life —

A songless wood, a bee-hive still as death,
A mourning land. . . . saddens the sun itself! —
Creating joy is then a king's great work!
Opening the way for joy he brings in peace,
Law, liberty, light, right, prosperity;
For this he lives, to give his people joy:
Joy in the happy monarch of a race,
Invincible, that in unbroken strength
In the first freshness of its juicy shoot
Firm-rooted, storm-proof, rises up to meet
The coming centuries with their suns and all
Their harvests, — full of blossoms and of fruits;
To be a king — supreme paternal joy! —

OPENNESS.

LIVE open to the world, as to the sun.
What thou dost hide is, sure, to some one's hurt,
What drives thee into corners is thy fear,
And surely fear is to thyself disgrace.
A mystery, of itself, is half a wrong;
It is a shame to thee if thou so liv'st
That all the world may not know how thou liv'st.
'Tis a disgrace to thee that thou dost set
The things of men so high . . . art so their slave,
That they ingloriously imprison thee,
That they have power to lame thy tongue and arms.
What not even decency can fairly chide
Thou need'st not blab it in the market-place.
Yet worry not thyself if haply one
Or other know of it whose name is man,
And who will soon forget it in the grave.
The shame of being poor, and seeming thus
To be unhappy or of no account—
Oh root it out! We are but beggars all,
'Fore God; and few rich men live justified
Throughout, but many silently despised,
Either for how they gained their gold and goods
Or how they spend them,—live like wretches, fools,

A shame and burden to the poorer, who
Stupid as *devil's-servants* court the rich,
And count for honor insults from the great.
Nor, if thou canst not cut off others' heads,
Take to thee shame as wholly powerless!
Power is withheld no less from all the rest,
Who wear their chains. Power is nothing else
Than one man borrowing the might of all,
Most awful of responsibilities,
Most deadly; to the *one* made tolerable
Only by this: that many share it too
Whom God may punish with him for misuse.
Be Pope or Mufti, Emperor, King, or boor,
Thou dost begin that day a better life,
And only then a God-like one and free,
On which thou dost renounce all privacy
And dar'st be as heroically great
As that frank hero is, the polar bear,
The Elephant, the Lion in the woods,
Who with a genuine God-like consciousness
Walks, with his naked hide, so all content,
And has no secret weighing on his soul.—
For be a man ever so good and great—
Hardly the best shall match himself with these,
The holy creatures made divine through God.
Treason is shameful, monster among crimes,
Traitors are the most formidable foes,
Yet always has the *thing* betrayed been good,
Wholesome and safe and saving to the world.
And whoso now with harm to no one, save

Cheaters of men and traitors to their God,
Lays bare a mystery of iniquity,
Him oh revile not — him dishonor not!
Lest thou revile — disgrace thyself in him!
Wrapt in a few rags shall the grave one day
Receive thee naked, and thy naked soul,
Proud man! shall stand up shuddering before God.
Man is already here a *mask* of God;
Man is a mask even to his fellow-men.
That which thou hidest is but thy disgrace;
Whoso lives frankly fears no judgment day;
And openness disarms all enemies;
He who is honest can be no man's foe.
Sinners in secret call him "void of shame" —
He *is* ashamed: to be small-souled and craven!

THE BIRD OF WISDOM.

"WHOM callest thou thy master! Noble man!"

I? None but God alone; He is my Lord.
Spirits alone have masters; bodies none.
He whom I love not, hate not, yea despise,
My master surely is not, cannot be;
For even the mother calls her darling child,
Whom *she* loves, fondly calls him *little lord.*
Force has not over spirits any force,
And might o'er men has properly no might;
For men *are* not the bodies that they wear,
No, not the very beggar in his rags.
If robbers should fall on me in the wood
And bind me fast — are they *my masters* then?
Robbers they are, my robbers, — nothing more!
And if they slay me, yea and bury me
Beneath the sand — are they my masters then?
Murderers, my murderers, are they — that is all!
"Whom call'st thou then *thy* master, noble race?"
The Master of mankind, the Lord of earth,
Of sun and stars and all the heavenly host!
To Him the whole soul cleaves as loyally
As all the rivers hasten to the sea.
Leaders, wise legislators, benefactors,
These well may claim to have earned the people's love.
Primeval peoples of the better stamp,

As the Chinese, rested their government
Upon the corner-stone of fatherhood,
And gave to every sire of every house,
The power of the great father in the realm,
Authority over the life and death
Of all his household, wife and children ; next,
Gave, to the eldest son the father's power
Over his brothers and his sisters, yea,
Over his mother. — Fair beginning that
Of government, methinks, and a wise break
Of man's perpetual mania for sway
Upon the shore of each paternal heart ;
A wise arrest of brethren's rivalry
In the affection of a brother's heart,
Trained to a father's rule and loving them
As nearest blood relation, honoring them
As children of his father and his mother,
Thoroughly happy when he makes them so,
And grieved to bitter tears when they are grieved !
But of all rule the heaven-appointed end
Is liberty for all, the ruler too,
The father and the brother, — every man.
And plight divine and right divine, these two,
Are the twin-bonds that make a people one
Which will not live on grace and sufferance,
And should not, — for the poorest beggar has
His rightful claim to every human heart,
And every giver only gives his due,
And parents' love and children's truth have been
From immemorial eld, for Gods and men,
Both right and plight, and will be so forever !

No ruler can be wiser than his age,
Than the humanity from which he springs:
From *it* comes all he knows, to *it* he does
All that he does: he is a man, like all.
No book, in the most secret escritoire
Of rulers lies *concealed* that tells how they
Should guide the nations through all future time . . .
Or to what goal the nations all should come!
And had there been such book, it would long since
Have, by humanity outgrown, become
A jest book. Free must be the ruler, free
Must be his rule and free his people too.
Your rulers, then, ye nations, first release
And make them free! Free from the very need
To punish, by your wise and righteous life!
Free from suspicion, by your upright will! —
From superstition by intelligence! —
Form to yourselves a true and absolute
Judgment of life: know where you would arrive;
What is the will of all, is straightway done.
Bondage lies at the slave's door, not the lord's,
And with the herd the herdsman perishes.
He guides the herd where he thinks good for them,
Humanity points out its shepherd's way;
Whither it will, thither will he go too.
Then only fares it well with him and his.
So the wild goose herself who leads the geese,
Though at their head, is but a goose * like them,
Herself as full as all the rest of them
With yearning toward the Spring across the sea.

* The Bird of Wisdom with the ancients.

SOLON AND SESOSTRIS.

THE bloom of spring, the summer's glowing pomp,
The gorgeous autumn with fruit-laden trees,
Are they no more, when the stern winter comes,
And covers hill and vale with drifting snow?
True they are gone, but they had long been gone
Already. They had lived their life out first!
Of the least rose-bud not the smallest bit,
Nor lily, which has never seen his face,
Has winter in his clutch — he came too late!
When thou hast, with thy friends, night after night,
Drained a great cask-full of delicious wine,
And in the cask the lees are vinegar,
Is therefore the sweet wine thou and thy friends
Have drunk, turned in your veins to vinegar?
The dregs alone are vinegar; the rest
Remains a sweetness in the memory.
The flowers have bloomed before stern winter comes —
Whoso is happy, was, before his death,
And late misfortune, even an early death
Takes not away the earlier, fairer years!
Nay, should'st thou, in delusion, deem thyself
Happy, and the delusion be dispelled,
Thy wisdom only *ends* thy folly — not

Annihilates! Whoso for eighty years
Should roam through fragrance over flowery shores,
Then plunge into the sea and sink and drown,
Still roamed his eighty years on flowery shores.
He who grows happy must have been before
Unhappy; and the man *who has become*
Unhappy, could not have become so now,
If he had not before known happiness.
Mutable is the lot of man on earth;
Let each see how he may continue happy,
Yet not proudly defy misfortune's shaft,
But in good fortune be compassionate.
Sesostris gave to seven kings the boon
Of life and liberty. And one of them,
When harnessed to his chariot with the rest,
Saw in a spoke of the wheel that now was up,
And now was down, an emblem of the lot
Of man, and even of the fate of kings!

THE END OF ALL THINGS.

THE end of all things is deplorable —
Of love and beauty, wedded life, all, — all!
All flowers that bloom and shoot up into seed,
All birds, when on their twig in the still wood
With hushed and stifled throats they sit and die,
And the wind sweeps them dead from off the tree.
All things that live come quickly to an end.
The unnumbered and innumerable things,
Day after day, are coming to an end:
The trees, the houses, cities, nations — all!
The earth itself shall one day pass away.
The sun shines down from heaven *before* his end:
The stars are only flowers that bloom and fade,
They live *until* they all come to an end!
The end of all things is o'ercast and sad —
And what has had beginning has its end;
And all has had beginning — everything
That ever eye has seen or ear has heard,
Nay even what has issued from the mind,
That has its life and also has its end:
The song expires upon the singer's lips,
The tender flute-note dies upon the breeze,
The crash of thunder and the peal of bells;

The pictures fade and die upon the wall;
The words of wisdom die upon the earth;
Custom and usage die, and manners die,
The holiest love dies with the hearts it blest;
The gods themselves perish and pass away,
Like marble statues gnawed by teeth of time.
The end of all things is deplorable.
Oh how much beauty, how much gladness ends,
For which all angels never ceased to weep,
Nor all the dew of nights had tears enough;
For it transcended tears; man, none but he,
Must mourn, instead of angels and of clouds,
The beauty and the loveliness *once his.*
Quite inconsolable, unbearable,
Were daily, hourly grief for all that ends,
All, all the precious things each soul must mourn,
Not one or two or three alone, but all
The wealth of beauty and of loveliness —
How happy then that Love too has its bounds
And limits! only strength to mourn its own.
Else man were earth's most wretched type of woe!
But now, within his bosom's narrow bounds
He bears his burden, even though it be
As great and heavy as his love itself.
The shock of sorrow stuns, (as death begets
Indifference) and so brings with it relief,
And constant thunder makes men deaf at last.
Man, like a child, awakes as moon and sun
Exchange their watches — and his heart is glad!
He sees his dear ones fade by slow degrees.

For even his little children pass from him
Only by imperceptible degrees,
Year after year *into still greater forms*
And fairer — yet they *pass away*, and so
Inure him softly to the daily end :
For lo ! insensibly *the little ones*
Are snatched from him, exchanged — and yet still there !
The radiant *bride* is in the *mother* lost.
And in the weaning undergone by man
From all the beauty and the bliss around,
New beauty thousand-fold *each day begins*,
And like an airy shape floats round him still !
New things come ever, bright and beautiful,
The old resembling, and replacing it,
For eye and heart yea and for heaven itself.
And as the fair and gladsome blue of heaven
(Which, with the sun and moon, does not the less
Glide by forever imperceptibly)
Seems to *stand still*, and in the eternal round
Really remains eternal ; *so the world*
Stands before man ; who calls it *mutable*,
And *fleeting*, half in earnest, half in jest ;
Harshly upbraids, yet blesses secretly,
Because it brought him all he ever loves
And brings new things to beings ever new,
Which they in turn can love with all their soul.
And that wakes pity . . . magnanimity :
For others' happiness, to lose his own !
Beginnings, therefore, no man deprecates,
No mother ever does her new-born child —

The man begun, — that yet one day shall end ; —
And only the *beginning* could be mourned,
Because it brings with it the end of things.
The world's beginning and all love's, God's own
Beginning, or God's being, that alone
Must bear the blame of sorrow and of death.
If *this* is death verily : that Love weeps ;
For without love no tear would ever fall,
And love through death alone grows passionate
And real, — and becomes the soul of God
In the vast universe, the changeable
And fleeting, — only by its fleetingness.
Only in man, then, does the spirit of God
Not contradict itself, in his own spirit,
And so it quietly accepts the still,
Tranquil, divine beginning of all things ;
And yet it says, fulfilling its own law :
The end of all things is deplorable.
*And glorious is the strong and god-like soul.**

* One is reminded here of Shelley's lines : —

"All things that we love and cherish
Like ourselves must fade and perish ;
Such is our rude mortal lot —
Love itself wou'd, did they not." — T.

THE DUTY OF THE OPEN EAR.

"'TIS critical to tell a prince the truth;
Twice it is harmful, and once profitless.
First hurtful: thou exasperatest him;
And a king's wrath embitters his whole day,
And well may harm a city-full of men.
Then hurtful: for it gets thee stripes and grief.
Then useless also; for thou changest none;
After each quarrel, even the better men
Only go on more stiff in their own way.
Reformed men, better men, are only born,
That is the hope and comfort of the wise.
And hence it seems superfluous, once for all,
That thou and all the people in the land
(Who think and live more nobly from their birth)
Should even *say* and publish honestly
What their soul knows and what their hearts have felt.
What in this generation's heart lay hid,
That in their children comes upon the scene
Living and visible, head, hands, and feet, —
And will inevitably be *lived out;*
As all the children carry on their games
So will the parents, risen again in spirit,
Stand as new creatures and create new things."

This word is keen and true ; yet cowardly.
Must thou then say to no one what will be
Tomorrow, what hereafter man shall live,
Which a true ruler with wise forethought may
Prepare for ? Frankness honors the good man,
And pouring out his soul refreshes him.
'Tis a man's glory and his duty too.
And were his coffin the reward for it,
And for the voice of truth the hush of death ; —
Yet the Chinese carry their coffins with them
Before the palace of their emperor,
When they must tell him an unwelcome truth,
But one that shows the land a higher good
Than he can see or haply will confess.
Yet 'tis the Ruler's duty to hear truth,
It is the only indispensable one,
The availing one that God requires of each,
Avenging each to whom it is denied.
And so when one has said his dying word
There in his coffin sitting all the while,
His faithful head sunk mutely on his breast . . .
Another straightway with his coffin comes
And utters in his ear the wholesome word.
And when he, too, has said his dying word
Within his coffin sitting there the while
His faithful head bowed mutely on his breast . . .
Then with his coffin joyful comes the third,
The fourth, the fifth, the tenth, the twentieth . . .
Until at last the word's not only *heard*
As duty bids, but also *listened to*

As right demands. — Say now: is not the weal
Even of the stubborn host himself . . . is not
The weal of a whole race which he is charged
At God's great golden banquet board of earth
To entertain with gifts — is it not worth
Ten coffins and ten noble hearts therein
That felt: "O man! thou only liv'st for men!"
And knew: that word-seed is the seed of work?
And whoso stirs in us a noble sense
And free, that man creates both God and freedom
For the divine race called humanity,
Of which God makes the Princes * only *hosts*,
The *Principals* and Marshals of their feasts;
For not a mad-house or correction-house
Shall he perversely make God's house of joy —
Of the glad spirit of his beauteous world,
Which nothing knows of sin or evil-doing
Save his, who poisons his own joy of life.
For knowledge, truth, refined morality,
Glow but to crown a glad and beauteous life;
And not to fire and fill, one day, a hell,
That has no place in his pure palaces.

* In German the *Fürste* (Princes) are properly the *First* men, just as the *kings* are the men who *can* (können).— T.

WHO EVER PUT BACK THE SUN?*

THIS the world teaches: the authorities
Have an authority above themselves,
The silent one, that smiling like the sun,
Lets not that seed spring up, but silently
Perish, that held dark fates for coming men,
And ill-assorted with the world's new year —
And with still care raises the seed to light
Which a good man, though least of all, had sown.
But fall not into *one* mistake, O men!
Whatever sin offends *against the past,*
Against the transient and the life gone by,
And therefore now lies dead among its dead,
That hold to be a lesser crime by far,
Yea, hold it even as naught, compared with that
Which might presumptuously against the high
And heaven-clear future of this god-like race
Have been committed, yet shall never be!
For these poor children, sprung of this poor race,
Are the *true masters of the future age*
And every day therein, and all its lore.
They who live after us shall be the heads
Of the dead myriads and of every past;

* The German title: "Who ever arrested the march of the sun?" appears to be a line from some song. — T.

And no one born on earth has leave to make
A testament, that flatly contravenes
Or even so much as fetters by a hand
The will, the wisdom, and the liberty
Of future souls to all eternity!
Honor, ye living men, them that shall live!
Corrupt not, drown not, lay not waste the soul
Wherein shall grow the thing that none e'er saw;
Just as around us here upon the earth
Blooms that which elder eyes had never seen.
Rather hand down the earth, a well-tilled ground,
And for this child — the human race — let him
Pass from your hands *ripe for a higher school* —
No Cretin!

COMPULSION.

WHAT is enforced, humanity repels,
Because enforced, how wholesome and how good
Soe'er; humanity wants first: *to will;* —
That right it guards with holy jealousy.
For he is never wretched who may will;
Happy he only who can choose, and does.
Bring now a slice of golden honey-comb
And harshly bid the child: "This thou must eat!"
He'll turn away from it; and wouldst thou fain
Force with the spoon the honey down his throat,
He'll shut his little teeth together tight,
And cry with tears: "Father, it makes me sick!
Oh why wilt thou torment me so?" For truly
'Twas *gall*, not *honey*. — But let father now
Go set his pot of honey secretly,
Without a word, without a prohibition,
Then will the child go gladly of himself,
And taste and in three days have eaten up all.
Nor think thou to catch men as men do asses,
By false decoys, making believe to do
What they shall do, shall practise, after thee,
As when thou washest *thine* eyes with clear water
Before the monkey-people looking on

And set'st before them then a dish of paste,
That they with glued-up eyes may be thy slaves. —
Enactest thou before man *even the best*,
Which he, confiding in thee, imitates,
That should be called : to allure, to lead astray,
Yea to corrupt God's children's lofty souls !
Set thou the food before the hungry man,
The water set before the thirsty one,
And speak no word, not even to bid them come.
And need I tell thee what will then take place ?
That is to honor both one's self and man,
To lead along his yearning to the truth
And light, and help the free and god-like soul
That lays its hand on all *befitting it.*
So the Lord sets two starlings out in spring,
Provides a hollow tree, provides dry stalks,
And soon a brood is twittering in the nest !
But cage them in, and make a nest for them,
With food and drink, and comforts rich supplied, —
The pair looks on dismayed and pines away !
The set example is a thing for asses —
Things daily babbled in our ears we hate !
What is enforced, humanity rejects !

THE SAVIOUR: IMPOSSIBILITY.

IS that so very sure: "Might, only, *tells*,
And only might makes right, is always right?"
But then a man might still go on to ask
The highest of all questions (for the question
Of slavery or freedom does concern
Humanity, in which God's life takes form). —
This must one ask: *What* might alone prevails?
And *what* right has it? Since a right it has;
For God himself could not, with all His might,
Much less the lord of some small strip of earth,
Maintain a wrong of his for many years.
Yet even the feeble and defenceless snail
Maintains a right within her house, until
The gardener tramples on it — and her too.
The bravest of all dwellers on the earth,
The marmot, has his right too in his house,
Until the marmot-digger comes upon him,
Beats him to death and takes his household goods —
"Takes" — says the man: "No," the marmot: "steals.'
"Man," he would say, "thy right is mastery!
Right of the stronger!" So superior strength
Slaughters the whole; superior strength no less,
And only that, hurls rocks into the sea, —

Not violence, not human tyranny.
The rocks devoid of sensibility,
Without a will, know naught of violence ;
Man, above all that live upon the earth,
Most keenly feels the hand of power ; to *him*
Can violence be done. Now then *what* might
Does really prevail ? Of evil men ?
The evil power lasts out its evil time ;
It can hale men to prison, rob their sons
Or murder them, make mothers mute as stones,
And men as stiff as rocks ; it *can* do all
Through abject hirelings and will-less tools,
So long as it counts *one man* more than foes ;
Two men will soon be masters of the one,
Whoever he may be, if they but *will ;*
For with a naked sword one constable
Shall hold in awe a panic-stricken town.
Yes, might does tell indeed on will-less souls,
On *frightened* ones ; not on the *marmot* who
Turns on his foe and boldly tears his face :
It tells but on his body and his life ;
Yes, might does tell, *but it endureth not* —
When it is violence, and when all souls
Do not and freely yield to it their will.
For if in any stillest nook there dwell
A simple man, a better, wiser one
Than a self-willed and headstrong hundred men,
The one shall be the little magic storm-egg
Round which come trooping all the thunder-clouds ;
That one shall be the little lump of leaven

That over night leavens the meal for men.
The might of the good man and reasonable
Alone endures, that lays no human heart
Under constraint; (for not to be constrained
Is any heart of man, it scorns constraint.)
Odious is force, as to the tender maid, —
Who yet to him she truly loves will give,
Yea offer up freely and joyously,
Her all, because her will inspires her.
That is the free, the holy might alone,
Might which has right, because it is possessed
Of God's own right and strength within itself.
Whoso feels violence quivering *in his hands*
Convulsively, in vain thou say'st to him:
"If thou hast power, and if a worm submit
Thereto . . . tread him not down beneath thy feet,
Because thou canst, — all people *can* do horrors;
Yet do thou not! . . . and is the worm a man,
A child, a woman . . . oh oppress them not;
Nor make one moment of their beautiful
And holy life a joyless thing to them."
Power hears it not and understands it not,
As no *wild elephant* will heed a word.
Naught saves us from the senseless lightning stroke,
But iron that hinders it from hitting us:
Naught saves us but impossibility,
That only — and all other means are vain.
Naught saves us but impossibility.
Impossible it must be to cheat the heart,
Impossible no less to enslave the mind —

The very purpose is a *blasphemy* —
Impossible it must be to fetter reason,
To spell-bind thought and the free soul immure
In old, dark, melancholy dungeon walls
Wherein the *tree of life* no more may bloom
And put forth freely all its heavenly fruits.
And to this blest impossibility,
Two are the roads by which God leads his race.
The one, the open road the people take:
To make the mighty, honest, wise, and good;
Then power is resolved into good-will
And good-will is the very joy of power;
For if in His own person God should reign
Upon the earth, *what freedom would there be,*
Freedom to teach, to live and to believe;
As He even grants it to all people now
Whom, as dear children, smiling He allows
To call their Gods by names themselves have made
And talk with them as children with their dolls. —
The second way half helps to shorten that:
To make the stupid wise, and wise ones strong,
Girt round with purest, never-conquered wills;
For if in a whole people each one were
A boy-Achilles and a man-Achilles,
In courage, only a Napoleon,
And in ambition, before such a one
What could a thousand heroes do but slink,
Scorned and disgraced, into a coward's grave!
Against that noble wife Penthesilea
What could a host, each an Achilles, do? —

Naught saves us but impossibility;
Whole nations and *each one of us no less.*
When 'tis impossible for *us* to be
Stupid and bad, because we have *the power*
To judge, because we are discreet and good . . .
Impossible for *power* to be rude
Because resolved into meek modesty
And silent awe before the *Spirit of God;*—
What blessed life noble humanity
Will live, as calm and steadfast as if God
Were walking million-fold in Paradise!

Make possible and real to yourselves
Impossibility; and just so far,
No farther, are you prosperous and happy!

DIVINE SENSE IN CHILD'S-PLAY.*

A SOMETHING unmistakably divine
And holy, and eternally unique,—
So has man's life no other, narrower aim,
No end beyond itself, no far-off goal.
Subject to none in the wide universe,
Not to the Spirit of the universe,
For through it lives the Spirit of God Himself
Out from Himself, for His pure blessedness.
And nothing can subject the Spirit of God.
God has no end but simply to be God;
And live as God throughout the universe.
Else God had some one greater than Himself,
And of *that other* God would be the slave,
For whom He worked at service in the world.
The ideal life of man is then: pure joy,
Forever ending, rounding in itself,
Self-bounded, self-sufficing, self-enclosed.
Yet though our life is thus a god-like play,
In the most pious and exalted sense,
By its uniqueness inexpressibly holy,
Still it is *bitter earnest to mankind,*
As children find grave earnest their light play.

* "There lies deep meaning oft in childish play." — HEMANS.

The heart beats loud with joyous expectation,
When on the eve of entering childhood's play
In the green, blooming, glittering, sunny hall:
They throw into it all their bodily strength,
The soul is all attention keen and quick;
Courage, determination too, they need;
And who disturbs them is their greatest foe:
Naught so momentous as their feast of joy;
Nothing so holy as their holiday:
And what the flowers, and what the trees, and what
A shadow on the greensward mean for them,
That none could ever say; none could translate
The words a mother whispers to her child:
"Ah! *whom* I have in thee, there's no man knows,
And who thou art, none can express to me!"
No lovelier play of God's than this our life,
So simple, of so few ingredients;
Of *coming*, growing, wooing, marriage-making,
Baptismal festivals, and every spring
Tending the garden and arranging crops,
Keeping the house in order, reaping, resting;
In winter thinking fondly of old times;
From year to year growing older; being old;
And then at last to bury, and be buried; —
That is so entertaining, innocent,
To the pure, true and innocent childlike soul,
So healthful to the body, to the mind
So rich in lore and profit thousand-fold,
That none could ever have conceived a play
That would demand of man more *watchfulness*

And animate and strengthen courage more,
Fill the whole soul with growing interest
And make one weary for a good sound sleep —
In open air beneath the golden stars !

Only the man who by a sad mistake
Has forfeited all this, who must look on
Alone and with morose and crabbed mind,
Is shunned by all that in their gayety
And joy forget themselves — forget him too —
He only has no comfort day or night.
He looks upon the sad, deserted play-ground —
Old earth, — with lonely, melancholy gaze !
And unappeased his soul within him pines
For weary longing, yet with *longing filled* —
Fulness of rapture in the spell-bound heart.

PROVIDENCE ARRAIGNED.

"THE spirit is charmed, infused, into the world,
Grown into it, and never can be free,
While yet a breath, a spark is left of it.
And all, all spirits, all the lesser beings,
Man on the earth, the others on the stars,
Have all of them as hard a time as he
To live and bear the burden of the world.
They have if possible a harder lot
Than he : Birth and all life's vicissitudes,
And finally to meet and live through death.
A great by no means enviable play,
The master-piece, the eternal tragedy,
Given on rehearsal by the manager,
Before no public, no dramatic judge,
At his own cost, out on the world's broad stage
As quietly as in the stillest depths
Of the remotest woods exhibited
To the blue spaces of the empty heaven. —
I sicken ! I, too, am a player here
Since yesterday and for a few days more.
And were I but the only one ! Had I
No fellow-players ! — Were there none I loved !
Then would I sleep sound as the stolid rock

And blissful as the wave beneath the moon." —
Such are thy words, poor friend! and thy complaint
Is bitterer than thy *words. Thy wife lies sick. . .*
Thou fearest that she may return again
The way of spirits, and her lovely form
Melt in the undistinguishable element.
Be of good cheer! Muster that courage now
Which in the hour of play thou didst not need,
No, but where each one day has need of it
(Even he who gayly swam the wave of life
Wafted along in peace by fortune's breeze) —
In the stern hour, the great and holy time
Of the immensely great and ancient soul!
The ancient men have nowhere said to us
One word of our own true, eternal life,
A few words only have they left to us
Of the great Hallelujah; they have proved
Nothing; have only fancied, only dreamed
What other dreamers in their turn should dream.
There is no hold, no ground for confidence.
The solace must proceed from man's own soul,
Our own existence is our only stay.
Of old-imagined wisdom naught is left,
Yet it has clearly dawned in us at last: —
The spiritual lives, and thou too art
The spirit, the self-same spirit, that lives and moves
And stirs with joy through all the universe,
That lives forever and can live with joy.
Only let every shape be lightly worn!
Each live his life out in calm confidence!

Each one, his life completed, be content,
And satisfied to meet a tranquil death!
Never too soon! untimely death is woe,
A breach of life; life breaks in two with pain!
Pain seizes on the great Eternal Spirit,
Who forfeits and for naught a form of his, —
And this same pain the *sufferer* must bear,
The *dying man*, and calls it misery, wrong!
It burns the loving ones, who gather round
The sick man and the dying man; they call
Him wretched and *themselves — now*, for this once,
And through each coming hour, forevermore.
It was a singular, unnatural woe!
And if it is repeated myriad times
In others, then are *all* as signally
Wretched in this their little day of earth.
The dying has no solace left him then,
None other have survivors left than this:
To teach men — Harmony with God; to live
In harmony with Element and Spirit.
So the bare doctrine of the earthly life
Became the very highest spirit-lore,
And of none other is there need, in this
Or any future world, — than everywhere
To live in pure and glad tranquillity.
So lives he in eternal blessedness,
So dwells the spirit calmly in his world
Spell-bound, and more and more grows into it,
While yet a breath, a spark remains in him;
Yet is this breath as tranquil as a child's
Or an old man's who sinks bowed down with age.

And seems it still a wonder : mark it well !
Live it and learn it by experience !
It is so *still*, transpires so still in thee.
And if the spirit is in itself content,
What can it suffer ? what can grieve it more ?
And though it had to walk through flaming fires,
Or over red-hot iron with naked feet,
What harm, what grief could thereby come to it,
If once it knew the magic recipe :
Touched by no breath of all the flaming fire,
Across the glowing iron to walk its way,
Through terrors which to it no terrors are,
At which it only smiles, nay, counts them joys.
But lo ! the spirit has this magic spell :
'Tis, *its own self*, the inviolable life,
The deep repose, the inalienable bliss !

Now go back to thy home more tranquilly,
And with the eyes of God behold hereafter
Whate'er may happen. *But there's naught so bad*
As it appears ! Beginnings are not ends.
Always to fear the worst were something great
Didst thou not *fear* it. Danger 'tis that brings
The coward courage. Courage makes men free,
And freedom clears the soul ; clearness of sight
Brings us the needed help, and help in turn
Brings health to us, and love, and joy in love.

MAN'S GRIEF AND MOTHER'S LOVE.

DRIVEN to and fro by speechless restlessness,
Yonder I see a man, now hurrying on,
Now stopping suddenly, as lost in thought;
He flings himself face downward on the grass,
He stretches out his arms to heaven for help,
Then lets them fall as one who sinks to sleep.
Now he starts up again, and through the brake,
Strides to an overhanging precipice.
I see him plainly, see his pallid face,
I hear his voice, as the poor man complains:
"Now hear me, O thou sun, and mark my words;
I say to thee, I have as yet a wife,
My children, too, have still a mother, while
Thou standest in thy place to-day in heaven!
And when thou diest, they and I, perhaps,
Shall see her too — irrevocably — sink,
And her eye close never to look again,
Like thine, a cheering sunrise on the world.
To thee I tell my tale of grief and woe,
For I, I know no throne of God; or where,
Or whether, He in yonder heaven sits throned;
Or, if in the wide universe He has
A throne, I cannot tell the way to it:

I have no wings, and had I, they would fail,
Before I reached Him : heart and strength would fail.
And should I haply come and kneel before Him
What could I stammer out ! . . . What would He say,
Should I demand of Him to wipe out Death,
Death from His universe ? Would it not be
As if one begged Him to annihilate
The universe itself? Bade Him enact
The cruel tyrant to the old-time dead,
Myriads whom He already had let die —
Nay, should He, for my sake, extinguish death,
I must, from pity for the wretches all
(Who, by an unjust doom, had suffered it,
If I were not to suffer it as well)
I must needs beg Him not to spare myself,
Nay more, and even to send the stroke of death
To her, alas ! my wife, — whose eyes must close
In this bright sun to open nevermore !
So justified I feel, so justly grieved.
Nay, righteousness itself I see is naught,
And is, like Love itself, a grief to men !
And so my wishes die within my breast,
The thoughts all take their flight from out my soul —
O sun, with thy great look make me, too, strong,
Thou that hast seen already millions die,
That lookest all around on trillion graves
Yet never in despair hast rushed from heaven,
Nay, still shone on, and smiled with friendly ray.
Three ways are open to me, wretched one : —
I care for *naught!* cast all away from me,

I cease to love ; ah ! I have loved so long,
And felt so long the bliss of being loved —
And now, with love, is all my sorrow gone ;
The dying one, she had done naught to me,
I breathe a blessing on her harmless soul.
Nor am I wroth with death, nor him who has
Death in his pay, for bitter daily wage ! —
Yet if the memory of blissful love
Torment thee, and through all thy waking hours
And nightly dreams the world afflicts thy soul,
Then weep and wail, and never dry thy eyes,
And pine away in speechless, holy woe ;
So ends thy grief — and thou and life are quits. —
For a *third* remedy — forget ! forget !
Console thee with another woman's hand —
On her soft bosom rest thy tear-worn face — "

'Twas the last word I heard, for suddenly
He flung himself *with horror* from the steep,
Before my cry, my foot, my hand could reach him.
I found him dead below. I called to aid
A peasant, and we bore him tenderly
Home to his poor sick wife ; she heard me tell
How he had loved her, her and her alone.
Oh what a shriek of agony was hers !
Then with a passionate cry she clasped her children all
And found her only balm in — mother's love.

COMING HOME FROM THE BURIAL.

FAR worse than in a ghostly, ghastly tale
At which thy hair in childhood stood on end
And tears rushed to thy eyes — far worse it fares
With thee, whom death has robbed of darling ones —
The tale thou canst believe, or not believe;
The deeds of horror thou hast never known,
And no one else has seen them with his eyes,
That he might testify and swear to all
The things his senses witnessed, how soe'er
Incomprehensible a miracle.
But thou, poor man, hast seen with thine own eyes
The cold and cruel miracles, fulfilled
By an invisible and cruel Power,
Whom thou dost modestly call only *Death.*
But every master answers for his man.
Yet now have both of them appeared to thee,
Though only in their horrible, monstrous *work*,
All the more monstrous: in *thy loved one's* form!
Thou, watcher, wide awake, with shuddering hand
Thyself could'st touch the dead! Bones of the dead,
Dust of the dead in their old sepulchre:
Dust of thy father, and thy mother's dust.
Thou sawest the sun shine on the ghastly place,
The old familiar sun, thy childhood's sun!
Thou sawest the earth bloom round it with her flowers,
The false, deceitful mother — childhood's earth!

And now the awful gloom enshrouds her form . . .
They loosen from her head the flowing hair,
At their cold touch her arms, her feet drop off,
The beauteous eyes, like great and lustrous gems
Out from the sockets cruel fingers steal,
And roll her fleshless head upon her lap.

"This is no fancy—*this is naked truth!*
This is no fable, no — *this is the world!*
And the torn heart, *that is thy very self;*
This horrible sensation *is thy soul*,
And this great child awaked out of the world
Of legendary wonders, who rejects
With detestation, scorn and impotent rage
This foul and most malignant sorcery
And yet beholds and long must witness it,
Till it shall seize him too —*that is a man*,
And this grim nightmare dream of man is thou,
Thou that hast gazed thy fill on Deity.
And never shall a future make that good
Nor ever from thy soul efface again
What has befallen thee here in her thou lov'st,
As truly as the world exists, be *that*
Whate'er it may: — a veritable dream,
A noonday sleep, a show, an empty nothing,
A winter storm to an eternal spring — "

So say'st thou, staggering backward from the grave,
And all thou say'st is true — *to thee to-day!*
It has been and it will be o'er and o'er.
Yet learn by this with free and fearless heart

To entertain the great and cheering thought:
Not all that happened before witnesses,
By actual witnesses seen, heard, believed,
Recorded — even could men believe it too —
Not even all *that* is therefore made out true.
Nay, it may haply be the thing that's *false*
In man and word, to be cast out as false.
The truth dwells in thy soul and there alone!
The meaning of the world is in thy heart!
Intelligence, that only makes things true! —
How deeply, how profoundly thou, poor man,
Wilt have to understand and grasp the world,
Ere thou canst *calmly* recognize such horrors,
Canst breathe a *blessing* on the dead and Death,
Nay, feel a pleasure in the "hellish work"
As now it seems to thy woe-tortured heart!

Yet thou wilt bless it, thou must bless it, if
Thou art a man; and now thou art a man!
The meaning of the world is in thy soul.
And is not then thy soul the Spirit of God —
Which with the Universe and thee is one?
And now if that wise Spirit should say to thee:
"What can no longer live must simply die.
Begrudge not death to her who goes to rest
From life's hard burden, nay, enjoy that rest
Thyself; then thou hast loved her, lov'st her still."

"— But was it needful then, the early death?
And the hard life? — That is another thing." —
Search out that too, and thou shalt find the truth.

The present generation must needs bow,
Must even bow despairingly its neck
Beneath the yoke of that necessity
Which ignorance alone has laid upon it,
That cannot comprehend the laws, nor yet
The scope and spirit of the universe;
Whence knowledge only by degrees sets free,
The knowledge and fulfilment of the laws
Of the universe and its indwelling Spirit
Which, as its guide, dwells in the very heart.
Man's future also lies in man's own hand,
For God's own Spirit is man in man's domain.

"— And yet my dear, dead love is lost to me,
And holy wrath consumes me unto death! — "

It is the very wrath of the good Spirit,
It is naught else than goodness, love itself.

"— And yet my dear, dead love is lost to me,
And human woe is God's own Spirit's woe,
Felt for man's sake and shared in man's poor heart.
For naught else is, indeed, and lives, but God."

O man, then bear it worthily, divinely,
'Tis only life thou bearest, and the soul!
And therefrom is no living man released,
And no dead man through all eternity!

MAN CAN DO HIS PART.

THAT gainsay not, — *that* thou thyself hast seen ;
With tears of admiration and with awe
And mute astonishment thine eyes have seen —
Deny it not : There is a spirit in man
That *can* depart in peace ; calm as a child ;
Serenely as a God ; sated with life :
So glad to see an end of earthly life,
That to take leave forever of the earth,
Of house and children, while the sun shall run
His long, long race — *is but a shadowy*
Emotion ; a light waving of the hand,
And hardly more than a sweet, holy smile —
And in a smile the soul has passed away.
And thou who hast beheld it, thou whose heart
Was broken at such God-like peacefulness,
Such superhuman, sweet serenity . . .
Oh deem thou not such sweet serenity
Is superhuman — such a peacefulness
Is human weakness ! Nay, see clearly this :
With what exalted, God-like freedom God
Lived in His human image here on earth !
How too His very death : is holy life,
The silver glance upon His own still life.

And oh! do thou prize high the human form!
Esteem it blessed in its sweet repose,
That it can say with tranquil sense of truth:
In morning's holy dawn *my end* shall come."
And in the holy dawning comes the end,
The true end of the human form. *That* ends, —
But not the peace, which deep within itself
Shut up the human heart, and took to itself
The key, as if it were a coffin-key.
And when so cleanly one has closed his life,
And now reposes in such godlike peace,
Oh not with tears of *bitter wrath* bewail
The life, the leave-taking of such a one!
No, but with tears of *heavenly wonderment*
Which holy awe forces from earthly eyes!
And follow not with groans the smiling form
Into the vault that hides it from thy sight,
No, full of warm devotion, burning love,
Sigh after it into that holy heaven,
Whence it came forth and whither it returned,
Even though its *life* had never been before,
And though itself were all dissolved therein.
For what men name the Past is a great realm
Like the great Future, only stiller, fairer!

TO THE WIDOWER.

YES, all the dead are canonized ; thy dead,
She too is now exalted to a saint,
The lofty, unattainable, divine
Image, which nevermore thy hand may touch !
And scarce thy thought may follow her from far
As with an angel's all too feeble wing.
Aye ! in the dead all miracles come true !
There is not one that remains unfulfilled
In them, and every aureole crowns their head !
And greater wonders shall thine eyes behold . . .
When the loved form, so near thee in the flesh,
So long illumined by the self-same sun
With thee, that spoke with thee so tenderly —
Mysteriously is wafted from thine arms,
Is borne away as a transfigured saint,
Away, aloft, through all the heavenly spaces —
And thou, thou lingerest here on the same earth !
Still pluckest fruit from off the self-same trees
From which she ate, still claspest to thy breast
The very children she once bore to thee,
Whom with her love she nurtured and trained up
To stand around thee like the forms of gods,
And weep with thee for the sweet, gracious spirit

Which in the heavenly form of loveliness
Their mother was even here upon the earth.
Then shall the ground waver beneath thy feet,
The solid earth shall seem to thee a skiff
That sways to break its moorings and launch forth
Out on the world-wide sea, its anchor weighed
And all its white sails flapping to the breeze!
But look abroad . . . those are the clouds there still,
The solid earth still stands beneath thy feet
In its accustomed place, and thou, thou still,
Art standing here by the familiar trees,
Thy children round thee, clinging to thy hands,
In long, deep yearning inexpressible!
The world has now become to thee a clear,
True miracle, and with thy human heart
Must thou endure the burden sore of heaven,
The holy load that killing, quickens thee,
That weighs thee down, — yet gives thee angel-wings,
Thou man of earth full of the spirit of heaven!
How one who stood before thee in the flesh
Could from such sunshine vanish out of sight? . . .
That by the grave thou sadly ponderest,
And over thee the rainbow fades and dies.
But take, now, wonder for wonder! joy for grief!
How one, who was so long invisible,
In such a sunshine can at length *appear?*
That by the infant's cradle ponder thou
With glad amazement! Lo! for the first time
He opens to the light his wondering eyes!

THE DEAD SON.

THE dead of night! the stars are bright in heaven.
A father sits and watches by his dead,
The darling only son of his old age.
He turns his eyes from him, away, on high,
And cries, after long silence, to those lights :
" *Ye are worth somewhat*, ye stars ! Not many thousand
Times more are *ye* worth than the earth here is,
Because thousands of times more numerous, —
No, worth so many thousand times the *less*,
As ye are numerous, innumerable —
Like spiders, worth the less, the more ye count —
Like snakes, worth less, the more there are of you —
Like poison balls, the more, the terribler !
Even to a God will I resign the task
To sit and watch like me, beside a son,
Whom He, like me, could never more awake,
Whom with this sweet and gracious countenance,
Incarnated in this angelic form,
Neither in time nor in eternity
Long as He lives shall He behold again.
He too, like me, would swoon away ; would dream,
Would sleep a death-like sleep beside his dead,
Then would he wake, would look away from him,
Away, aloft, and say to those high lights :
" Ye are worth somewhat, O ye stars ! all, all

More, — vastly, fearfully, — than this one here !
Only one fault have I committed : — this,
This only — that I ever made the world !
No one but this ! yet this one is enough,
More than enough to break my ancient heart.
It is no dream — he lies before me here
So plainly visible, so palpable,
With the calm, stony look that dead men wear —
Dead nevertheless ! and I alive withal !
Alive, and with my old love-burdened heart.
At love's door must be laid, and there alone,
The blame of all this sorrow for the dead,
This bitter anguish over dying beds,
Wringing of hands and sobs from breaking hearts ;
Love only sheds these tears ! Love only mourns,
Will mourn, refusing to be comforted ;
The tears of love let no man think to dry !
That I bestowed on man *Love unto death* . . .
Oh ! what a crime ! how infinitely hard,
Inexpiable, if the loving one
Might not himself die of his very grief
Over his dead, his dying, all dear forms
Whom death has swallowed up ! But now, indeed,
A mortal, dying, may forgive me still !"

So, the sad father in his musing thought
Would God, in his place, sorrow for His son.
But other help was yet appointed him :
His wits that carried him *beyond* himself
Had left him utterly *beside* himself . . .

He dreamed that he was God, the aged father,
And all untouched was now his aged heart
By that dead man whom he no longer knew . . .
Whose fate concerned him not, was not enough
To draw a tear or even a sigh from him,
When now the dead was carried to the tomb!
Whom now he not so much as wished to see . . .
Still less to meet him in another world.

To his amazement, he himself grew sick,
To his amazement died: he closed his eyes,
And raised his hand, as praying *to himself.*
That man I knew — I saw — amazed I saw,
And for a moral spoke to you of him;
For pain and death are only for Love's sake,
They would not be, if Love itself were not,
And whoso loves, to him they too are Love
And nothing else! Only that Love may be
No mere delusion, no mere nightmare-dream
Or dream of bliss, from which a man shall wake, —
Ah! this is why death is, and sorrow is,
And dust and ashes shall be for all time,
As truly as this whole great universe,
Truly as God is, who is all Love!
Not to *create* Love, is this world made fleeting;
Were there no world at all, Love would exist,
But it would slumber; *now it wakes, it glows,*
It loves, *yet sees no longer what it saw.*
It is the blest blind spirit of the world,
Which, all unseen itself, loves on forever.

JOB: OR MAN.

WHERE is the man, has lived his eighty years,
And is not weary at his heart of life?
So tired and sated that he dreads no more
To lay his meagre hands and fainting feet
And breast and head down in the darksome grave?
The soul shall vex and harass him no more;
The sun may go his way, and Spring with him,
To join the rest of all those old dead suns,
That shall henceforth on life's long pilgrimage,
By him, gone hence, be willingly forgot,
And he be glad that they are dead to him,
As he is glad that he is dead to them.
The dim and purblind eyes shall see no more,
The deaf ears hear no more, . . . he is not left
To wait out all the years of lapsing time,
As children wait to see the stream run out,
And weave them wreaths: till nightfall calls them home
To sleep away their idle, childish wish.
Ay, and how many, many weary youths
Would be content, yea, glad to lay them down
To their last sleep; and not to rise again
To-morrow morn or any morning more.

So very slenderly do men esteem,
Yea, even despise this world—so deemest thou.

Men do not think thus lightly of the world,
Do not despise, not even deprecate it:
The universal spirit is content
With human life, then most content — enough
To give up soul and body peacefully,
When it so willingly will part forever! *
That is the comfort that the spirit needs
On its long, long, eternally long flight,
That all who here have rightly lived life out,
Shall leave behind with joy the shell of earth;
Else life would be God's highest punishment . . .
Upon its road a thousand hells would blaze
Forever breathing out new poisonous flames.
But blest by life, the spirit *once for all*
Is satisfied with his eternal bliss, —
Just as a child that on its mother's breast
Has drunk its fill so eagerly, that now
Its eyes stand staring open, and its lips
Tremble — like those of the worn-out old man;
And both of them sink down in *one* sweet sleep —
The child to wake again to-morrow morn,
Upon its mother's bosom, still a child;
The soul of the old man — as child again,
To wake upon a greater mother's breast,
There spell-bound by the charm of blissful love.

* Does this throw light on a couplet of Gœthe's:
"*Thou wouldst be pleased with death?* Then why with life
Makest thou always such a strife?" — (?) T.

THE GOOD GOD.

WHAT is the highest goodness of the spirit
But this — to be content with all the world?
First with itself to be content, and then
With the whole world's existence, and its own;
With both, just as they are, to be content.
Can, now, *self-will* attain contentedness?
Can holy *purpose:* saying, I will be so?
Can the mere dream: oh I will be content?
Joyous? Then joyless, if perchance the world
Should ever thwart it, or it thwart itself!
One only dreams while sleeping, not awake.
Truth is the only way to goodness, then,
Self-satisfaction with the universe,
If all that holds its place as true, allows
Yea even constrains the soul to be content.
For should the soul in this world find itself
Nailed like a very martyr to the cross,
Without the power to live or power to die . . .
Should find itself so fastened to this world,
Then could it rightfully bewail its being,
Nay, 'twould do well, to curse its very self,
In imprecation then *would be its strength:* —
It suffers wrong, is *better than its fate,*

And if the soul could not annihilate
Itself, forsake itself, and sink to naught,
One way were left: to hold fast *on* itself
With all *its might*, and only be as good
And fair and true as *it could ever be*,
As He Himself would be, and say to the world,
"Thou art not! Thou to me at least art naught;
Thou shalt be but the ship whereon I sail!
The flute through which I breathe my sorrows out!"
If neither the ship nor flute were worthless now,
If the whole voyage and all the songs were not
Quite miserable; if not blind and wretched
The eternal and unborn abortion lay
In utter darkness, moaning after death!
And thousands of sick men do wish for death,
Even at the price: never to rise again —
They lived, and now they die; for *dying weans*,
By its pangs, from all desire of further life,
The unhappy ones who *here*, irreparably
And irretrievably, *have suffered it* —
Even though starving ones with all their children
Were buried in a mountain full of bread!
They have, without one word, sent hope back home.

Goodness is then the very ground of life,
Even if life did not need it for its aim;
For in the coffin it would come too late,
Like morning's meal — after the fall of night.
Hard, hard it is even for one to be right good;
Even to *see* suffering, rends the good man's heart!

Only the happy are at last the good;
Only into a happy race, the king
Pours joyfully his will and heart and mind;
Man's kingdom is the whole wide universe!
That is his fair and gracious fatherland!
There shall no dust lie on a blade of grass,
No rose-leaf rest upon a dead man's lips!

GOODNESS.

WHAT has not issued from a man's own will,
That which without his will has come to pass,
Without his toil or skill, yea even without
His knowledge, — *that*, one says, " befalls " a man,
Is something " done to him," " takes place " with him.
And so the child is born without his will;
Without his will he lives; he sees, he hears;
Grows day by day, at last is full-grown man.
He sees not to it that his heart shall beat;
He has not so contrived it that his blood
Should journey through his veins and home again
Faithfully from its circuit to his heart —
Still less is it his will the sun should rise,
The moon and all the stars; that spring should be;
That so much as a blade of grass should shoot;
A tree should blossom, or a fruit grow ripe! —
All this goes on around him, this is done
To him in this his nearer body-world —
And round about him in the earth and heavens,
Just as his body is a work going on.
As quietly, without his thinking of it,
His bride befalls him, sweet and gracious presence;
His wife befalls him now; his children, too,
Sweetly befall him, and the years of life,
Without his toil or skill, without his thought . . .

Till age and death befall him, too, at last.
All that he has to do with all is this:
Truly to *feel* and clearly *think* it all. —
The inner life — that is the work of man,
His holy business — so indeed it seems!
Yet what he ever is to feel and think
This plainly is prefigured to him, too,
By living forms made manifest to him;
In pictures, as to children, clearly shown.
How he shall feel and think — is this alone
Not something happening to him? done to him?
When not his body only makes a part
Of his experience, but the universe
Around him is itself lived by him too?
Each smallest cloud and every drop of rain,
And every flower and shadow of a flower? —
Nay, even the soul is something lived by him!
Life is breathed into him and out of him,
Him — his profound and very self: the spirit,
The universal spirit that lives all lives.
The spirit has power to give in its will
To all that happens round him and within him;
And if he has the wisdom to do this,
Then do we call him *good;* and even the spirit
Of the universe men therefore call the Good.
And "*goodness*" can to none mean or be more
Than this: as calmly to resign one's will
Into his own existence, life and lot,
As a child does into its growing frame,
Peacefully, as a tree into its shadow! —

TO THE WIDOW.

POOR wife, who standest bending o'er the grave,
To see the coffin slowly sink, and hear
The dull earth's dismal rattle on the lid,
O thou, thou art at thy most bitter hour!
Earth's type of woe, to suffocation full
Of deepest agony; thy bosom sobs;
The tears rush down in torrents from thine eyes —
Yes, from *thy* eyes indeed, — but ah, their source
Is the great fountain of the universe, —
The fount of Love; — yea, they gush forth from God.
God, only, sheds the tears that flow from thee,
For God is all of life, and all of love.
God only does all living and all loving,
Where life is, and where love; and only He
Is there, where sorrow is, Death and the grave.
Love — Life — Death — God hath not *invented* them,
He from eternity was Life itself,
And will be blissful life in love and death
While He abides — that is, eternally.
Thou gazest still into the grave which never
Is full, and shudderest to think that soon
That too will close, and this sad hour be gone!
That even man's yearning, too, is transitory.

Thou soul of God, look up, bethink thyself
Where — where, then, they have buried thy best friend!
"*Where?* — in the *earth*!" thy look disconsolate says.
But now, consider, then, — what is the earth?
The silver-dew, from all the ethereal virtues
Of heaven distilled, the holy, heavenly drop,
Precipitate of all the elements,
Aye, 'tis a tear of God, that from His eye,
Moistened with tender melancholy, fell.
And as the glistening drop of silver-dew
Out of the rose's cup exhales again,
So will, one day, the drop of earth exhale.
And, mourning wife, thy dead man's tranquil face
Is buried in the bosom of the heavens, —
Aye in God's hand — in the blest head of God —
Ineffably more sacred and secure
Than underneath a perishable shrine,
Though smoked with incense of a thousand years.
God is man's grave, and is his monument.
And if man must be buried and shall be,
Begrudge him not for holy sepulchre,
God's Spirit — the only holy, blessed one!
And in it thou too shalt one day find room.

God is man's grave — thou dear humanity!

THE BEGGAR-MAN.

LET thy great heart, I pray thee, be content,
Thy God-like heart, too good and all too large,
Beloved man! Set every thought at rest
About the future fate of yonder sun,
That roams through heaven above there like one lost,
Or of that starry flock that nightly strays,
As if it had no shepherd, through the skies.
They live, each one, their several, single lives,
And every life comes to a perfect end,
Even when it breaks off, goes down suddenly;
Each up to the last moment was divine.
How it shall fare, too, with the human race
One day, with all the women and the men,
The old men and the children numberless,
Who yet shall come, all on the self-same earth,
Pass over it and disappear again. . .
Make not thyself uneasy about that;
The million deaths will all pass by through time,
As lightly and as softly, as thy hand
Passes with gentle motion o'er thy eyes.
What troubles thee, that is not trouble, nay,
It is the blessedness, great and complete,
Thou feelest for all, to think that each of them

Shall feel it also, as thou feelest it;
That all shall yet be rich, as thou art rich,
In this great beauteous mansion full of dreams,
Where under heavy blossom-laden trees
The dead are softly carried to the grave;
Where by the side of graves and over them,
The mothers stand with infants on their breasts;
And where his dirge is sung even at the grave
Of the poor beggar-man, — then no word more
Is said of him, the sun tells nothing of him,
All knowledge of him perishes from earth;
And yet he daily came with hat in hand,
And begged and prayed, with his old withered face —
And thou, thou gavest him, and he gave thanks
And breathed a prayer, and thou too joinedst him
In praying for a higher, holier thing —
Which no one heard, no not the sun himself!
Each knows about himself; that is enough.
Each lived his life, and so, divinely lived.
Aye, let him rest! as rests the beggar-man,
So shall the world one day in blessed peace,
Nay, — even to-morrow! For all future time
Is nothing but one great to-morrow! nay
Who names *to-morrow* names eternity!

THE CAUSE OF DEATH.

THE cause of death is birth — and nothing more,
And nothing other than a holy one;
For what has once begun, must end again.
So is there only a good ground for death:
The holy spirit's yearning to be man!
'Tis clear: to have been born in *no disgrace*
Nor *any punishment* for a human child,
That had not been, is just beginning *man*,
To finish him again, when life shall end.
To inherit *sin* is quite impossible,
And if one should entail it, 'twere a shame.
For sin is something each who does it does
For himself alone; for every soul is free;
And taking sin away is impossible.
Each has a burden of his own to bear —
And none can take my *seeing* to himself,
And none can take my *hearing* to himself,
And hear twice over and see twice at once,
And none can take himself the pangs I feel
From burning coals I carry in my hands.
Naught can take sin away but to *know this:*
That error is the school-time of right-doing;
That every one is good as God's own Spirit.

That no one sins, but freely *struggles on*
(Oft-times through direful deeds) to a God-like sense
Of his own being and a God-like life.
A father's poverty one *may* inherit,
A mother's woe, their very blood, their fate,
Their evil passions, and their enemies,
Their friends no less, and their good works as well,
The *fruits* of sin, — but never sin itself.
But *death* is not one of the bitterest fruits;
Early, too early death may only strike
The child of parents who have gone astray.
But not parental only, no, all faults
Of all mankind from immemorial time
Must ever weigh upon each race and child;
For no one lives from earliest childhood up
Who has not reproduced, *inherited*,
And as a man enjoyed all good, that men
Have ever brought to pass in olden time;
And no one lives from tenderest childhood up,
Without experiencing, *inheriting*,
And expiating all evil as a man
That overcame his people in old time.
So we are suffering to this very day
For the old superstitions of the *Jews*
And for their hope — we Germans, who, in sooth,
Have never cherished fear or hope of theirs —
And of the *old Greek* child's-play of the Gods,
Their priests and priestesses and their Pythia
Who still transforms herself into a boy;
And for the *ancient Roman's* lust of sway,

Although twice shattered on the German rock.
And all the nonsense, all the slavery
The *mind* has ever suffered, 'tis our task
To do away, and feel as truth of God
The mighty universe, and clearly feel
Its spirit as our own. — Yea that is what
Shall to all nations be our legacy.
The entire human race is one, one man,
One spirit dwells diffused throughout the whole,
And in the human form the spirit gains
A *longer* and a *happier* life indeed, —
But not *exemption evermore from death!*
For all the race of innocent flowers — die!
The woods in all their innocence — they die!
The ever innocent tribes of fishes — die!
Yea even the holy stars themselves too — die,
They that have never even harmed a child!
That never did a wrong, but only lived!
The spirit's "mind to live" and "mind to die,"
That is the only cause of death! 'tis God!
And blesseder or fairer know I none!
And none more devilish than revenge and sin!
Poor Jew, thou that inventedst Paradise,
Farewell! Farewell to thee forevermore!
I let thee go, for God and all the heavens!
The death of the whole human family
Confounded thee; fain would'st thou make it clear;
And as the death of such a multitude
Of innocent beings to thy mind appeared
The horridest of all barbarities,

Thou wouldst derive it (thought of horror fit
To strike men dumb!) not from a Father — no,
But from a tyrant of such monstrous type
As thou didst need to serve thy desperate turn;
A Father, savage tribes could scarcely match!
'Twas his delight to *tempt* and to seduce
His host of children to a tree of Life!
Instead of murdering them all outright.
Never have been created mortal men;
No living pair was ever cursed with death;
Immortally in ever-changing forms
Heaven's blessed spirit lives its proper life.
And everlasting all are that do live,
Or ever shall live. That is the redemption,
Thine own redemption too, poor, trembling Jew!

LIVE AS AN IMMORTAL.

WHEN a young mother and a blooming bride
Mourns her dead child — when from the lover's arms
Death tears his darling — from the man his wife —
Then do they weep and sorrow piteously.
But why then do they weep and sorrow so?
One thing is sure, they would not weep and wail
If they had courage to *die with* them. Then
They would be calm and restful as their dead.

. . . And wherefore have they not the strength to die?
They count this life the highest, sweetest good,
Which they would fain possess and cling to still,
(Theirs is not then the very highest love)
And which the dead have lost, who now no more
Enjoy the love of dear ones left behind,
As they, the living, do henceforth no more
The love of their departed ones — this pains,
This crushes, kills their courage . . . *and they weep.*

But mark! men never weep these coward tears
In heat of battle; weep not for their dead,
Nor for their death shed tears even when they fall —
They *know*, 'tis true, no higher thing than life,

— *Only they quite forget to think of life;*
They seek for something as immortal men,
Quite fearless, reckless, — so they do not weep;
They neither weep nor wail; they fight, they conquer.

Whoso will conquer must forget his life,
And, as immortal, battle joyously.
The daring man who leaps into the sea
To snatch a drowning woman from the waves,
Lives in that moment only, wholly; not
For yesterday he lives, not for to-morrow;
Things great and good and beautiful and brave,
Are done, each one of them, beyond all time;
And he who feels himself apart from time
Feels himself quite beyond the reach of power;
This only makes man free and glorious.
Nor is it among men so rare a thing —
This feeling of the eternal; 'tis possessed
By all who ever look into man's eye,
Who look upon a loved one's radiant face
And hear the true and tender words of love.
And fearless would defenceless children be
Before the mightiest tyrant, did they *not*
Think of the morrow! Living in the moment,
That makes men Gods. Yes; in the moment — *now* —
All virtue, all things great, appear to thee;
The sun pours through the moment all his fire —
And the day's hirelings are the evening's slaves,
Whom over night the morning binds anew!

PERFECTION.

WILT thou charge God himself, as Death, as murderer,
When the ripe apples fall from off the tree?
Pluck'st thou not the ripe clusters off, thyself,
And do not the fair, innocent children pluck
Ripe strawberries with unstained consciences?
"They are perfected!" Let the holy truth
Whisper the magic word, to give thee peace,
And even to cheer thee, when thou seest the tribes
Now coming to perfection, perfect now,
And gone like all the fair things once perfected.
Perfection has itself no further aim,
It is the end of all things, pure and clear,
The Heavenly consummated on the earth.
Nothing comes after it, — when once the rose
Moulders, and man's dissolution comes,
Which is no more, which leads to nothing higher,
Nor can lead. 'Tis to vanish out of sight,
Become invisible, yea, cease to be,
And give God back the spirit and the stuff
For the sublime completion of new works.
For all must be completed that begins;
The spirit, too, must as man complete itself.
Thou marrest, man, thy God's own holy life,

Disturb'st the holy blessed perfecting,
When thou dost violate thy human form,
So that the holy blossom it contains
Never blooms out nor ripens into fruit.
For know thou this: that the divine perfection,
(And even the strawberry and the purple grape,
The very violet also, has its own
Divine perfection, fair as perfect man's) —
Yea know thou this: that the divine perfection
Is bliss; the *struggle* for completion is,
Itself, before it comes, and while it lasts,
Not afterward, when the completion's past.
Even so the mother feels in her new-born
And perfect infant, the divine perfection,
And bathes it with still tears of ecstasy;
She faints with bliss; her child cries *in her stead;*
Perfect, complete, *as child*, which will, as *man*,
Henceforth perfect itself through coming life,
With help of all the influence and power
And blessing of the earth and sun and sky,
The magic virtue of the starry heaven
That shall thrill through him to the very heart,
Through all his holy frame; shall call to him . . .
From all old days of God in a mild voice,
Laden with fragrances of happy hours,
As airs waft up from vales the breath of spring.
And as the mother o'er her child, so thousands
Rejoice over the perfecting of thousands —
Thousands who filled while living here on earth
Complete existence; even as these rejoiced

While here, in the perfected work of art,
The picture or the statue born complete,
Out of the marble ; or the master-piece
Of poet, or the singer's witching strain.
Yet every thing that is complete, is dead
And gone, as any thing beneath these heavens
Can be, whether it be the frame of man,
The spirit, even the life, the past — which also
Is gone, softly and sweetly borne away
On every morn's and every evening's wings . . .
Yet to the spirit that has *lived it once*,
A sure possession for Eternity !
Just as a master of his art lives on
To ripe old age and still perfects himself,
Who in his life wrought many a perfect work,
Which came from him, a portion of his life —
Nay which he was himself, and *which he is*,
Like that great Master of all things, which here
Are called the works of God . . . *and are his life :*
The fruits of that gigantically great
Immortal orange-tree which evermore
Stands full of blossoms, full of little grafts,
And full of glowing, ripe and golden fruit —
The tree of life — not the great poison tree.

SORROW.

THE sorest sufferings grief alone can heal
And make the miserable endurable, —
Yea, sweet and precious, — till the noble man
Would scarce exchange it for another good.
Grief is not powerless, weak, it nourishes
A mighty strength ; for sorrow none can feel
But he who has his heart filled full with love,
Beauty, truth, freedom and fidelity.
Only as these are precious goods to him,
Living realities and energies,
So only can great sorrow too be his, —
As these are stirred within him mightily
And shed a burning and a shining light.
Her sorrow makes the dead child more and more
Dear to the mother's eyes, felt more and more
As something indispensable to her life,
The more it throbs, and burns and pains her heart.
Sorrow is next of kin to joy itself,
Health, honor, freedom and the sense of right:
It is itself all they that feel themselves
Vitally wounded ; sorrow for disgrace
Is wounded honor ; sorrow for untruth,
Love disappointed ; were not *they* aggrieved,

The heavenly ones, who then could suffer? None
Could without these feel sorrow, none complain.
Then all were well and all things right and good,
Naught could be lost from life, nor could there be
Aught to desire; for who could miss aught dear,
If he had ne'er possessed a precious thing?
Knew nothing noble — were not so himself?
Honor thou every one's pure sorrow, then,
As his most holy temple, as his soul!
Honor another's sorrow as thine own!
The husband's from whom death has snatched his wife;
The wife's, who lays her husband in the grave;
The little roe's that moans o'er a dead dam;
The starling's, robbed of his dear little ones;
The bee's, whose hive the bear has broken through.
Respect it, oh respect a people's grief,
That cries for rescue from the oppressor's sway,
Whose tyrannous hand has grasped its highest good,
And keeps them barren to himself and all.
But the most cruel of all men is he
Who shuts the mouths of holy sufferers
Against complaint, murders the soul's desire.
— To stifle righteous wishes is a murder,
A fouler one than killing living men,
Who have a rest and refuge in the grave.
He drives out love and God-like sentiment,
Scourges the sorely wounded till they bleed;
He tortures dying men with burning tongs;
He tears the tongues of angels from their mouths.
Be tranquil, O my brothers; for your grief

Has to the most high God a sacred worth :
He gave to sorrow to be *dumb*, and so,
And only so, to do its utmost work
With men, who then can rescue, help and save ;
He gave the least as well as greatest grief
Intangibility, that so no tyrant,
No villain should discern, should rob man of it ;
That by its very magnitude and might
The sufferings of all men it should heal,
Break through for mortal men the gates of heaven
That they might freely enter in to God ;
That it might stir their love into a blaze,
That it might superfuse them with its grace,
And fill their hearts with all its energy.
Sorrow is terrible — when it descends,
Girded and harnessed with an angel's strength,
Transformed to an avenger, God's own arm,
Raised above every sorrow of its own,
Yet flying to relieve the suffering worm,
Not to say, all its living, kindred souls !

Grief is a coming home to the old Heaven,
And thus it heals all human suffering
With bitter wailings and with thousand tears.

BE CONTENT WITH THY LOT.

ONE thing be warned against, my brother man:
Take not the griefs of all men for thy grief!
Abstain from heaping up, nay, dragging down,
The fates of all upon thy single head,
As a child pulls the boiling kettle down
Upon his head and scalds himself to death.
Of *all* misfortunes only one hits one,
At most, and rarely two: of *all* the host
Of countless maladies, each one attacks
But one, proves fatal but to him alone:
Not all the goods of earth can fall to one;
Each one must find some flowers along his path,
And though they should be only few and small
And common, such as grace the common road.
The dying and death of generations past
None feels and none remembers any more;
Only the death of dear ones stirs his heart
And harrows the friend's heart — that is enough!
Brings tears from out his eyes — and that's enough!
Yet neither grief nor floods of tears avail
To lift the poorest man to man's full bliss,
That he may live in manly dignity
In his majestic, beauteous, heavenly realm!

Even if it be our doom to *weep* and *wail*—
Even if renunciation sad and long
Is *part* and *parcel* of the life of man;
Perhaps makes up the sweetest, wholesomest
Part of man's life and gives it inmost worth
Bequeathed from the primeval world, from God,
And given to man, that he may be a man;
And without which he were no genuine man,
How rich soever and how prosperous;
How strong soever and unfortunate;—
Do not for that double, nay multiply
A thousand-fold thine own, thy proper grief!
See not thy lot repeated *on all stars*
In all the universe a million times!
See not up yonder, in those countless worlds,
Thousands of millions lying sick to death!
See not ten thousand suffering every hour,
Closing their eyes in death . . . see not the earth
Heaped o'er the grave and sodded with fresh green
And in the sunlight gleaming drearily!
Thou seest scarce aught, *save Death*, the all-destroyer,
Thou seest not *Life*, the inexhaustible!
Thou dost not see and feel thy living self!
And all thy dear ones, round about thee, glad,
Thou seest already as men doomed to death,
And so even now as scarcely living men;—
Not glowing in the fulness of their life,
In the fresh spirit of the living God;
Thou seest not the miracle of their sweet,
Serene, content, and beautiful existence.
Thine eyes have played thee false and made thee see

The universe as one vast charnel-house ;
The Spirit thou hast *dreamed* a murderer,
And God the great, only self-murderer !
Save for thine own thy love, and spend on them
Thy grief, thy pity and thy holy sighs !
Love to thine own, that only is no dream,
Sorrow and lamentation for thine own
Alone is true, alone will fill thy heart !
Only what thou canst truly, wholly feel,
Sincerely in thy bosom's sacred depths,
Is worthy and is right for thee to feel,
As pith and kernel of thy inmost life,
Its solid strength and noblest ornament !
Thus, only thus, thou dost not dissipate
Thy heart, but gatherest all its energies
Into a life worth living, made more sweet,
Sweetest of all, by sorrow's bitterness !
Let, then, thy little dwelling be to thee
The busy workshop, the divine abode,
Wherein transpires in full and heavenly truth
What anywhere and any time * takes place
And ever can take place. Then hast thou work,
Divine employment in the life and weal
Of those that God has given thee, hast enough
To fill thy soul, in a divine concern
For their misfortunes, aye even for their death !
And one thing more is given to man : 'tis this —
Though he should miss all private happiness —
Though he should have none but unfortunates,
Always and only sufferers in his house,

* In the German : *anywhen.*

He would have labor, sad and feverish toil,
Care urgent, constant, indispensable —
Yet even in sorrow love remains to him;
Sorrow itself shall by the magic power
Of kindly deeds be wondrously transformed,
Transfigured utterly *to love, itself,*
Through patient practice, ever ready help,
And cordial sweet reward of grateful looks;
So that good, anxious neighbors round about
Would have to bear him off with violence
And drag him with barbarity from his home
And his sick wife! And he with bitter moans,
Would die far off, because his dear ones now
Had him no more . . . no more his faithful love!
This is the human heart in all its fire
And courage on the day of life's great fight;
So simple, modest, and divine a feeling
Has *man*, and every one of *woman-kind;*
Whose only merit in her own eyes is
To make the father and the children glad;
Who, without any pride, dies of pure grief
That without *her*, her darlings will be sad,
Ah! will no more have *her!* — and so she sinks —
Her soul has passed into the heaven of love,
To power and glory and eternal life!
Hold, then, good brothers, only to *your own!*
Let each one cling to his own kith and kin,
Behold them live! and live for them alone!
So shall each heart and every home be blest,
A blessed, heavenly kingdom on the earth.

THE LONG NIGHT.

IN sleep thou hast but empty images
Of all the friends who ever lived with thee,
And have been torn from thee since childhood's years ;
Thy very mother is a shadowy shape :
Nay, all that round about thee live to-day,
All that goes on around thee far and near,
A thousand star-lights unperceived by thee,
The clear full moon up yonder in the night,
The child that lies there sleeping at thy side —
All these have but a phantom-life for thee,
They are not the expression — the express
Image they make upon thy soul, but only
The *impression* they have made upon thy heart,
Have left behind ; the feeling (nothing more)
With which thou ever hast felt, hast taken them in,
And now in silence still retainest them.
The whole world now is nothing else to thee
Than what thou dreamedst it in waking hours ;
The temples and the Gods are all to thee
Only a dream, thy dream ; powerless now
Are all of them, on thee and on thy soul :
The priest and lamb are both alike to thee,
And lamb and wolf are one, and sun and spark.

Thus art thou even now by night a spirit,
Exalted far above all mortal things,
And half of all thy lifetime thou art this ;
Thou hast existence without God or heaven,
So wholly without will and without blame,
Without belief or even superstition,
Or wishes, which by day lead men astray,
Which only serve by day, by day avail,
As light, again, serves only in the night.
In dream even love itself is naught to thee ;
The withered leaf then wrings out tears from thee !
Thy mother dies and gives thee not a pang !
A shining pebble is a great full moon.
Thy very child is a *strange* child to thee —
And in the night — explain it as thou wilt —
All the night long thou art but half of life,
The spirit in repose, calm, colorless ;
And as night evermore returns to thee,
No one can tell thee whether with the sun
Thou shalt arise to higher, better life,
Thyself be better, when thine eyes once more
Chain thee to busy day's vast circling stir,
Whence each successive night releases thee ;
And *even* the very best and wisest men,
The mightiest and the most aspiring kings,
They all are in the night what thou too art.
And every one of them night after night
Repeats it million ways one half his life —
O Death ! thou longer sleep ! thou long, long night !
How fair thou canst and wilt be ! how divine !

THE SUN-SICK.

[A PEGUAN EASTER SONG.*]

HOW will the great Somebody be amazed,
When He one day awakes from His long sleep—
And sees so many beauteous, God-like works
Wrought out and gloriously perfected,
Which He in His long sleep had thought upon,
While His old *sun-sickness* lay heavy on Him,
Whereof men call the short and fleeting share
That falls to them their "waking hours," their "life!"
How will the great Somebody be amazed
On waking from His drowsy sun-sickness!

That glorious resurrection would I share,
I surely in that festal joy shall join!
What is a rising from the grave, to that?—
A bitter memory of the ancient woe;
And bliss comes only with *release from woe!*
But thou hast all the world for recompense!

* The Peguans believe that God has gone to sleep in the world, and will not till a future day arise upon it.

THE COMPLAINT CLEARED UP.

WHEN thou behold'st how the old people mourn
And hear'st how with one voice they all complain
Who are for ever and for evermore,
Changed from young children into sad old men,
And breathe out imprecations on this life,
And curse the day that ever gave them birth,
And wish the sun and moon and all the stars
Were not and never had begun to be,
Rather than that they should so spend their days
In vanity, having naught of life but death —
Give them mild hearing then, yet understand
The meaning of their passionate, sore complaint;
This understand: It is not *life* they curse,
Nay, properly they imprecate not *death*
In any wise as their deliverer
From sorrow, or as only ending it;
This understand: they only rightly curse
This old, worn-out and good-for-nothing frame,
Which serves even God no living purpose more;
Wherefore He breaks it up and lets it die.
Note well: this plaint wrung from the human soul,
This wail from all humanity around,
Is mediately the wail of God Himself
And is the earnest of eternal life.
Then rather welcome it! it shall be hushed;
And all the young life in the universe
Has in its joy forgotten it again!
And thou forget it too, beloved soul!

OUR GOD.

GOD only lives, the ever busy force ;
And had there ever been a human spirit
That had, in man's form, lived eternally
So without God, as if itself a God,
And thereupon this man had one day died,
And nevermore henceforth could anywhere
Be found in all the boundless universe,
When he had once lived out his earthly day,
And done his work as man, and closed his eyes
Forever on the light of sun and moon —
Then would a man only have lost the man !
That man of an eternity gone by,
The second God, the self-subsistent man,
He would have had his going down, he would
Have forfeited his *future* — nothing more ;
Even as a blossom shaken from the tree
Loses its fruit ; and yet 'tis not the bud
Loses the fruit ; the tree, the garden does !
So, too, the man who has already lived
Half an eternity, would not have lost
His future, for when he was now no more,
There could be no one, no one left to cry
And make a moaning sound : " Ah, I am lost !
Woe ! I have lost myself." Not one ! Not one !
Nor could a God cry : " Thou art lost to me ! "
For not to Him this *no one* could belong.

And in like manner would it also be,
Had man been first created at his birth,
For at the great counter-creation: death,
He would have been extinguished and unmade,
Nay, would have been made *over* then forever,
Yet would he not have lost the future then,
The second half of his eternity,
For then there would be no one who could cry
And moan aloud: "Ah I have lost myself!"
God only, the great Gardener, He must say:
"Lo! I have lost a fruit!" — But never thus
The gardener speaks, when from the bending tree
He gathers the ripe fruit in baskets full;
The end, the consummation of the fruit,
That is the very joy for which he longs.

A hard, unmerciful poet of old time,
Only as an apology for death,
Created once a "Master" who made man,
As potter's work from clay of Paradise,
And sternly warned him from his Tree of Life,
Lest haply this His *ware* might live forever!
Might be forsooth immortal as Himself . . .
Thus kindling in man's breast Himself, the first
Real ambition to be of the Gods!
Then, others feigned a "Father"* of mankind
But half as jealous, and so lenient
As to give man a spark from His own self,
That should enable him to see the right.

* The Heavenly Father: before Homer.

And others still, who honored high as heaven
The tender love of mother to her child,
And grudged not to a *mother* a whole world —
Adored a *Mother** both of Gods and men
And all the stars that glittered in the heavens,
And of all creatures, even the woodland roe.
But the great Spirit is not *Father* or *Mother*.
He is the very Being in all Beings,
And if we should not count it robbery
To be like God, and no disgrace to God
(As even many an ancient sage himself
Deemed not, when he divinely looked on things)
So God counts not for robbery and disgrace
To be a man, and be all gentle creatures.
And must *we* too be perfect as God is,
Then should we men *be able to do this:*
Partake the self-same nature, self-same spirit;
And then, and only then, will it be true:
Whate'er thou dost to men thou dost to God,
Thy father is thy God, humanly near;
The humanly near Goddess is — thy mother;
Thy wife — the heavenly Queen on earth is she,
She in thy arms, the mother of thy children!

Now; this *our God who has at last appeared*
Himself on earth, to all men gives Himself
And to all creatures; all who come to live
On earth and in all regions of the heavens,
And even the wondrous body of the bee,

* The great Mother.

The rose is not too small or mean for Him ;
The cloud, the very shadow, not too fleeting —
For *He is everlasting!* and the world
Is holy, and all beings in all worlds
Are holy, for the Holiest dwells in all !

And He who in His fulness dwells with all,
Through all and in all, one and whole in all,
He never yet, upon His heaven-wide way,
Through His long first eternity till now,
To this bright sun-lighted To-day of earth,
Has lost a single flower, or leaf of flower,
And least of all a single human child
— Which by his being and spirit lived indeed —
He has made all — yea, all of them *His own*,
With all their joys and all their love, His own
With all their beauty and with all their works,
Upon His broad and boundless heavenly way
Through His long first eternity till now
To this bright sun-lighted To-day of earth . . .
And on His broad and boundless heavenly way
On through His *second* long eternity
Still will He make all creatures' life His own
With all their pleasures and with all their love,
With all their beauty, all their blessedness.
To see Him with thine eyes, His life, His ways,
Until thine eyesight fades into His light, —
That now, O man, is thy felicity ;
That is His tranquil blessedness in thee,
His inly sweet, serene self-consciousness.

REDEMPTION FROM LIVING DEATH.

THIS is no more the question, whether thou
Shalt live and last, long as the heavens endure ;
Thou *shalt* last while the heavens endure. But this
Should be for thee the question, this thy care,
How from it all thou shalt come out at last ;
How thou mayest yet be free and rid of life
All coming time so long as heaven endures,
Which must endure, even though the stars, one day,
Should bloom *out*, wither away and run to seed —
— As the mere flowers of the heavenly field —
That *thou* no more shalt rise again in that
New, *greater* spring-time, when the same old power
Whose impulse stirred the dust to its first bloom
Shall kindle it to a second bloom, and yet
A third, and so forever, till it soars
To shine as constellations in the heavens.

But tell me now : who then is tired of LIFE ?
Who ever could be ? and who really is ?
(Since naught e'er finds existence tiresome,
As sea and water tire not of each other.)
The Indians — the best minds and purest of them —
They have in use an *opcn sesame*,

Once and for all to free themselves from life,
That so they may attain to a dead calm,
(Which is just what God shuns and hates and flees,
And plunges ever young into young life.)
And how do they get freedom from the world,
From power and from the very hands of God?
By living pure in spirit, pious, good,
Despising gold and goods, and property,
More than they need for clean and holy lives.
For holiness, and holiness alone,
Can set them free from God, the world and life.

Thus do they dream to be released from life,
And only live divinely human life,
Without ennui, as the divine life is;
And their delusion: to be rid of life —
Is the unconscious yearning: to be man,
As pure as God can be, to be a man:
They know no master and acknowledge none,
As consciously both freemen and divine;
They know no slaves and they acknowledge none;
They reverence flowers as the mute gods of earth,
Respect as equals all things that have life,
That fly or creep or stand like rigid rocks;
The very temple is to them a beast
With giant feet reposing on the earth.
Woman is not, with them, distinct from heaven,
Nor yet from earth — as being a nearer heaven,
The Mother Earth, only so sweet and fair,
That they are fain to clasp her in their arms.

They teach their children piously: to flee
From life (that is, satiety of life)
For, but for *that*, they would be glad to live.
With weariness of life even God Himself
Appears to them a slave, the lowest slave,
Who *must* exist, whom *nothing can release*,
Since neither rope nor dagger can he find,
Nor poison-cup for his deliverance,
Nor coffin, grave, nor vault for his repose.

This holy yearning understand thou well!
For wouldst not thou too, gladly, then, be rid
Of all the weariness of life, its load
Of flesh, and the soul's heavy burden, too,
Of shame, servility, and servitude,
And be as free as a God is — *who can die!*
I know a man, who well can teach thee this;
And if thou wishest nothing more of him
Than what shall give thee overflowing bliss,
And what shall, day and night, and near and far,
Fill all thy soul with holy impulses,
What, when possessed, yea most, when torn from thee,
Shall be worth more than sun and moon and stars —
Thou wilt have cause to be content with him!
I know him by experience — hear his name;
It is the man veiled under *woman's* form,
Who as fair virgin loves thee ardently,
Whom thou so lovest, that thou wooest, win'st her,
And clingest to her bosom blissfully . . .
Till *little* men and *little* women soon

Crowd thee away from it, young blooming gods,
For whose sake thou dost lift the fervent prayer
That heaven's high house may stand for evermore !
This earth forever like a garden bloom !
The very strawberry and apple-tree
Which they enjoy, may never die nor fail,
Much less, the mother with her children perish,
Nor thou — that thou mayst see their heavenly life,
And hope through them eternal life to win !

The heart — that is thy home, and not the earth !
The *home* is all thy fortune — not the world !
The blessed saints, are : ***husband, wife and child.***

LOVE TO ALL, FAITH IN ALL THINGS.

THE highest faith is to believe in all —
All things ! as highest love is love to all !
All things have always been and ever are
Believed on ; for whatever is, is true.
And all things always have been and will be
Beloved, as little fishes by the fish.
But that in *thee* love lives and loves, in *thee*
A lofty moral sentiment is throned,
This is thy *knowledge* only, 'tis no faith —
Thy knowledge : that love lives in all who live,
And fair morality in every heart.
Just as thou *knowest that thou art*, and not
Merely believ'st it ; *else were thy existence,*
The holy feeling of existence too,
And even self-consciousness, only — a dream
Of thine, about — some other than the dream : —
Thyself, (say,) the believer, who believes
Only that he believes, and nothing more ;
And is no more, *for he himself is not.*
But only from conviction faith can come,
For faith has a fixed object to believe,
For faith is only a belief in God,
In *all* His wonders, might and majesty
And glory in all worlds for evermore !
But then, the more thou learn'st and knowest of Him ;
The more thy knowledge takes from thy belief ;
The *more securely livest thou*, all live,
In the true light that lights the universe.

THE DESPERATE AND REPROBATE.

GOD is a Spirit, is a thinking thought,
For He it is that lives through all that live,
And He is they, and, they are none but He.
God is enthroned in no one single place ;
In the whole boundless space there is no Heaven,
Secluded and partitioned to a hall —
His Heaven is the whole boundless universe.
No door-keepers has He, no worms of earth
For champions and patrons of His Heaven ;
All who are born already live therein.
If they *could* shut up heaven against one soul . . .
Or grant it to one soul as boon of grace,
Because it had on earth obeyed their mind,
And disavowed God's holy majesty ;
Oh, He would crush them with a thunderbolt ;
They would not be, were they not powerless
And vain against the better sense of man.
The Spirit of God is full of His own truth.
How graceless were a God, who must, by prayer,
Be reconciled to His own *very self.*
How shameless, if a single creature should
Have superfluity of righteousness
Enough to ransom others out of hell,

If one soul *could* be righteous for another.
God's Spirit would renounce the God with scorn;
And does renounce; for God needs not a God!
Only let all who live know this full well:
God's Spirit lives the self of all who live:
Let each revere himself then and all others,
Then all the world has freedom, joy and peace.

PUT AWAY THE SWORD!

WHY can a bear never become a Turk?
A Christian, Fohist, Jew, or minister
With his black coat and his blue stockings on?
The holy answer lifts thee with sublime
Sense of thy worth above the slavish word
Of excommunication on thy race,
Which flouts in fearless freedom all such bans,
Annuls and flings them on the old heap of lies.
Had it been possible, how gladly would
Mahomet have transformed with his Koran
All lions, bears, wolves, serpents, into Turks;
He would himself have armed them with the sword,
If they could otherwise have grasped his sword,
Than with their teeth, indeed, and their sharp claws.
No one can change the nature of a bear!
While bears exist, no one can take from them
Their skin, till they are dead, slain by his hand.
No God has given the lion God-like gifts;
No sword, no book, *brings* them the Spirit of God:
No sword, no book, can *take away* from men
Reason and wisdom, honor and the sense
Of things divine, of God-like quality.

Who, now, is man? and Who, who lives his life?
Thou knowest, and all acknowledge it with joy.
What does he give, who cannot give me God?
And having God, I learn of *Him* to know Him.
Lo! this is why no bear can be a Turk!

This, faithful mother, let none take from thee,
That *thou* art thy child's mother, thou *alone;*
No other woman of all other women
Could be his mother in the whole wide world,
None but thyself; none other owns thy child,
And thou his only mother art to him.
Let *this* move thee to sweet and sacred tears!
Who now of *human* teachers were so blind,
Conceited and presumptuous as to say
To any mother . . . as in mockery . . .
"O mother, love, I pray thee, love thy *child!*"
And to the child, "Love thou thy mother, do."
Himself had *learned it from the mother* first!
Himself had first beheld it in the child!
The very ox and ass, dumb brutes, have seen
This at the crib; the ass has learned it too
And understood it by the foal his child!
Who could *give love* to the wild ass and foal?
Who could *give* love to the maternal heart?
Who in a child's heart could awaken love?
Only: "the way" in which one could love best,
That, haply, a wise person still might show,
Who had experience of his own: a *father;*
This the unmarried knows not, knows not thus! —

This, thou true mother, let none take from thee,
That in thy heart thou cherishest a love
At which thy child's eyes sparkle with delight!
And if thou weepest — makes it weep with thee!

That one has loved, now, and has rendered help,
That was his own good luck and merit too;
No man becomes on that account his slave;
Sure, no one is the slave of his own love!
Not to say, slave of any other's love,
Of living men, and least of all, the dead.

This, faithful father, let none take from thee!

ANTIQUITY.

OF this one childish error clear thy mind:
Thy reverend antiquity is not
That of the old, *eternal universe!*
Thy ancient times are only the young days
Of the earth's childhood; for the earth itself
Is nothing but an out-blown water-lily
Floating on that enormous ocean-pond
Which, never-wasting, heaves eternally,
"The ether," sprung from the primeval seed.
Naught e'er began; the self-repeating life
Goes on forever in the self-same place.
The earliest grass-blade, withered now long since,
Once it was green! the yesterday, now torn
In shreds, and lost, was once bright as to-day!
The first weak word of the first human child
Was a primeval, an eternal one,
But seeming new as coming from new lips!
And every thing the ancient folks believed,
Was nothing but a new-born childhood's faith;
And all that was divine in its own breast,
That every race imputed to its gods.
It is not that all gods were but one God —
One God was all gods, one god was all men;

And where they worshipped God, the gods too were
In bodily form, like man who worshipped them.
The being called man was but the wondrous eye
To see them first, and see them in such way
As his eye shaped them. *God eternally*
Contemplated Himself in His own world.
And this self-contemplation was man's life.
Not, that He may, in all His changeful forms,
Himself be ever guessing — "why He is"! —
Does God exist. God clothes Himself with forms
So to enjoy forever His sweet being
And all His beauty in the realm of light;
Among the dying, yet untouched by death,
Still with the new-born, yet Himself unborn;
The great eternity in the great heart,
He sees His fore-time imaged awfully
In the dead bones of giants down below,
Swept away long ago by mighty floods;
He sees His future shining yonder high
Up in the fixed and starry firmament.
In every being to do well to each,
There His own God-like nature recognizing,
Greatly and purely as a God to live, —
That is for all and each of human kind
Religion — godly life and contemplation —
And godly vision and life is blessedness,
For blessedness is seeing and acting God.

TO-DAY: THE KEY-STONE OF THE WORLD.

TO quicken or retard his rate of sleep
No one has power, for all things have their time;
And neither can one hour make good a night,
Nor can you crowd a day into an hour;
To sleep beforehand, lay in a good store
Of sleep, is what no one can do. So none
Can *live* ahead, or live with greater speed.
Each apparition of yon morning sun
Is but a throbbing of the mighty pulse
Of the world's body, yea the sun itself
Is only a blood-globule in its veins.
And if thy soul lives not in place and time,
Yet is thy body introduced by life
Into a constant series; as a wave,
Curled by the wind, drives on the wave before,
Driven on in turn by that which follows it;
Just like the nodule on the stalk of grain
Which by the others keeps itself erect,
So grew thy forefathers, so growest thou,
So will thy children, children's children grow.
And all of you make up a human stalk,
Which always was in seed, always bore grain,
And so in each successive summer lived.

But the beginning of our human stalk,
And likewise of thy human body too,
Was something out of all the range of time.
After a long, immense eternity,
Before a long, immense eternity,
Sown in the midst, as if 'twere sown in air
Like a thin phantom floating in the skies.
But thou shalt in past generations see
The spirit's endless life made palpable,
And in those yet to be the eternal *being*,
And in those yet to come the eternal coming,
The fair procession out of being's depths
Into this sunny day, this human life;
And in the vast, unending starry heaven
Shalt thou with joy immeasurable learn
To recognize the great eternal home,
(Forever open both to thee and all)
For ever-new and ever-nobler life;
With God-like joy shalt see thy temple there!

When a good mother fitting out her son
Follows him with her blessing, when a father
Weds his good daughter with glad willingness,
That is the *eternal love* of this vast whole,
For this eternal love itself could not
Bring forth one day the thousandth generation,
Without *this generation* on the stage!
Nor could it bless a single one of them
Did it not pour out its full horn of blessings
Into this single generation's lap.

Already, of old time has it ordained
This generation, through mysterious nights
Cherished and reared, and through mysterious days
Led it along up to the present hour.
Thus is the love of mothers, then, the old
Primal, eternal love of this vast whole,
With which it swells well nigh to suffocation:
The gladness and the laughter of a child,
The singing of a lark among the clouds, —
That is itself a fruit of all the stars,
Their blessedest product and best influence!

THE WONDER-WORKERS.

AND were there, could there really be one
Who even made an ox out of an ass,
Who could so much as change figs into thistles,
Or glue a torn-up frog to life again,
And did not die himself, even when a shell
Had struck and shattered all his entrails out —
And had he both the will and power to teach
All men all these and even greater acts,
Till God's fair world should be a bedlam now
For every crazy man and every fool —
Then should I hold him — well — "greater than God?
. . . A mightier than the Almighty One . . . ?"
Thinkest thou so perchance? nay, *weaker*, *worse*
Than the first plain and simple pious man,
Whose faith firm as a rock on nature rests,
Who lives by her divine, eternal laws,
Who knows that sun and sunrise, flying clouds,
The growth of grass upon the meadow lands,
And bleat of lambs, and herdsman's mellow song,
And people's little children plucking flowers
In the bright sun beneath the clear blue heaven —
That *these* are greatest of all miracles,
And as the being of God unsearchable.

He only, who beholds the universe,
With all its stars, the sun that moves through heaven
In majesty, the earth spread at his feet,
On these and on all men, and his own heart,
Looks, as a child from out his cradle looks;
Regards them as mere things of every day
As commonplace and customary things,
Because he needs must be accustomed to them,
And live in them, to be content with life —
Takes every fool's-trick for a miracle,
(Not for mere nonsense and absurdity,)
Because God-fearing wonder stirs in him;
Only, instead of wondering at God's *law*,
He stares with wonder at *wild fancy's dreams!*
Far better is it in the universe
Never and nowhere to see any thing
Except with the mind's eye by custom sealed
And blinded, holding every thing to be
The grossest and most bald of commonplace
— The potter — nothing round him but a great
Convenient potter's field; the countryman
Nothing around him but a mighty farm —
Than one's *own nonsense* in a wizard's glass.
For man is called to this — for this one thing
Has he been gifted with the highest spirit,
That he might hold with fair and holy nature
Such *genuine, confidential* intercourse
As with his neighbor's daughter a man holds,
When he has taken her for his darling wife;
And look on this great body of the world,

As the great body his own soul inhabits.
For God will not do witchcraft, He will *live*,
Freely and simply as a cradled child
Uses his little eyes and hands and feet!

The Germans swept away the witches first;
Then swept away their cruel sweeping act.
Through God ye banish wonder-mongering faith
And by the use *of power* comes joy in power.
One, only, knows no miracle: God! and the mind of God:
And every man who has the mind of God,
Who feels himself to be the spirit of God,
Who looks upon the beauteous universe
With all its glory, as his property
And his possession, as the snail her house,
And as the little throstling does his nest,
And as the brown bee does her honey-tree.
How shall a hair on *thy* head be to thee
A miracle! an eye beneath *thy* brow!
How shall the mother call her new-born child
A miracle, — herself a greater one?
Can spirit be a miracle to spirit?
How canst thou talk of wonders, when thou art
Thyself a miracle, the greatest, thou
"*The wonder-seer*" thyself, the wonderful!
Hast thou, then, entered into thine own being,
Hast thou into a single grain of sand
Entered in silent thought, thou hast thereby
Entered into the vast ethereal seas
With all their constellations; all the stars

Are not more wondrous than one little grain
Of sand beneath thy feet; the multitude
Makes not the wonder greater, rather less;
Just as the value of the greatest pearl,
Or the crown-diamond, lessens in thine eyes
If mountains of them lie in every street,
And all the children, making playthings of them,
Scatter and squander them about, as men
Squander and fling away this wondrous life —
Their only, their irrevocable one!
The oftener the familiar sun returns,
The longer yon blue heaven is flushed with light
And every night the stars shine through the dusk,
The stars grow more and more *every-day* things,
And by such long familiarity
Even life becomes a common thing, and *death* —
Uncommon only, when in some strange shape.
Whate'er is strange *about* them startles us,
But death and life themselves wake thought no more.
But *labor* does away all miracles,
Work, at the blissful tasks of the old God:
The task of washing the dear new-born child,
Of dressing him in his first little clothes,
Of putting on his first sweet little cap —
Joy makes all wonders soon to be forgot;
His mother with good right forgets them all,
His father does, and every genuine man.
To make the new hedge round his meadow-land,
To cut the hay and drive the wagons in,
Quite other, truer human work is that,

Than to stand wondering there at all the flowers
That so mysteriously came, lived, died.
Thus is man's labor, every smallest task,
A work of holy, healing blessedness
For him! and with the human *heart* man lives
More blissful than with stiff stupidity
And staring wonder in a hollow mind,
Blindly believing all things *but itself*,
And from the master of a thousand powers
Degraded to be slave of its own fears.

Wouldst know the greatest wonder-worker's name?
'Tis *Labor*, the deliverer of man
From memory's dream of dead and buried things,
From fancy's idle dream of things unborn,
From frightful emblems of decay and death;
And even if all should die and melt away
Beneath the grasp of man and disappear
Like the cold snowball in the child's warm hand—
Labor remains forever fixed and calm,
Above the wreck of every fleeting work,
Even as the eye rests on the fleeing clouds;
And even the children find the soft snow serve
For balls, for the glad fling, the merry game!
Labor alone makes man a genuine man,
It makes the world yield lasting joy to him,
Though all he did were naught but nothingness.
But man by labor makes himself a life
Secure and free and goodly, of his own,
And every tree he planted once in hope,

To him and to his children still bears fruit.
Through busy, thoughtful and clear-purposed toil
A man, whoe'er he be, grows clear in heart,
And every day of the vain, hollow world,
Through labor, has for each its worthy end.
At morn, it gives to each one *his desire,*
At evening hands to each one *his reward!* —

Long have I wandered round with true, sharp eye
Among strange peoples over all the earth,
And none but the vain idlers everywhere
And the proud *idle women* have I seen,
Distrait and wretched; for extorted gold
They bought themselves sorely repented joys;
Lived without pleasure in an empty world,
And dying with a yawn, were laid away
Into an empty world — the grave: — the long ennui!

LIFE — A BATTLE.

CLOSE by the side of *those few moral sayings*
Which the old sages of the ancient time
Have left us, deeming they bestowed on us
Thereby the world and all its blessedness —
Beside and all around those well-meant words
There still remain abysses full of night
And gloom, and mountains full of trouble too;
There's the old human heart still full of woe, —
Here's the new road of life, full of new thorns!
God is to-day the same old riddle still,
The starry night is still the same old night;
Death is to-day the same old terror still,
The grave is still to-day the dismal hole.
The deep abyss is not yet filled up, though
So many thousands hourly fall therein!
We have not yet strode forth from man's estate,
Man is this day and hour the *first man* still,
And will remain the first to the *last man*,
Saved by no God and never to be saved
From chasing after ever-growing truth
— Which like the rainbow still eludes his grasp;
From striving for the growing sweets of freedom
— For still he drags behind him his old chains;

From ever deeper, clearer, broader knowledge,
— For ever deeper grows the human mind ;
From adding beauty to his earthly home,
— For more and more *well being* means to man ;
And never from his mortal body saved
— Which still remains exposed to every fate.
From earthly trouble man is never free ;
The spirit, from the stuff in which it dwells ;
In which it is *at home*, as is the soul
In the body, and *the body in the soul.*
And the mere task of conquering as he should
All the crude elements, that is the gist
Of man's whole fight life long, even to the grave.
Nay, only by it is he kept so great,
So free, so noble ; it belongs to him,
Makes up his very life,.and gives him work
In daily little victories, —*victory*, never,
Long as he lives ; and man will weep so long
As he has eyes ; and he will mourn so long
As his heart beats ; and feel anxiety
Long as he loves ; and man will love so long
As God shall fill and animate his frame.

Ye pious and ye proud ones, all of you,
Begrudge not God, I pray you, His hard life !
Hard for *you* only, if you had to bear
With *your own* strength the immeasurable work.

THE DEAF AND DUMB MOTHER.

HE who has never thought, ay never could
Think of his life, has yet enjoyed his life
With better, haply more complete a sense.
Thoughts draw us off from their materials,
Thoughts are a special and particular work
Other than life is, and the sense of it,
The inner sense that wholly fills the heart.
So may the lark then well and sweetly live!
The bee may live in gladness and in joy,
The lily too, the modest violet!
Thoughts do not constitute morality,
They are not *love:* thoughts do not constitute
Honor or happiness; nor can they make
Man blest; nor needs he them to be divine.
Thoughts, to the artist of this earth, the rich
Poet, whose name is man, and who is man,
Are the material for his *human work;*
As, to the lark, tones are, for utterance,
As, to the bee, his hum, for rallying-cry
And note of recognition on the mead!
The young bee when it hies for the first time
Forth from the hive out through the swarming-hole,
As if *omniscient,* flies with lightning-speed

Straight off to the red clover ; not the rose,
Which has in store for her no nourishment !
She builds her cell as never man could do,
With all his cunning ! and each cell is glued
Fast to the middle of its counter-cells.
And if the bee *has* not science and art
And wisdom, *she herself is wisdom*, then,
The highest, and the very truest art ;
And if she does know nothing, she herself
Is, in *her* mind, *all-knowing*, in so far
As the well-doing of her work requires ;
And all, who never had nor could have had
A teacher, are both *teacher* to themselves
And lesson ; without word and without thought
Grasping and using their own faculties
And living in their own accustomed life. —
The fair young human mother, deaf and dumb,
And poor as any pigeon, *feels* nathless
Deep joy and rapture by her husband's side ;
A blissful rapture in the new-born child,
Which even now with pride the kindly nurse
Lays in her arms, which blessing silently,
And almost weeping, tenderly she feels :
How sweet the *little guest ten minutes old* . . .
The little friend, the darling son from heaven,
Upon her breast drinks eagerly the milk,
As if he came from a long pilgrimage !
She feels the mother's natural agony,
When in the night her child has passed away . . .
When in the morning's beam she sees it dead !

When now in the green earth they bury it!
And through her tears now is she forced to smile,
When with such sweet, imploring sympathy
Her older little boy clings to her breast,
Looks in her eyes with such calm confidence,
That she can almost read it on his lips,
When now he says: "Ah, mother, do not weep! . . .
No, dearest mother; no, *I* will not die!"
And seals his naive assurance with a kiss. —
The spirit is not blind, nor deaf and dumb!
Not half, no, *wholly does it understand*
Itself and life! for *into every life*
It brings with it in full what life contains,
And what the sun could not have given it,
Nor earth, the grave nor death, can ever give;
For even its destiny, its blessedness,
Its sorrow and its joy it brings with it;
For all is to the spirit *only* what
The spirit feels withal — and nothing more.
Thus is the spirit perfect in all points,
To him life is but opportunity
To feel himself, and is enough for that —
And if his life were richer still in griefs,
In joys still poorer — he is rich indeed;
Needs must it be a transit, — nay, a flight.
So only is it to the eternal spirit,
The all-conscious one, — the genuine stuff of life!
And so is God's eternal life, and thus
He lives forever in His universe.

HOPE.

HOPE is no child of heaven by any means ;
  Hope is unknown to its inhabitants ;
The blessed wish for naught and hope for naught,
Nor yet expect they aught ; for evermore
Content and tranquil, every want supplied.
So say mankind because they wish it so,
And what man wishes, he believes ; all else
He disbelieves ; his faith means first his wish.
He asks not after truth, *that* he rejects.
To his own terrible hurt, he cannot see,
He cannot hear, full of his misery
Which stupefies his heart and makes him dream.
Fear wedded Sorrow once upon a time ;
Then in the ruddy dawn she had this dream :
That what she suffered would be all transformed
To joy and bliss ! She even lost in sleep
Her paleness, and has long since worn a smile.
Whereon she bore him "Dream," and every day
Bore him the self-same offspring, which she reared,
And gave to every one the name of "Hope."
To every one who suffers, every one
Whose heart the shadow of calamity
Congeals with fear, she in compassion sends

One of her daughters for companionship,
Who transforms fear for him to a light dream,
Herself only a dream of pallid Fear.
He dreams the bliss he pines for, which he needs,
Which wishes' wings bring ever nearer to him.
So, like the rainbow, Hope appears to stand
In different spots and over different flowers,
To different eyes, and seems to every one
Of different hues, like the chameleon;
To every troubled eye she shows more bright,
All heaven around her grows more radiant;
To each afflicted man she waxes more
And more enchanting, with his deepening woe,
That he may calmlier bear it, and endure
And struggle toward the day of new-born bliss
With wondrous, though delusive energy.—
Man feeds and nourishes, himself, his hope
With his own heart's-blood, with sore pangs of soul,
While it still hovers round him, while he still
Needs it to guide him to his happiness.
But when the clouds no more obscure his heaven,
She grows more pale; as *he* more tranquilly
Sleeps through the night, she *softly steals from him*
To lay herself for once down at his feet
And rest in sleep from all her wearying arts.
The sick man named his sweet delicious hope,
Health! But when *health* herself now came to him,
Lo! he no longer knows his hope again;
She has gone from him like a phantom-light,
Wasting away like the disease itself!

The poor man named his dear delicious hope,
"Bread! Labor!" But when labor came, and bread,
He knows his hope no longer now, that, too,
Has vanished from him *as his poverty.*
Every access of fortune ends its hope,
Scares it away; as the enfolded bride
Her bridegroom's empty longing, who henceforth
Clasps tree and stake, belike, instead of her.
Every misfortune conjures to it its hope
Just as the sun does shadows round its path.
With every piece of fortune dies a hope,
With heavenly-rich o'erfulness compensated,
By no one ever missed henceforth in dream!
And happy will the whole of human kind
Be made at last one day when *not a hope*
Early or late comes to a bed again,
Hovers alluring o'er a wanderer's path,
Or sits again as scarecrow on a grave;
When toil, intelligence, content and love,
Shall wed the glad soul to the universe.

MEMORY.

MAN is each morning new ; day after day,
Early is he new-born of the whole world
(No more his mother's child alone) in soul
And body. And because he has this power
Of constant renovation, and his soul
Was never destined to be petrified
In any single narrow feeling's mould,
In any single narrow groove of thought,
Therefore each feeling with the moment born
Dies with the moment, and so on forever,
All his life-long, to his infinite gain,
That so he may become what man on earth
Was meant to be : *a prover of all things*
And *self-experienced* in the whole rich world.
Memory is but a dream of having known
The immediate taste of an enjoyment once,
Only reminding man that he once lived,
That the time was when earth was bright to him.
For if the *memory of a strawberry*
He had once eaten, satisfied a child,
Then he no longer need eat strawberries,
Only remember : how they tasted once !
And if the *memory of bread* sufficed

The poor, then would all poor men have their fill,
The everlasting, still satiety
Would spoil all viands for the rich man's taste,
Would spoil the zest of every dear delight
Of each new day with each new gift it brought,
A flying pang, of some new sorrow born
Within our breast, which we in childhood felt,
Now spell-bound to us and immortalized,
Would turn to gall all after-joys of life
And petrify in the eye the bitter tears.
One transient feeling of a beautiful
And stirring moment, made eternal in us,
Would snatch from us the rich o'erflowing horn
Of plenty, brought us by the coming years.
But joy and grief are only meant to feed
The heart with noble good against their days.
If all the fragrances of all the flowers
Still lingered with us . . . and if all the bells
Mingled their sounds within us, what a jargon
Would deafen us to our own spirit's voice!

The ancient spirit of the world who dwells
Within us, when we come into this world
Brings with him naught from his eternal life,
That with a clean and open heart he may
Receive a human life beneath the sun.
The thousand sorrows and the thousand joys
Which he has surely, surely, once enjoyed
Are now with him no feeling, not a dream!
And if life's perpetuity is precious

In those most precious and beloved heavens,
Still he takes nothing with him from this earth,
Of all its joys and sorrows, in his heart
(No more than in the coffin) save his own
Pure primal soul, as a chaste flame of love,
With the capacity of endless bliss.
Thus is life worthy of the God-like spirit,
Worth in itself man's best fidelity,
Meeting the spirit's wants in all its worlds !
Each meeting here on earth is a reunion,
Each new acquaintance is a recognition ;
For long the ancient soul has known it all.
Who loses not himself, gains every thing.

VIOLET'S-BREATH AND HEAVEN'S SPIRIT.

WHEN thou explor'st the heart, the deep well-spring
Of life, of thoughts and feelings, how much more
Art thou amazed and awe-struck at its wealth
Of goodness, love, truth and fidelity,
Than men are at yon holy heaven above,
Full of great, busy, living starry fires!
Thou didst no more than show a boy, who sought
A doctor for his poor sick father's life,
A wrong way through the woods, where thou hast learned
A shorter, better — *how that grieves thee now!*
Thou only wouldst not help a beetle up,
That lay beside the road upon his back
Struggling with all his might to right himself,
So much as just to bend one blade of grass
Towards his feet — *how that repents thee now!*
The ploughman too, who, with his children, ploughed,
Last moon, thy field for thee, — from him thou still
His well-earned daily wages keepest back;
Who now in modest silence passes by,
Greets not, nor even so much as looks at thee,
That he may not remind thee of thy debt
And of his need — *oh how it shames thee now!*

Am I then nobler than the lofty heavens?
I better than the fairest star of night?
And in my soul, because I am a man,
A new divine emotion now first lives?
Not rather, has just sprung up like a flower
Out of its seed? Not rather, has just risen
As from a mouldering body! . . . But was I
Always of old a man then? Nay, is not
The form of man old as the earth itself?
And as I feel to-day, have not long since
Whole blessed generations also felt?
Is it not then of immemorial age,
Ay, even eternal, that which comes to me
The new-born man, as a new thing to-day?
And is not that a common property
Which in thy heart thou holdest for thine own:
Goodness, love, truth, and fair fidelity!

Then wonder at thyself, no more, O man!
But wonder at that mighty universe
Wherein love, goodness, truth, fidelity
Are but the *common heart's blood, common dew.*

And so the violet brings not up with it
From earth's black mould its fragrant violet's-breath
Nor yet its beauteous tint of violet blue —
It comes a *white* bud to the sunny realm,
Which paints its little chalice violet-blue
And fills it full with violet perfume
And fills the rose for us with rose-perfume,

And fills man's bosom with the soul of heaven,
Wherein love, goodness, truth, fidelity,
Sleep silently, to wake in thee as child,
And silently sleep with thee in the grave,
Free, and at large again for evermore,
As heavenly spirit of the universe,
The violets perfume when its violet's dead.

Revere thou then, O man, that heavenly spirit,
The all-pervading, universal soul,
Old as the stars, and new as newest flowers,*
Within thee ! honor, follow Him who fills
Thy soul, as goodness, love, fidelity —
So that to every creature *thou* art good !
So that thou lovest wife and children more
Than thou canst love all on the earth beside !
That thou fulfill'st the promise of thy hand,
And thy great debt to all, fidelity !
For know : thou art thyself the heavenly spirit.
And what thou hast that is thy property,
More than thy hand thine own, and more thine own
Than are thine eyes, than is thy human head.
Yet mark no less : the gracious heavenly spirit
Belongs to all and gives itself to all,
And in its love itself inhabits all.

* *Sternenalt* and *blumenneu* (star-old and flower-new) are the bold and beautiful words.

THE HIGHEST SPIRIT.

BE not impetuous, vehement, over-loud
Where there is no necessity ; it spoils
The tone and whole complexion of *the house*,
Spoils for its inmates all their tranquil mood,
Stirs up too violent an answer, spoils
The very ring and color of *the land.*
What dost thou call necessity ? — the cry
For swift and vigorous help, when suddenly
Harm and disaster threaten any one,
When a good thing, if it is done, must be done
Quickly, and when delay is danger, letting
A spark grow up into a mighty fire.
Spare, otherwise, thy treasure of heart's-strength
Which, like thy days, was measured out to thee
For the long works and uses of thy life ;
Spare even thy breast the needless draught of breath,
The arm its muscular strength, the eyes their sight,
When thou wouldst only spend thy force for naught.
But keep thy energies well gathered up,
As thy life's treasure, wasted by no rust,
But ever ready in a wakeful soul
For service : to be willingly brought out,
Yea, wholly given up, for him who needs

The good of it, that he may do thee good.
So, sweetly, to divine maturity
Grows day by day the maiden's tender form:
Her modest virtue spares her gracious limbs,
Refrains from giving away a hair, a hand,
A word out of the heart, or even a look,
Till the right time comes, and the right loved man
That she may be to him the perfect wife
Who shall, in blessing him, herself be blest!

My child, *the greatest strength is gentleness;*
It rules the child with one kind, faithful word,
Rules man and wife, people and neighborhood,
It even controls the beggar's vicious dogs.
But the *weak* heart is not the gentle spirit,
The *strong*, full heart alone possesses spirit
Even to heroism and martyrdom,
Like the still sword that tarries in its sheath.
Scream not, then, like the bell that cries out "Fire!
When only fire-flies' sparks are trailing by,
But when the alarm-bell calls to earnest work
Fly as the storm flies roaring to the fire.

LET NONE OFFEND THEE!

THOU wilt not *give* offence, I can believe;
And so far, therefore, rests no blame on thee:
But circumspectly stand upon thy guard —
Never to *take* offence from other men!
Then only art thou wholly free from blame;
Then art thou wise and good; art a just man,
Well-poised, secure from harm; thy life a joy
To others and thyself. Live like the sun,
Then shalt thou no more take offence than he.
For lo! *how many daily take offence!*
The richest, mightiest! — know then in thy heart
Thereby: what they must be and how they live!
Then shun, as thou wouldst death: *taking offence!*
So shalt thou flee life's worst, most poisonous plague —
And surely hasten to the heavenly arms!
To life majestic as the sun's on high! —
Meanwhile the very murdered man himself
Bears often more than half his murderer's guilt;
Nay, who provokes the sin, has all the guilt.
This I say softly. But thou, take 't to heart,
And circumspectly stand upon thy guard —
Never to take offence from other men!
Thou wilt not give offence, I can believe.

TO THE MEEK MAN.

THOU dost not well to be content with all
Thy neighbor does, who lives with thee and needs thee! —
His tongue, by *silence*, grows degenerate!
His very patience breeds impatientness!
Then overlook them with a generous eye,
Smile on them in a *good* and *faithful* heart,
Yet tell them firmly and without reserve
Thy honest mind and their vainglorying.
'Twill make them wiser, *even better men*,
Make them more reverent for the man in thee;
Enhance thy worth with them; for they would tame
The very speech and action of the king;
But whoso says the truth and does the right
Secures respect and freedom with his kind:
To do his own work, live out his own life,
Not to say, wear his hair as pleases him!
Walk his own gait, quick step or old man's pace;
For what his heart does, he does royally. —
Thou dost not well to be content with all
Thy neighbor does, who lives with thee and needs thee, —
A kindly spirit rules by right divine.

THE MIGHT OF LOVE.

SAY not: The ancients left behind such deep
Unfathomable words, that all the wise,
With all their wisdom, are but shamed thereby;
For should a simpleton pronounce to-day
The mere word "magnet," or a child say "goose,"
There would be prophets whom the mystery:
"What is a goose?" would likewise put to shame,
And to *make* one — that would defy them all:
A work that eats, flies, waddles, swims, lays eggs,
And has these countless years renewed its youth!
Then comes the child, — light-hearted, cheerful faith, —
Laughs at the fooleries of all the wise,
And briskly clears all mysteries at a bound,
Exalts, exaggerates himself, makes light
Of hardest things, and, unexplored, unproved,
He lets things pass, that he may pass — may *be;*
For he himself would not be, were they not!
He gives the wonders, all, convenient *names*,
And hangs them up as *pictures* on his wall,
To pay them, following custom, on set days
A loud respect, then hang them up again.
Thus has faith painted over for itself
The world, and cunningly sealed up its eyes.

But thou with vision cleansed and purified,
With clearest understanding and best knowledge,
Shalt look on all the wonders in *all* things.
God's being is eternal mystery;
Fathomed, He could not be the Infinite!
Holy *astonishment* alone can bring
Thee near to Him, and lowly reverence
Shall bring Him near to thee, and make Him thine;
In ecstasy descending on thy soul,
He shall inspire and lift thee to Himself.
So too, wouldst thou draw near to *beauty*, thou
Canst find no other way than that of *love!*
Love lifts thee up to beauty on her wings,
Love draws her down to thee — down to thy heart!
Through love art thou made like to her in worth!
And if *there are* divine and beauteous wonders,
The greater wonder still a man can *do:*
Through love and reverence all highest things
To win, and to possess them as his heart.

Behold, such power alone sufficiently
Attests the true divinity of man!
And every child attests it day by day!
Reverence is only a live consciousness
Of all the glory that lies round about
And weighs on us, because we are and feel
Ourselves so glorious; and the *love* that yearns
Within us, is the power: to make it ours.

THE WORM AND THE SUN.

OH not from magnanimity, but oh,
From wisdom and from prudence shalt thou give
All hate, contempt and malice to the winds !
So shall thy soul be with itself at peace.
This proves thee not magnanimous forsooth
Not to feel hatred : for the *love* that wars
Against all hatred, *is no virtue :* nay
'Tis the soul's daily food and common bread !
Contempt, however, the sincere contempt
Felt for the world by a high-minded soul. . .
That seems sublime, the sole deliverance
From this our slavishly inherited,
Inevitable existence ! It alone
Has power to lend a show of liberty
And God-like elevation to the soul,
Which, like a king deposed and exiled, feels
Itself in silent equanimity,
And conscious of its own intrinsic worth,
Smiles the more tenderly and tranquilly,
The more the insignificant populace
Scorns and despises it ; the more the world
Sinks in the scale of worthlessness, the more
The spirit that contemns it, feels itself
Exalted and sufficient for itself :
Itself a world and kingdom in itself !

But when contempt comes in, respect goes out,
And pity slips into the place of love.
Whence could come pity, didst thou not believe
All beings suffered in the world like thee ?
But how could suffering touch thee, didst thou not
Love thine own self and others as thyself,
Whom by the self-same spirit thou seest inspired ?
But thou shalt love thyself too as thyself.
So love thy fellow-men then as a mother
Loves her sick child, already doomed to death,
Resigned by her — and yet loved on — nay, never
So truly loved and cherished until now !
For : death, disgrace and wrong excepted, all,
All things can Love love truly to the end,
True to itself, not the beloved alone.
This is the mother's holy, heavenly task,
To nurse the child, to lay his little toys
Upon his bed, to let his tiny arms
Twine round her, to caress and comfort him,
At last to let him die upon her breast,
Then close his little eyelids, and once more
To bathe his limbs, and then more carefully
Than if he were still living, comb his hair,
His golden hair, and never once upbraid
The little wildling, — then to dress the still,
Submissive child in his best Sunday clothes,
And lay him in his coffin sweetly wreathed,
And watch by him securely sleeping there,
As faithfully as once by his sick-bed !
What else has Love to do with fleeting things,
Decay and death, the living and the dead,

But just to love! if she can only love,
Then no one dies to her, then none is dead;
Love lives and Love keeps its own fire alive.
And therefore call not love a foolish thing,
As if it soiled itself with death and graves —
Love scents not the dank mould of noisome graves;
The grave is scented by the rosy hands
Of Love, and touched by her the dead all shine
Transfigured!
Be a spirit then, the spirit
Of Love, and hate thou nothing, hate thou none.
For were the very universe itself
Worthy of hatred, and its spirit too,
Which, coffined in the grave-mould, still lives on,
And still must live to all eternity —
It feels itself withal, it feels its shame,
And glorious, great and noble must it be!
So, too, be thou for hatred all too great;
Hate is unprofitable; it embitters
The heart — for rotten nuts; for every thing
Deserving hate is many thousand times
Inferior to thee; as the dead worm
Is to the lofty sun. And yet he shines
On the poor worm and with a pious touch
Transforms it to the holy dust of earth.

Oh not from magnanimity, but oh
From wisdom and from prudence give thou then
All hate, contempt and malice to the winds!
Then shall thy soul have peace within itself!

THE WEALTH OF WISDOM.

WITH her own hand the mother wove at night
A garland for her child, while yet he slept,
Which he to-morrow is to bring to *her*. . .
And she, what joy she has in braiding it!
How will the child rejoice too in his gift!
The joy is certain, and as beautiful
As to bring thanks to God and offer Him
A grateful tribute of *the gifts He gave*,
Or to send up a prayer upon the wings
Of *His own breath* into the pure blue heavens —
The joy is certain and so beautiful!

And piety is — like a childish play
Between a good child and the child's good mother.

The clear perception of this magic work
May well restrain thy eye, heart, hand and knee;
Yet well thou markest and thou feel'st it well:
That *knowledge* too is a no less divine
And holy beam, and is as true, as fair,
As when a mother takes, at the child's hands,
The offering of the wreath she wove for him!
Who said: that wisdom was a hollow, cold,
Vain thing! Nay, wisdom is so full and glowing!
The soul is rich as the heart never was —
Man *is* all that he *has*, bound up in one.

THE INNER WANT.

LIFE'S genuine goods prove thou not by the old,
The worn-out, dead-alive, nor dying men.
What one enjoyed not, in his youthful days,
Of youthful bliss, he never will enjoy.
A hatful of red cherries gives the boy
A sight of heaven ; and a hatful of diamonds
A dying man esteems not worth a smile.
The inner want supplied alone insures
Man's happiness ; and this his inward need
Is always changing, in that he himself
Is never for two moments like himself.
Of all good things man tastes on earth, *the first* *
Is the most precious ; to the little child,
Lo, even the first pear is a new world !
So the first stream that glides before his eyes
To him is just as great a miracle
As if the tender ether from the height
Of the blue heavens were flowing here on earth
And bathing him in all the bliss of heaven.
The repetition of enjoyment is
In part a reminiscence, not a first

* *Per contra*, Shakespeare: —
"Like the *last* taste of sweets, is sweetest last." — T.

Fresh and exuberant joy. Things oft enjoyed,
And though it were the day or the full moon,
Grow stale through custom and breed weariness.
To the best things that ever fell to him,
The experienced man will ever cling at last,
The man who growing older, grows more wise.
The old man in the end finds each *last thing*,
The thing he last enjoyed, a saddening thought . . .
As: the last cluster which the sick man plucked
And laid before him, more to look at it,
And taste yet one more grape from off the bunch,
Than to find joy in it; for no more joy
Is the last autumn . . . the last day — to him!

CHILDREN'S JOY.

MAKE beautiful to children their young days !
Despise not nor neglect the smallest joy !
Thou mak'st them for the time as little gods,
Nay, for their lifetime thou implantest in them
A gladsome mood, an ever cheerful heart.
The pleasures of their youth will pass away,
The time will come when of these pleasant days
They will know nothing more ; of the ripe nuts
They knock down from the tree ; the leaping-pole.
No more they know the smile their mother wore
To see them bring the baskets full of grapes —
Yet has all joy struck down *into the soul*,
They always hope for kindness from the world !
That which was once so fair may yet be dark !
Yet a glad spirit shall bear bitter things
One day with its first strength, nay even feel
The first bright sunbeam kindle gratitude.
But a sad, weary, dismal childhood hour
Makes serious, sombre faces, makes a dark
And cloudy eye. Thy heavy-laden child,
That once so pined for want of doll and dress,
That was begrudged even its dance in spring . . .

The poor great grown-up child, he hardly smiles,
In turn, upon *his* child who smiles on him!
Oh *childhood's joys* yield highest interest;
Man needs them to meet life with cheerfulness;
The spirit of the universe himself
Needs them, that he may feel within himself
A heavenly joy amidst his beauteous heaven.

THE THREE TREASURES OF LIFE.

ON holy Christmas Eve, long after dark,
Bending beneath a heavy load of wood,
From out the silent forest a poor man
Trudged homeward to his hut. Keenly the stars
Sparkled o'erhead; the river smoked with cold;
And pale and ghostly gleamed the silvery snow.
Yet in his hamlet seeing now a light,
He leaned against a tree by the wood's edge,
And cold and weary soon had sunk to sleep.
Then a glad dream came o'er him. His young wife
At home had found a treasure. Eager now
To help her lift it, he attempts to rise,
But, weighed down by his load, sinks back again
Against his tree, wakes up ashamed, and starting
Thinks of his seven little ones at home.

Within his little cottage all is dark.
His load laid down, he steps into the room.
"Husband, is 't thou?" his wife's familiar voice
Calls from the bed.
"Yes, it is I: where are the little ones?"
"Around me, — all asleep."

"But thou — I dreamed —
Hast found a treasure."
"I — a treasure?"
"No?
Then we are just as well off as before."
Just then he heard a new-born infant's cry,
And scarcely would he have been able now —
Even if his poor light had not given out —
For tears, to see the little guest from heaven.
"Ah!" says the mother; "yes, I see now, I
Have found the treasure! . . . such a treasure, too,
As we poor people, who have nothing better,
Have need of, — yes, and such as we well earn!
And such as God gives His beloved ones!
We must be dear to Him, full well I feel!
Now we have more anxiety, more toil;
But what of that? more love, too; ah, full measure!
Two little boys are lying by my side;
Only feel here! . . . the little infant heads. . . .
Here! touch them softly! — One — and here the other . . .
And see! the little brothers and sisters there,
Worn out already with the very joy,
Have gone to sleep around them; but my heart
Is wide awake: and, oh, it makes my eyes
Sparkle to see thee, how thou weep'st for joy!
I thank thee, God! for *Labor, Care, and Love!*"

And in the starlight there he prays aloud,
His hand laid softly on each infant's head:
"I thank thee, God! for *Labor, Care, and Love!*"

FOLLOW THE LORD UPON HIS WAYS.*

HEAR'ST thou, O just man, good and noble things
Of human kind, and of its life on *earth*,
Which sorely tried it, and yet gave withal
Much opportunity for worthy deeds ;
And thou, at the recital, in thy soul,
Hast full assurance that thou wouldst thyself
Have in like case, done every thing just so —
Then in thy bosom dwells the same good Spirit
That wrought those works thou seest on every side,
Only with other hands, not yet with thine.
And wilt thou then be quite amazed at this,
As at a thing unheard of — never known ?
Thou wilt not be amazed, nor even surprised,
Not even give thanks or praise, not, surely, doubt.
Thou wilt not doubt the Spirit of the Good
To be the same in all and in thyself,
When conscious to thyself of one good work,
Which once thou diddest all unconsciously,
Without a thought of self or of thy life.
That memory is enough for all good works
For thousand deaths, if only thou wert One
Endowed with thousand lives for such an end !
Who doubts a moment that *the worst of men*
Would gladly stay an utter stranger's tears
By raising his dear dead one from the grave ?

* "Begleite du den Herrn auf Seinen Wegen :" the beginning of a familiar German hymn. — T.

Who doubts that the *most miserly* of men
Would gladly, for the hungry beggar-children,
Change all the stones around his house to bread?
But unless other men have faith in him,
The best man cannot do a miracle.
Still, if thou didst no single miracle:
Thy pious mind transcends all miracles —
The poor with water keeps his marriage feast,
The beggar, without stones, has bread to eat,
And God lets never a dead man die twice;
A good man all the time does miracles:
God did them — and to man's heart 'tis as if
He himself did them also, did them with Him!
How gladly makest thou the sun to shine . . .
The flowers to bloom and all the birds to sing . . .
The ears to ripen, and the rain to plash —
O doubt not: *a good man is rich as God,*
And feels as rapturously blest as He,
For his soul does as glad a work as His!
Each man can, in his soul, do, with them, all
The good things, all the others ever do;
Each man can, in his soul, behold with them
The beauty that irradiates all around;
And thus the spirit of the universe
Is richer countless myriads of times
By all the countless myriads of hearts,
And gladder, than alone! The living hosts
Are evermore God's blest associates,
His glorious reduplications all;
And therefore lives He in the thousand beings,
And therefore is He life and is the world.

QUIET GREATNESS OF THE GOOD.

THE sun were still the sun though prisoned close
In a great dungeon-vault of solid stone,
Where not a ray could find a chink to pass ;
How wide a circle feels his light and heat —
That only shows, but not creates, his power.
The poison of the serpent, though concealed
In a slight bag beneath his hollow tooth,
Is poison not the less ; the poor dead child
That it has bitten, only shows its *work.*
The musk, while still shut up within the bag . . .
The fragrant incense in the silver box
Is even now the perfume, ere it fills
A temple, and all streets, the city through ;
The fire does naught but set its spirit free.
The camel, sleeping still in morning's light,
Is even now the tireless, willing beast,
Ready to bear his burden through the whole
Of the long day, whose gray dawn streaks the heavens.
The flute's sweet note is the same gracious tone
Even in the dungeon of the prisoner.
The air but wafts it airily away
From herdsman's lips, from mountain-crag to vale —
And so the good man is the good man still,

Though he had never yet opened his mouth,
Nor raised his hand to do a single work.
The shepherd watching faithfully his lambs,
The mother loving heartily her charge,
The father, who with vigor rules his house,
The helmsman true and tranquil in the storm,
The man who, like a general, cool and wise,
With nothing but a wooden king and queen,
And wooden pawns for peasants,* wins his fight
Upon a field no bigger than a dish —
These are the noble, great and good of men,
Incarnate only in contracted space,
With little influence near and visible,
But still the spirit of the great itself.
Give them a little knowledge quickly learned,
They were the very heroes of the earth ;
Only arrayed in somewhat greater forms,
And furnished with far-reaching, God-like arms,
They would be even exalted, God-like ones.

Mark this ! see clearly and believe it well,
For thine own cheer, and faith in all men's *worth !*
A heart which yields in goodness to no God,
A soul fair as the soul of any One,
As clear, as mild, as strong in love's own might,
A spirit that, God-conscious, conquers death,
That dreads *no man*, but only its own wrong,
Its own disgrace and its own slavery,
Is equal to the very greatest powers

* *Bauer* in German means *pawn*, as well as (primarily) *peasant.*

That live on any one of all the stars —
A longer, a more prosperous life, perchance,
But not a blesseder or more divine.

With this conviction now look out once more,
And see the toil-blest bees go flying by!
And see the blest industrious spider spin,
Yea, look upon the tranquil, restful flower,
See the song-gladdened lark soar up to heaven,
Filled with her joy as with the bliss of Gods —
Then look upon and weigh the prophets all,
Weigh all the princes and the emperors,
In this eternal balance, through all heavens
Acknowledged — and behold: *their influence*
Only through others' lives is visibly
Greater than the good heart of one poor man,
The pith of life, its worth in thee is like
That of all men, it is the heart of all
The beings of the universe, the heart
Of the great spirit of the universe;
Appearance does not truly make men *great*,
But only visible; *and many great*
Appearances are only soap-bubbles.
Gold, hidden in the mine-shaft, still is — gold.

TO WHOM THOU DOEST GOOD.

MAN, hast thou done kind service to thy friends ;
Hast thou through all the days and years she lived,
Been true and tender to thy wife, so far
As lay within thy power, made her life glad,
In her last sickness nursed her faithfully,
Put to her lips the last refreshing draught,
Pressed-to her eyes, adorned her lifeless form
Within the coffin, borne her to the grave
With honor due, and planted o'er the mound
Roses, to make a sweet and fitting rest —
To whom hast thou done this ? Answer I pray :
To *whom* hast thou done this ? Thou know'st full well ;
None — none but God alone can be — a man —
A human soul, the wife, the noble mother,
The loving, virtuous and beautiful !
No prophet could, poor man, so much as be
Even a kid, still less could be a child,
Not to say all the human race entire !
A man, a man — none can be that but God —
To none of all the prophets hast thou done
Thy good, — no, but to God, to God alone !
Not by the strength of any prophet, thou
Hast done the God-like work ; no, it was God,

And He alone, who did it for Himself,
Though by thy hand and from thy faithful soul
Which knew and reverenced God within itself.
And what of good thou doest to a child,
A beggar, that thou doest to God Himself,
That dost thou from the God Himself in thee.
Do it with zeal, then! with meek piety!

To set one's *single self* in place of God
Were shocking! even in thought were blasphemy!
Man, believe simply this: what does believe
Through thee—nay more, what *lives thee*, that is God.

THE GODDESS NEAR AT HAND.

SUCH darkness would not come upon thy house
If thou hadst quenched the sun ; — thou hast not *then*
Done such an evil thing, when thou hast set
The poor man's house on fire above his head,
As when thou sorely hast aggrieved thy wife !
She is the gladness of thy soul, the peace
And comfort of thy heart, the children's joy,
And, briefly, the good spirit of the house,
For whom thou livest and canst live happily
As for none else thou canst in the wide world !
What the beloved one has sanctioned thee,
To that the spirit of heaven has set its seal !
That dost thou cheerfully through sorest pains.
She says : "I am contented !" and thy lot
Is no more hard. She says "I feel no pain ;"
And thou, thou too art well. And if she bends
Her head to thee, and honors thee, then all
The excellent and honorable dames
Of earth have justified thee, have approved ;
For beauty, goodness, grace and love, themselves
Have smiled on thee in a now living form.
Afflict thyself then, rather than thy wife —
One's own distress is never great nor long

And never can it stay at the sweet word:
"Oh for my sake grieve not! it gives me pain...
I weep"—— such true and God-like power *that* heart
Can gently exercise upon thee, which
Thou lovest, and which loves thee heartily.
Then let thy wife's love be as dear to thee
As holy as the holy Queen of heaven,
As thine own goddess—and thy wife herself!

HOME, THE SACRISTY OF HEAVEN.

THE earth, and day with all its stores and works,
With all its treasures and its properties —
They too have life, like a vast body — they
Are to the man another *wife*, as good
As ever his own wife was! to the wife
As good a husband as her own e'er was.
The wife is to the man a nearer heaven,
The earth brought near and in a narrower form,
For his embrace, and to bear children to him,
The little ones, which earth and heaven then rear.
The earth is to the husband but the great
Eternal wife: who brings forth all his works
And rears and trains them up to demi-gods.
The wife is to the husband his own body,
The man to her is her own body too,
Answering as egg to chicken, cell to bee;
For daughters are descended from the man,
And sons, likewise, descended from the woman,
And both, when wedded, are *one* man of Heaven.
The Home is not "the little world" alone —
It is the mighty sun's true mother-house,
It is the Holy Heaven's great sacristy;
For without fruit the fig-tree has no use,
And the great tree of Heaven is good — for naught.

THE TRUE LIFE.

THE faithful sun brings each betimes his day;
The sun with every four and twenty hours
Brings myriads of million days to men.
Each one goes home at nightfall with his day:
Each rises with his day at morn. The lamb,
The tree, the flowers — have all received their day;
The blooming poppy and the violet
Have equally received their night and dew. —
The sun gives also, through the broad expanse,
To *many stars* peopled with countless souls
Innumerable days, to each its own!
And the innumerable suns that shine
In the immeasurable realms of space
Give to innumerable constellations,
Swarming all over with inhabitants:
The one great day of the whole universe,
The one great night, the hour of blessedness.
And all of them are giving this great day,
And all of them are giving this great night,
Forever — ceaselessly and endlessly.

And is that nothing? Is it no great gift?
And is it not the true kingdom of Heaven?

And is *that* nothing? all an idle lie?
And is not that *the true eternal life*
Which our One Spirit of the universe
Gives in such countless, boundless, endless forms
Of beauty and of bliss ineffable?
And can there be out of the living God
Who fills all space and each remotest nook
Completely with his truest, highest being,
Can there outside of him be anywhere
A private life? Beside his blessedness
Poured out already, — an o'erflowing sea, —
Another blessedness! — a future bliss . . .
One faithlessly withholden from this earth,
Saved for the world against a future day —
Of the great God that were the greatest sin;
He would not *be* God, if He hoarded it
Just as a miserly and senseless father
Saves for his children his most precious gifts
Against their death! and yet the world's great spirit
Whose life is all that was, is and will be . . .
Has saved, has starved *himself* out of his bliss
At his own spirit's, his own body's cost,
At his own life's cost in the life of all?

THE HALL OF SPIRITS.

THAT seems to thee so odd — so laughable :
That thou shouldst be a spirit (a ghost) yet breathe,
And body it and live, have head, hand, foot,
And feel the solid earth beneath thy feet ?
Well, wilt thou be a shadow, then, which none
Can touch, and through which every man can walk ?
So wilt thou be a dead man then, whom naught
Can stir in his immovable repose,
Who neither hears, nor sees, nor speaks, nor smiles ?
To be a shadow or a dead man, then,
Is all too thin for thee, and yet thy life,
As spirit, is disconcerted by the sun
In whose refulgent daylight thou dost walk
Visible to all the children ? — Oh the sun
Is half a farthing-candle to the dusk
Of the great night in all the universe :
Appearing here below in sunshine, thou
Art only walking in the shades of *night*. . .
A midnight apparition — hard on cock-crow !
Thou only hast come up for a brief while
After the lapse of an eternity
Out of the shadowy kingdom of the dead,
The holy grave of the old former world —

Thou tarriest here one turn of Uranus —
To look about thee, just to weep here once,
To love once, and to have men weep for thee —
Then disappear again for evermore
From out this earthly scene, this ghostly hall,
So full of juggling shapes and frightful masks,
That to the very mother her own child,
In his mysterious strange and fairy shape,
Only by use grows a familiar friend,
After a long, wild, wondering stare at him
And proving shyly all his little limbs,
As all young mothers secretly will do, —
And while thou tarriest here, does not thy glance
Climb the far mountain summits ? Soar by day
Up to the sun ? at evening to the moon ?
By night up to the stars ? Dost thou not dive
With ease into the old world's earliest depths
And its last distances ? dost thou not pierce
With wizard's might the souls of other men,
And fetter cunningly bliss-breathing shapes
With silken chains of love to thee forever ?
And is then *he* no spirit by whom the world
Was not created ? Then there is no spirit.
And thou hast come too late ; then none has here,
Not even the master, any more to do ;
And he may fold his hands, like the old dame
Who has spun off her wheel long hours ago ;
Nay, but all spirits have a spirit's work, —
(Thou too both hands full,) when they touch this earth,
Both hands full, when they vanish from it. Thou,

Thou knowest what spirit's work and labor is:
Creating life! free action, ever free —
The spirit's watchword! the old sacred rite
Valid through all the spirit's boundless realm,
The ancient gladness and the ancient love,
The Beautiful, that highest of all spells
By which spirits rule the world and other spirits,
Which calls all good that is but beautiful —
And thereby thou createst it to be
Thine own, and thereby *dost create thyself!*
And wert thou not, thou wouldst be made, a spirit,
By such existence, by such magic works,
Such beauty shown during thy earthly stay,
Such pangs of agonizing woe, such tears,
Such yearning sorrow when thou vanishest,
Before all eyes going down into the grave,
And by the midnight torch-light of the sun
Convoyed thou sail'st out into our great night.
This with clear faith hold fast: thou art a spirit
In human guise, with skin and hair, with bone
And marrow, only so a genuine spirit;
Else were thou but a shadow, but a dream!

PERFECTION.

O MEN, count not your gifts within yourselves,
Nor carry on heart-reckonings with each other;
When God sends rain from Heaven, he does not count
The drops, but pours them out in plenteous showers.
But say'st thou: "God owns all things! all forever!"
I answer thee: well, yes, and God gives all,
So, only give thou all! For *every man*
Who gives his all is just as rich as God
And even *more blessed* — were it possible —
Since what is given away he has no more —
Yet gives away what is not his, but God's,
Who gave it him to be his heart's delight!
God *lends* for a short time — man *gives* forever.
God lives and never dies: he cannot give
His life a sacrifice — lo! man gives his
Joyfully for his loved ones! Thus does God
First become perfect and complete in man,
Man whom He blesses with the soul divine.

OUR OWN.

WHAT means: to give thy life up for thine own?
To leap into the well . . . strangle thyself?
And leave the written words: "behold my love!" —
To give thy life up for thy kindred means:
To consecrate to them sincerely all
Thy days, to toil, to care for them with joy,
To bear them in thy heart continually
As thy choice treasures, reverencing them
Devoutlier than the images of God;
To gain the days by losing them in toil,
To gain the nights by gladly losing them,
The Springs, the Summers, Autumns, Winters all:
And all thy years to the last closing year,
To the last day and evening of thy life,
Still drawn and bound to them with all thy soul.
Thus giving, daring all things, sparing nothing
For their sakes, power or love or soul itself—
So dost thou give thy life up for thy kin.
Thy *life*, however, that was not thy *death*,
Thy dying long beforehand, thy last day!
Now go, and offer up thy life to them,
As they themselves do all their lives to thee,
The labor of their hands and even the hand

Therewith . . . The overwatching of the eye,
The energy of heart, the soul's affection,
The days of youth, the wisdom of old age,
The friendly and familiar intercourse,
And with all: Heart and soul! and world and life!

But all of this thy kindred cannot do
For all; for many; only *thee alone.*
All this thou canst not do for all! for many!
Only for thine! yet this canst fully do!
And in the doing thou findest life's reward.

Thus each man finds salvation in his kin.

THE REFUGE OF THE POOR.

THIS know thou: If thou hast an honest mind,
'Twill lift thee up above thy fate, and make
E'en poverty and hardship light to thee —
Thou canst be free in giving — *yet have naught!*
A miser thou canst be — yet very rich.
Be of good courage then! thy honest mind
Lifts thee above thy fate! Then labor thou
More busily than for mere gold and goods:
To gain a noble soul and glad, good heart!
Be not still worse than thy unhappy case,
Be always better still than thy best lot.
Who forces thee to *feel* within thyself
Only as in the world it *fares* with thee?
In such case all the poor must always weep,
And the good-hearted should be always sad.

THE BEGGAR-MAN.

AND fanciest thou, the poor old beggar-man
Roams round forever like a ghost on earth;
Because he glides so visibly to thy door!
He has been coming now these million years,
And in these latter days strangely to thee,
And haply, Saturday, will come no more!
Thou art to him peculiar; so to thee
Is he, now from a boy grown old and weak,
And grown so poor and feeble on men's earth,
And will so soon be a rich man again,
And no more suffer want — like all the dead.
Well then: now coarsely drive him from thy house,
And set the dogs on him, and laugh and hoot,
When in his haste he stumbles o'er his cane,
And lies there helpless, sprawling on his face.
But be assured then that thou hast in vain
A wife and child, — thou know'st not *who they are;*
Then be assured thy gold and treasures thou
In vain possessest — for thou know'st not *why;*
Nor know'st: *How short a time;* thou know'st not this: —
To God Himself his life is beautiful,
To man his life on earth is beautiful,
Only so far as by his spirit he
Breathes beauty over it and through it bliss.

THE SAINTS.

FULL many a noble man has had to bear
A dismal fate, — man at the hands of men, —
Their hate, their errors, their fanatic rage;
Suddenly, ignominiously they sank
Trampled into the earth with nameless woe;
They sank like water spilt upon the ground;
Yet still the story of their dismal fate
Lives ever on men's tongues; their image stands
As if in marble, weeping in the world,
And whoso hears of them or looks on them,
He also weeps, sorely bemoaning them.
O beauteous lot, to touch the hearts of men!
To wring out tears of pity from the eyes
Of unknown generations through all time!
To be a *man of sorrows*, that is sweet!
To be a sound of sorrow in the mouths
Of myriad men, and tears in myriad eyes.
The unhappy man is *really* the tear,
He is the sadness in them, he *himself!*
Nature creates not mortal ones alone,
She makes immortals also, like to gods,
Who sweep afar down the long line of days
And to poor mortals say invisibly:

" Be calm ! be glad ! thou sufferest naught ! But I
Have suffered. Look on me — and be thou glad ! "
Let him then who endures fate's hardness, whether
He suddenly or slowly perish, think :
" A solace thou shalt be to myriad hearts,
Shalt be their sorrow, ah, and even their tears ! "
And then, when sinks his dust into the earth,
He mounts as spirit, as a flame to heaven :
Heaven in the heart ! And as man felt himself
For the last time before he left the world,
He feels himself forever. Even in parting
His life all darts into its solid core
And shines forever a bright star in heaven.

THE RELICS.

RELICS . . . who ever lived that had them not?
Without these treasures who would care to live?
The heavens are all one great sarcophagus
Full of the holy dust of holy life.
Man gazes sadly at the ancient stars
Which in the dim old ages brightly shone
O'er every head and now shine down on his.
They have survived the world-consuming fire,
As if they were the sparks it flung abroad;
The stars are the most aged, immemorial
Old relics of the ancient God Himself;
The witnesses: that in the magic cave
He once has lived, and furnished forth all life,
As a great feast, a banquet of the Gods,
And there the torches still are burning on
In the new morning! And the sun hangs there
The true old chandelier to light our earth.
Earth is the holy altar where, below,
Heaps of once living bones, are mouldering now
In peace! Each handful of the dust thou tread'st,
A touching relic, of long-withered flowers
And human children, who saw fourscore years.
The earth abides forever — they are gone.

'Tis not the relics that are venerable,
They only *witness* what is venerable,
And chain our hearts in mute astonishment.
Yes, he who fell devoutly on his knees,
Before yon stars, yea, he who knelt in prayer,
He piously would feel the life they saw
With rapture, he would reverence that old life
Because he looked with awe on men to-day,
Because he loves *his own* and even respects
Himself as without duplicate for all time ;
To the unloving, God's a hollow spectre.
The *ashes* of *burnt straw* all men despise.
But to the loving, nay to him who only
Can feel astonishment, the childlike man,
Who sees in the first blade of tender grass
A miracle ; for him each relic charms
The spirit forth that first appeared in it,
The love that once expressed itself thereon,
The lovely soul, that raimented in dust
Still lived and loved — and vanished into dust,
As the poor roses and poor violets,
With none to save them, moulder into earth.
And with the wonder *melancholy* blends,
The truest relic of the universe,
That still is left of all that charmed the soul
With beauty, glory and divinity !
And so too are the great old temples all,
With all their many rigid marble feet,
Their ribs, the hollow sockets of their eyes,
The green and moss-grown *shell* of the wide roof,

Only the relics of a monstrous beast
Of the old world! And so are the old scrolls
All only relics, even the holiest,
On which that wizard of the world's great stage
With a light touch impressed his spirit once,
And then like violet-fragrance, in his springs,
Exhaled with it. And what but relics are
Whole cities peopled still with myriads
Of hermits swarming through their streets to-day?
A relic is thine own paternal roof,
The garden, which was once thy mother's care,
That mother's baby-spoon, her first year's shoes,
Which as a wonder of the holy world
At the glad marriage board are carried round
Upon a platter to the guests in turn:
To show the young lady as a *little child*,
And soon to be a mother, who will soon
Need such another pair of shoes again,
To put upon *her* little native gods,
Who will in turn sit at the marriage board
And soon have need of little shoes again
To put upon their little native gods.
For He who in this ever-shifting play
Of generations, still so gloriously
Lives on, can surely be none else than God!
And He *appears* to the glad marriage-guests,
And they are *mute!* and many a mother weeps!
But in his open soul the father sees:
That man himself is but the sacred relic
Of father and of mother; not alone

The precious lock which he with tearful eyes
And reverent hand cut from the dead one's head —
The very hair on his own blooming head,
The fingers of his hand which he beholds
As wonder-works and mysteries, they are relics
Of father and of mother, even as *they*
Were relics of their fathers and their mothers ;
And men are holy relics all of God !
Witnesses to attest His ancient life !
But holier be to thee the God who lives to-day !
Discern His presence in the present spring,
Which is a wonder once that no man sees !
Admire his beauty in the present rose,
And lingering dew-drops of the starry night,
Embrace Him in thy tender, blooming wife ;
Her eye be holier to thee than the stars ;
Richly reciprocate her love with love ;
Pay honor to thy children as young gods.
For thou wilt also with thy wife one day
Be to the generation yet unborn
A wonder and strange relic of the past.
For there are common relics that belong
To all, — the old heirloom of earth itself,
The mountains, vale and stream, and moon and sun ;
And then to each, peculiar, precious ones,
Valued and venerated more than all :
The plough which once the father drove a-field ;
The dear old pear-tree which his father planted ;
The old time-piece on the wall, the cuckoo-clock
That even above his cradle voiced its call,

And like the genius of their humble cot
Called blessings down for thousand happy homes;
The wedding-ring sent down from son to son;
Grandmother's little pearly white child's-tooth;
The glass from which the dear sick mother took
Full many a sip of water and her last;
The lamp that in the death-night gave for her
Its feeble glimmer and survived her still;
The last few threads of yarn upon the spool
Which her industrious hand so gladly spun;
The last of violets her child brought to her;
The old church-spectacles for Sunday use —
These are the holy things; whereby to see
God, if one can achieve it, and our loves
In Him! whoso has relics dear to him,
He whose eye gazes on them, till his heart
Is melted into the great reverence,
Needs not another's treasures — strange to him;
Enough, too much, for him to have his own,
He has enough in self and wife and children,
A sense of bliss transfiguring the world;
Honors himself, as breathing saintly form,
And lives a saint and honors *living ones!*

THY FAITH.

WHO, down in this deep cavern, then, has made
All in the darkness here, the tender moss?
Has the *whole God* Himself descended here?
The whole Great God from all the starry heavens,
To the last corner of the farthest space,
The whole Great God Himself with His whole might?
Not surely the whole God; for He remained
Himself up yonder in the starry heavens,
In farthest space filling the universe.
Who now in this deep cavern, then, has made
Down in the darkness here the delicate moss?
But tell me first of all: Why was this moss
Not made a star? So much even as a palm?
Who teaches then the little drop to fall here?
Who shows the little spider how to spin?
Who teaches the young bee to build her cells,
Small, yet complete as the great starry arch!
Who ever taught the little gnat to fly?
Hast thou then seen the teachers, hast thou heard
The instructresses who taught a sunflower
To rise into the air out of its seed?
The little apple-tree from out its core?
Not the whole God with His entire might

Has taught and done all this. Of the whole God
A portion full of God, a being divine
Itself, with power and magic virtue filled,
That lived and wrought here for its own delight,
Which it shares not with any nor can share,
Which naught despoils nor can despoil it of.
So every thing fulfils its God-like life
Encompassed by the magic potencies
Of all the rest, so far as it can stretch
Its arms, its twigs, for help. Yet by *itself*
All lives! Each *must* live by itself, indeed,
That so the proffered aid may serve its need;
Else all things, flowers and trees, and beast and man,
Yea, and the very *stars* themselves would be
Mere phantoms, mirrorings of all the powers
At work in the great universe around;
And even these powers themselves too all were naught!
But thou, O man, be of thyself quite sure,
And of thy spirit, which is thou! *Thou hast*
Nothing beside; through it alone hast thou
The fair rich world, and God so far alone
As love divine wells up within thy soul.
Hold fast thy God and on thyself believe.
Thy faith is thy possession, is thyself.

LOVE TO GOD—GOD'S LOVE.

THOU that hast lost by death a precious heart,
And seest the image of the form so loved
Stand mute and motionless before thee now—
Thou wilt, and thou alone canst worthily
Honor the sorrow of the men of old
Who kept the memory of the loved and lost
Immortalized in fair and lovely forms
Of brass and marble, had their images
Cut out in stone and wore them in their rings,—
Thus even when the holy ancients lived,
Even then innumerable forms called "man"
Profoundly, so profoundly mourned their dead,
Shed many thousand burning tears for them;
Ah how the human race has wept, has wept!—
—The human race?—Who was it then? 'Twas not
The human race that shed those tears, that mourned,
That was dissolved in bitter grief and followed
In death the dead so passionately loved.
Who were they then—who was that weeping race?
—*The Spirit of the universe!* 'Twas He
Who wept His tears out through the eyes of men;
Himself has He lamented, with the hearts
And lips of men has He bewailed Himself,

The forms which were Himself, He with their hands
Has buried, heaping up above their heads
Mounds, monuments, — memorials of life,
For signs: that ever His eternity
Subsists but by things fleeting, born alone
Of ever new and ever bitter death.
And even despair itself is better far,
By far more noble and divine than cold
Forgetfulness, iron indifference.
And have you not this long time far and wide
Wept all of you a Son of God, who died
A cruel death? Came not a whisper there:
That even God dies, that God Himself can die
And will, and that too though He *will not* die —
By force of *His* original primal nature,
Which He, by no compulsion from without,
Yet with an iron firmness bears and must
Bear in Himself eternally — He must
By virtue of this nature — ever die . . .
Only without once ever being dead,
That so He may *be able evermore*
To feel a holy melancholy, such
As no unbroken life, and though it were
As blessed as a child's, could ever give!
For to lose life in seeming, only seem
To sacrifice the highest rapture, *that*
For God Himself in man, and to the God
In all, is highest rapture, so first known,
So only. — And were not this holy cause,
This reason coming from the primal world,

Death's final cause to the primeval spirit,
Then would all thought, all knowledge, all research,
Then would all highest love itself — have *none!*
But now, by dying, by *beholding death*,
By such departing never to return,
Such disappearing from the light of day,
Such giving up for all the days of life,
Is dust itself transfigured to God's dust;
Dust moulded into shape grows into bliss
In human tears and human lamentations,
Which are the lamentations and the tears
Only of that forever blessed One,
The eternal Spirit of the universe,
Who pours them forth immediately, Himself;
For every shape is His eternal shape,
And every soul is His eternal soul. —
Those were old scraps, old sparks (those words of old),
Of the great Spirit of this universe
Who ever on the earth has felt and known
Himself, and long ago *expressed* Himself
In holy forms He wore in earlier days;
Old scraps, old sparks of Him, the words that said:
"Who gives to drink a cup of water, he
Gives it to God. Who looks on me, a man,
Looks upon God." Who to a dying man
Gives comfort, gives a joy to God Himself.
See God then in all beings near and clear,
And lo! ye see and feel Him in yourselves!
Do good to your own selves and all around you.
He who has honored, loved a living man,

He who has truly wept and mourned one dead,
That man has loved, lamented, wept for God,
All full of the sweet preciousness of death,
All full of the pure blessedness of love.
And out of God alone all love wells up!
And it is God alone whom all love *means*,
He from whom only, every breath proceeds,
By whom each finest dust-grain lives and loves.
Naught is but God, and full of Him is all,
Full as of love, so of His loveliness;
And even the beauteous, God-like frame of man
Is the deep, holy, honored reservoir
Of love, from which alone man learns and draws
And tastes of love, and from no other source
Divine than this clear, inexhaustible well!

THE PARTING.

TO each at last the earnest parting comes,
Beginning of the end of mortal life,
Harvest of all the loves and all the woes
A man's heart treasures up within itself,
Which earth and heaven have kept in store for him,
And now shake down upon him in a *shower*,
Just as the eastern kings, returning home
From victory, at the triumphal feast
Had pearls and jewels rained on them by hands
Of love, in welcome golden beaker-fulls.
The days, to suffering and to loving ones,
Seem now for the first time true holy times ;
Now glowing memory sees that all the days
Of life were just so holy, just so rare,
So matchless. Yet who thinks of this ! And better :
Who *should* not think of this : From forethought free,
So fearless, full of love and care, *these* days
Are the true life days. This is clearly seen
Now by the suffering and the loving ones,
And a faint gratitude creeps through the song,
And the grave's breath cuts chilling through the heart.
The beauteous, beauteous days are ending now,
They cease and never will come back again.

For the last time all things begin henceforth
So softly to transpire. For the last time
The almond blooms, . . . how sweetly, wondrously;
Itself a miracle; a miracle
The eye that looks upon it; the still soul
That sees once more that friend of youthful days,
Adorned with all the grace of *all its years!* . . .
For the last time, now, comes the father home
With such a friendly joy in *all his kin;* . . .
For the last time the sun goes down; the stars
For the last time climb up the darkling sky; . . .
For the last time on yonder moonlit hill
The children sing their songs to Easter night.
For the last time around the table all
The gathered loved ones sit. For the last time
The children tell the mother a good-night, . . .
The mother on each forehead prints a kiss,
And clasps them long in silence to her breast . . .
For the last time comes sleep, the friend of man . . .
For the last time a holy stillness reigns.
Till suddenly the *parting* startles all;
Hope flees abruptly from the sobbing ones;
Fear shrinks and cowers, and death, invisible,
Speaks the last word, well understood: Depart!—
Then for *the last time* is there *parting* too!
And bursts of more than childish tears are heard,
As ne'er before; yet not for the last time.—
For *parting's* sake alone was death devised;
On life's account it needed not have been,
But parting is the silver-glance of love;

Rich, and replete with all divinity ;
Then first the spirit feels fully what it is,
Had here, has still and takes away with it.
Calm and devout then be the parting hour!
For nowhere is there *greater* festival,
Any so high, so holy mystery,
In any temple, any realm of space,
As where love dwells beneath the lowliest roof.

THE END.

THERE stands in flower thy bed of hyacinths,
Thou seest them all bloom out and fade away,
They have gone out like bright and brilliant flames.
Thy friend, who comes to visit thee, finds none ;
He would almost be glad, could he deny
That flowers had been here — thou canst give no proof
To him that they have lived — but thou thyself
Must sadly own each flower has had an end,
And though they have fulfilled their *being's end*,
Their end has come. They're gone, and nevermore
Shall *they* return ! never these graceful heads !
So the sick mother feels and truly says
From her heart's depths : "When will my last end come?"
Though such a word will rend the children's hearts.
"His end has come at last!" the people say,
Of the oppressor though he has not harmed
Their bodies ; only, fearfully, their spirits ;
Who fain would not have left their souls free life,
Nay, would have stamped upon them all his head
As on so many coins, and yet could not,
For by God's will each human heart is free.
"*Who knows how near my end may be!*" So says
The aged father, and the children all

Believe his word and see it soon fulfilled —
He came — and he has finished, and he says
Justly : It is fulfilled, this brief, this vain
And transitory life, which for each man,
Speeds like a whizzing comet to its end,
Like meteors that shoot and fall to earth,
Once and forever lived, and made to tell,
Once and forever, then forever gone.
To cease, to make clean end of that which each
Has been : here, as a hyacinth, and there,
A violet; there as rose and here as man —
Such is the end, if in this universe
End there can be ; the only possible
And all-sufficient end for all that lives
And loves and wears a body and a form
And has a feeling of its days, and feels
For *other* forms, which it uniquely loved
And none beside in all eternity
And in all worlds. Living, alone, is life,
But even the violet puts its raiment on,
Made of old earth and of old heavenly dew;
It lived upon the ancient dew of heaven,
On sun and moon that wove its spring-time for it;
Now in its lifetime it exhales again
The violet ether into the old Ether,
The father and the heir of all the creatures,
Inheriting them all with all they are,
And all they were, for He gave them Himself,
Gave them His pure, original ancient spirit,
That they might feel themselves to *be* themselves,

And when they end, He takes it back again.
Thus He who is Himself without beginning
With heavenly bliss begins in them their life —
Thus even He the endless One, with bliss
Celestial, in them, with them ends their life.
And if the sun, when he has day by day
Risen at morn, when he has day by day
Expired at evening, still remains the sun —
The days themselves are nevertheless gone hence,
They *end* — they end, because they once began.
So violets and hyacinths and men
End, and forevermore. Their children only,
Their like, return ; *of them not even the shadow*
They cast on earth ever returns again.
For to be one by itself, precious and dear
To other forms, as sacredly themselves,
Invaluable, irreplaceable, —
For this that ancient force exalts, ennobles,
Glorifies, yea, even deifies itself,
Which, in its old familiar homely life,
Save for itself, has small significance!
Thus grows the smoke of coal to brilliant flame,
Thus the sea's breath to the bright bow of heaven,
The marble mountain to the form of gods ;
And all that lives, ye living ones, esteem
Far higher than all suns, all potencies.
And prize the heavenly soul *that loves you*, far
Above all love — that is but idle fire ;
And prize the enchanted creatures *that you love*
Higher than all the universe with all

Its contents, all its creatures and its spirit;
For not till in this single, special shape,
Was He so sweetly, blessedly *near you, in you;*
For only in *this unique form* are ye
So sweetly, blessedly *near Him and in Him!*
And love has no beginning, has no end,
And blessedness has neither bound nor time,
And life itself is love and blessedness.

THE HOLY WEEK.

TO every house there comes its holy week,
Haply its holy month, its holy year:
The interval that passes, from the day
When first we know, a loved one soon shall die . . .
Be buried . . . vanish from our sight, be gone—
Until the hour when he does verily die.
That is your holy time, children of men,
On which ye look with sad presentiments;
The holy time, too, of the sufferers,
The amphibious souls that in a dumb amaze
Hover between the earth, the grave and heaven . . .
Now, look already down from heaven to earth . . .
Now, look already from their grave to heaven.
They go to bid the vale a last farewell,
They sit upon the mountain-top till night,
Till moonrise, till the sparkling stars come out,
And love to hear a loud voice call them home;
They go to bid farewell without a word
To the old church; their childish plays; to take
Leave of the garden where the roses hang
Which are one day to bloom, the kindly trees
Which have so often dropped down fruit for them,
Beneath whose shade they rested on the grass.

By others unperceived, they touch the stem
Once more in token of their gratitude,
And the young trees in silent benison.
They bid farewell to *clouds not yet arrived!*
The snow that on the distant mountains lies
Sleeping, and will not melt till they are gone —
The fount that trickles down so silently,
The old, eternal, holy mystery.
The friend comes yet once more to see her friend;
The friend comes oftener now to see his friend,
Yet once more, as to one that soon shall be
A rarity, that only a short time
Shall longer bloom on earth — *the king of day.*
The children all lead and accompany,
With trembling joy at still possessing her,
The kindly mother, who so sweetly smiles
And seats herself among them all once more,
Not yet an angel, scarce a woman more,
Only a lingering shadow, not yet gone.
The pigeons all come fluttering to her feet. . .
The lambkin comes . . . and the tame magpie comes
And chatters oddest things, that make one weep!
The bees go buzzing by her to their work —
She folds her hands and lays them in her lap,
And shuts her eyes, the children all are hushed . . .
She hands them now the earliest violets
And weeps, good woman, as she looks on them . . .
The cuckoo calls — but once, and then breaks off,
And all look at each other and grow pale,
But she — she only *smiles*, and the sun — *shines.* —

At last it grows a sadness to go out
Into that tenderest, loveliest warmth of spring,
Into that all enlivening, balmy air;
She only shrinks and says: "I am afraid!"
— This is your holy time, children and men,
The holy time, for each one to the full
As holy, as was ever to a man,
Full as to *all* in all the universe;
Rich, as all kings together ever knew,
Poor, as all beggars know on all the earth
And through the heavens; in its sad sweetness given
Only to the departing and their loves;
By God 'tis consecrated, theirs alone,
Yet not alone to the now mouldering dead!
That time, like death, is the *one given to all*,
Which even the bird celebrates in the twigs,
When with hushed breath he folds his wings to die;
The time which raises mortals into Gods,
Transfiguration of themselves and God.

THE LAST PARTING.

NAUGHT *but a parting is the death of man;*
For other death there is not nor can be
In all the range of this safe heavenly realm.
Thus is the death of man the soft farewell
He life long dies, from tottering childhood up,
And onward every day through all his days.—
Each blade of grass lives here but once on earth,
Once for all time and all eternity.
In heaven there grows no grass and not a rose,
In heaven *that* grass will never bloom again,
Else would the holy earth not be the earth,
Nor yet would heaven be heaven, nor would the grass
Be grass, nor even man himself be man.
Never again lives *this* man here on earth,
Never again shall to his bosom clasp
The form beloved; never be husband more
Nor wife; for him no more shall children bloom,
No more the sun shall light him to his tasks,
The smallest of them he shall do no more;
Never a raindrop falls upon his head
Twice out of heaven. He never shall grow old
Again, not twice be mourned for as one dead. . .
Never again shall other mouldering bones

Of him lie in the grave! Each time a task
Is *done*, *there* also is a taking leave
Of it; to drain the beaker is to take
Leave of this draught; to rise from table means
A parting from the meal; to rise from bed
A parting from the sleep and from the dream,
Which man shall sleep no more, shall dream no more.
Every *completion* is at the same time
A final parting from it, as the artist
Parts from his work.— Yet to the *living* man
This constant and familiar leave-taking
Is his *life's joy*, for the farewell itself
Is pleasantly disguised by still new tasks;
But his past works ever accompany
Man in the spirit and work out for him
After well being, richly building up
Life as a house for him wherein he dwells.
The final parting is the real death,
The full surrender, utter letting go,
The blessing and resigning of all that
Which man has ever wrought from his youth up
Till now—till his last day. . . the holy hour
When on the sight of the departing one
His dead all rise again, stretch out a hand
And bid him welcome, when on lightning wings
Life's joys all weeping glide before his eyes.
Like dream-shapes to his rigid stare now seem
They that were once so real and so dear—
Those dear ones now as utter strangers close
His eyes for him. . . for *him*, as if he too

Were but a phantom shape from their life dream,
Now fallen dead and lying visibly
Before them there, all wet with burning tears;
And now all trust in that dumb, sun-bright world,
From which the truest, most beloved, believed,
Have melted into air. . . and *disappeared,*
Is henceforth rooted out and utterly
Dead and extinct, as the grave's tenants are.—
To feel our bygone life, our loves themselves,
The long since vanished ones — still with us here
Beneath *our* sun, strangely to know of them,
To know *them*, bear them in our conscious breast —
Is what we mean by "anguish" for the dead;
A greater wonder (greatest far of all,
Which it confounds the mind to comprehend)
Than if we had partaken henbane root,
Than if we had ourselves the philter drunk
Of death, *we*, and not *they*, the silent dead,
And verily the living, they alone
Do drink death's beaker, yea, and drain it dry,
Conscious! benumbed! while the dead. . . only sleep.
All that the *living* in his day of life
Was called to see already snatched from him
And vanish evermore, Youth, Beauty, Joy,
Like an intoxication which next morn
Is as a dream when one awakes from sleep —
Shall not the *dying* calmly let it go
For his death's time, the after dream of life?
Only to shake out nut-shells from their laps
Have the departing — to fling chaff away —

The bread has long been eaten, the seed sown
To spring and grow beneath another sun.
Not: thinking on this brief and fleeting *work*
Can be the eternal soul's eternal *life* . . .
On this still, everlasting leave-taking,
And on the final parting which is death.
The final parting is no endless parting,
It is as short as sundown, it creates
No endless *deprivation* and regret,
No infinite sense of something *missed* and lost;
For even the robbed-of-all soon goes himself;
The evening sun to the long shadows says:
" I vanish ; and ye vanish too. The more
Ye stretch your length out over field and vale,
The sooner shall ye disappear like me."
So also do our dead ones speak to us
When the time seems to us too long till night;
The sorest parting is the blessedest:
It is the witness of our truest love,
And of the highest worth in those we love.
Thus sweetest solace lies in saddest grief;
The happiest only reaches the blest woe
Of being the unhappiest, but only
Because he once has been the happiest.
Through tears he holds as by a magic spell
Before his sight the bliss he once enjoyed, —
A rainbow builded of his very tears ;
His *sorrows* — they are only his *past* bliss
Still living ! to the sad and sorrowing heart,
The sincere mourner, not a joy can die,

Can fade, for him who does not in his heart
Bury in cold despair a buried heart.
Vain is all thy ado about the dead ;
Can prayer, or mass, or penance bring them back ? —
One thing I know, and only one, that soothes,
That strengthens and that comforts. . .*grief !* Ay grief
Belongs to life as a sweet part of it,
As a constituent and essential part,
Oft even to youth through many a troubled year,
To age most surely, though for a short time ;
But all the deeper, richer, the more brief.
A child has not yet gained much ; only he
Who largely has possessed can greatly lose.
Therefore the richest loser is the old,
For he can lose the entire human world.
Who loves most, he can shed the sweetest tears,
Yet even righteous griefs are griefs no less !
Thus is our loveliest, our truest life
The *presence* of our friends ! their intercourse
With us : our seeing, hearing, loving them ;
Their hearing, seeing, feeling us so near
As spirits *nevermore are near* each other
For loud, exulting, and enrapturing joy,
For *blissful peace !* Bodily nearness is
The *nearest* neighborhood of souls, the heaven
Of love, the purest satisfaction given
To heart and eyes . . . filling them e'en to tears. —
— O ye who live, to you each hour brings joy !

THE EAGLE.

THE feeling of security, the sense
Of satisfaction as the well tuned heart's
Clear ring, man needs, that he may make his way
Onward with calmness, and with confidence
May do his work, and even freely breathe.
First and not least joy needs firm standing ground, —
He who is rich and well does ; and the poor and sick.
The upward, heavenward look shall strengthen him
As if he saw there thousands of the blest
Who comfort him with looks that gladly say :
There still is bliss ! somewhere up there on high !
Even though he toil and pine and suffer here.
But without shrinking, without fright to look
Up even to heaven, and down with sweet content
To earth, which now in stillness holds his grave,
That needs the sharp, discerning eye to see
What an immense, nay infinite realm of woe
The ancient Death up yonder does *not* sway ;
How he does *not* there waste, destroy, make wholly vain
The beings' life, and make the universe
A terror and a horror in its vast,
Frightful immensity and endlessness.
Sorrow is man's best teacher. The old father

And the old mother of my youthful wife
Had on one day both gently breathed their last,
Had on one day been buried in one grave.
And now she stood in the bright, starry night
Gazing from out the old tower all undisturbed
By me, as I close by her sat asleep.
I reverenced her grief, yea her desire
To cherish the blest dream that her dear dead
Were happy somewhere up there overhead
In heaven ; may even to behold them there
As stars ; for it is written that the good
With brightness of the stars shall shine. 'Twas yet
Long time to moonrise. — When at length I woke
Roused by gold blaze and quivering of my eyes,
There stood the moon high in the firmament;
But she — on the stone balustrade bowed down . . .
With low and agonizing sobs of grief
And with closed eyes she lay there fast asleep,
And I awoke her calling her by name.
Then on my breast she fell, as if a friend's
Breast were a refuge for her from all Heavens !
And when she had collected and composed
Herself, and knew me and herself, she said:
" How good, that thou still livest, that I live!
But scarce can I believe this greatest wonder. —
I saw in dream this night wide open stand
The true, the great, eternal house of death !
The house — it was the old familiar world
Where we had spent our lives from childhood up.
I sat upon a gold-brown Eagle's back

That hung there still, as if nailed up in air.
I knew: that *every seven thousand years*
One of his feathers only would turn white,
And when at last he had grown white as snow,
Then, when a hundred thousand years had passed,
One feather would grow brown . . . and all at last
At such long intervals! He could not tell
How many million times he had grown white,
And then grown back to brown again, with age.
Now he was brown, without a plume of white.
Then softly, slowly he rose up with me,
Glittering all over with a lustrous light
As if his flight were through a mine of gold,
And constellations above constellations
Came down to meet us, large and luminous;
Quite nearly, clearly, could I look on each,
Quite plainly could distinguish every voice;
And through all bloom and green that hid each disk,
I saw wide open many thousand graves;
And 'spite the swarming populations all,
Thousands of dead I saw lie buried there,
While mid the hum and din of funeral trains
We slowly swept along and soared aloft,
Till I compassionately wrung my hands.
And in the disk of every new-found star
Again I saw the graves stand open wide,
Heard the heart-piercing, agonized *alas*
On each one's dying lips! . . . What an alas
Forever groaning up from million souls!
And so we landed on the stars of graves

And so the dread alas ! still met my ear,
So long, long, such immeasurable time, —
Till of the Eagle's feathers one grew white !
Then to the right he bore me through the sky,
And in the sidelong sweep I also saw
The graves upon the stars all open stand,
And heard in tones heart-piercing that alas ! . . .
When, as in stern rebuke, the Eagle asked,
'*Hast thou created then the starry host ?*'
I, struck with awe, for answer only prayed,
But he swept onward. Mute I gazed around,
Still heard I the alas ! . . . and I too sobbed.
And when I now had dried my eyes again,
Then had the Eagle an unmeasured time
So long, so long, so far, swept on with me,
That all the feathers of his neck were white . . .
And now I shuddered as I thought: how many,
How many of the death-stars have we seen !
Then did he gently let himself descend,
Down — down — so many hundred thousand years
That all the feathers now on both his wings
Were white ; and all that long time while I gazed —
As if let down on a great amber chain,
Still other stars arose upon my sight
On which innumerable graves stood open
Wherein they lowered constantly their dead,
From each of whom came forth that sad alas !
The alas ! groaned out from the woe-laden breast,
The alas ! wrung out from the soul's parting hour,
The alas ! that made my innocent soul to quake.

Love had long since been stifled in my breast,
I had long since had no more tears to shed,
And as the sun, so still was now my face ;
My heart was ice and long had ceased to beat.
Then asked the dreadful Eagle, once again :
'Shall I go down a hundred thousand times
As far through the abyss ? Millions of times
As high soar with thee ? . . . To the right . . . so far ?
Leftward . . . so far ? We yet have time. Then come.
Yet hear me and believe : the living die
On all the stars with that profound alas . . .
Wilt thou have been the maker of the stars ?
Wilt thou then be their master, nurse and mother ?
Yet ere thou answer, weigh thy answer well !
Not only *is* it so throughout the vast,
The boundless universe, nay so it *was*
So long, long, such immeasurable time,
That I so many times have changed to white . . .
And brown, as there have raindrops fallen from heaven,
So many times as there are grains of sand
On all the stars, times so innumerable
That all, all water had a thousand times
Been tears already, and all, all the air
Already sighs, yea even the sore death groan ;
Of earth each handful had been . . . dead men's dust.
And wilt thou wait, canst thou endure so much,
Then shalt thou see, that it shall last so long —
So long, that I shall for so many times
As there are stars : have grown *now* white, *now* brown,
And inconceivably longer, — long ! how long ! ' —

Then I with horror from the Eagle plunged
Down from those terrors into the abyss,
Hoping to fall out of the universe,
Away from death and graves, away from love,
More willing not to be than full of dread,
When lo, thy voice called to me in the heavens,
Thy name rang through me with a saving power . . .
Then on thy bosom I awoke with joy —
Yet here am I in dream brought face to face
With the bare truth that like a nightmare weighs
Upon the universe in which we live! . . .
Live— did I say? Nay if I longer live,
I only wander round a death-pale ghost
As livid forms that leave the grave roam round, —
To all a terror, even the little ones
Who fear their very mother . . . till she weeps!"

And her whole body trembled as she spake.
When she had wept out on me all her tears
And passionately clasped me to her breast,
Me, as a wondrous shape apart from all
On all the stars she in her flight had seen,
I put to her that Eagle's question then:
Wouldst thou not then have had God make the stars,
And wouldst thou rather never have been born
And sooner when thou diest die utterly? —
That Eagle was the bird of wisdom, wife!
He has made known to thee the eternal life
Which in despite of death is jubilant;
He has assured thee of the eternal love

Which loves its dead, and feels them living still;
For naught can rend from love its proper heart.
But learn the vision's highest teaching now:
All death comes *after* life, comes *after*, not
Before it. Lo! to every one life lasts
According to his own peculiar time.
It is as blest as his heart's feeling is,
As cheerful, as the eye that looks on it.
Then look this one thing calmly in the face:
He who lives wisely, lives to good old age,
He craves repose, he asks a peaceful grave;
And they that love him, grant him the repose.
Life lasts the time of man's eternity,
And parting lasts but a few holy days,
And dying lasts only a moment's time —
Like the mere rising from the marriage-feast,
Like going to sleep for a long pilgrimage,
Like gently waking for the long, long sleep.
How short is death — how long and fair is life!

THE SCHOOL.

THE world's a house in which a man should dwell
With moderation ; yea, 'tis well with thee
If thou dost never make missteps ; transgress
Against the ancient usage of the house,
And *art*, *thyself*, *still good*, though *it* were hell.
For thou canst only feel thyself, not others ;
And what *thou wilt*, that which thou dost and wouldst,
That is to thee thy world, in its own spirit,
Which is peculiar in thyself and each.
'Tis the best thing for man to reckon life
A lesson which the universal spirit
Gives himself day by day, on to old age ;
And *what* he has to learn while in this school
— Where he still is, when tottering on the staff —
For *that* alone 'twas built (so let him think)
For that alone he came into it, and that,
And that alone, which he has learned, he takes
Along with him — hard, hard words oftentimes,
As : "Bury now thy father and thy mother !"
And : "Now thy wife !" "Now learn to take thy leave
Forever of this lamp, and close thy eyes,
And in the darkness open them no more !" —
Yet sometimes cheerier ones : "Take this fair maid" —

"Now make a wedding" . . . "A baptismal feast" . . .
"Now, go make merry with thy friends!" . . . and now:
"Visit thy son!" . . . "Thy daughter's home make thine!"
The will to learn, this power to do the right,
Makes glad the pupil and the old master, too,
As if a child should learn for him the names
Of ancient heroes, battle-days, and towns
Whose memory long ago had died away,
Which he will never visit, never need
To know again, — *but only this one day!*
And of such things the teaching shows the master —
And of such things the learning shows the scholar
As one exalted high above all time,
Whose only aim in life is to unlock
The holy feeling of the heart, to unfold
The heavenly understanding perfectly
To the large freedom of the realm of thought,
To the pure bliss of turning a full gaze
Upon the Right, the Good, the Beautiful.

And life is discipline — and nothing more.
Not with a thirst for *low* things does the spirit
Come upon earth; no, for the *highest* thing:
For life! and for the proving of its love!

CONTENTMENT.

NOT many fortunes has the world to give,
Only *to* many, ever different souls,
The simplest, shortest policy is best,
The wise men call it: quiet human life.
And gifts too are but few, ever the same.
On a few simple viands, milk and meat,
And creatures of the water, wood and field,
And garden fruits, on these and such as these,
The human race has lived, day after day,
From gray old times, and will till gray old times.
The same old light, the ancient solar lamp,
Illumines all the earth, and house and hand,
And work and faces, darling cradled child,
And each one's pathway graveward, and the grave.
The same recurring cares, and children, fill
The hearts of parents; all are moved and stirred
By the same modest wishes; each but gains
What others gain of goods — who gains at all.
The young man wooes and wins himself a maid,
The maiden likewise wins a youth; and both
Win children; and the child a mother, father,
Brothers and sisters, and a flower-garden,
And playmates, and a little play-ground, too,

The self-same yard in which his fathers once
Were happy children, and his grandchildren
Will one day take their turn at youthful sports,
Till *life's voice* calls them off to earnest work,
The self-same work that all have done of old:
To holy labor and to blessed love:
To thousand-handed labor, with its thousands
Of implements: loom, shuttle, plough and wheel,
Yet all of them twigs of one common tree! . . .
And love, the thousand-fold, itself with thousand
Heart-flames, and all: leaves of a single Rose!
So for themselves to live, then to take care
Of parents, nurse them, bear them to the grave
With tears, and then at last prepare themselves
For parting, bless the world and go their way —
This is, in all the wide, wide world, the whole,
Of human life among all peoples, when
It comes so far as this, when happily
Such term is reached. But thou — make this thy hope!
Thou canst not reach so far as other homes,
Scarce can thy *warmth of love*, thy strength, thy hand,
Reach to thy very kindred in thy house.
The others all would, without help from thee,
Utterly perish, had they not themselves
Their heart-full, each, of love, their wealth of soul.
Place firm reliance on the heart of men,
On every one, into whatever woes
His path has led him; man is stronger than
His heaviest destiny; in sorest need
He still possesses *that old cry to heaven,*

Still human pity, counsel, solace, help ;
He has, himself, in every wrong he bears,
The sense of right ; when wrongfully accused,
The shield of innocence ; when assailed — defence,
Patience, forgiveness ; yea, a man still has,
Even in the deepest woe, the refuge sweet
Of weakness, *lying low* and *keeping dumb*,
Nay more, *the drying up of all his tears*, —
And then, then first, within his God-like breast,
The mighty sense of triumph over all :
" Thou art a man ; and this is human lot ! "
Place firm reliance on the human heart ;
Surely : " in each one dwells the living God."
So look serenely out o'er all the lands,
O'er all the homes of men, for therein dwells
Power ! . . . Look abroad over all graves ; for there
Power *has* resided, triumphed, done its work ; . . .
Look round on all the children, all the birds,
On all the flowers, upon the sun — for there
Power *will* dwell, conquer, reign victorious !

THE PURE SOUL.

WHAT once is done is wholly perfected,
Wherefore should that be hoarded up and where
Keep it? and *who* should keep it, and for *whom?*
And could man ever use that thing again?
The breast with this new moment's feeling filled,
The soul preoccupied with other thoughts!
How could the old man use again the joy
With which in boyhood once his bosom swelled,
When for the first time in the stream he bathed
That flowed all rosy red in evening's glow?
What meaning has it for the mother now —
The laugh with which she laughed to greet her dolls?
What signifies the sleep slept yesternight
To-day, to the well-rested traveller?
What signify the many tears once shed,
That only from a present sorrow flowed —
To the encoffined sleeper smiling there?
The soul itself grows ever purer, cooler,
Only a few great things can move it more;
To treasure up the soul itself for man —
He scarce would thank one for it, as scarce worth thanks;
Man thus is made a mummy thousand times.
But every thing he was, *all that* he was

In every moment perfect and entire.
The ceaseless transformation silently
And sweetly shaped him to the man complete.
He *grew* upon the feelings he outgrew,
As the tree flourishes on the spent rains.
No maiden ever wept that she had grown
Up from an infant to be tall and fair!
Memory is a lightning-flash in dream,
Each thing holds good its moment and no more.
And joy and sorrow man contentedly
Dismisses from him, as the mother-lark,
Lets her young fledglings go from the still nest,
Be it left desolate ; swept away by storms.
The soul of man is like the mother-lark,
When without knowing what a rapturous joy
She was preparing for, instinctively
For the first time she busily built the nest.
In the new spring she builds it gladlier still!
She carries, in the sense of those light straws,
The heavenly feeling of the little feathers!
The pure, the loving and confiding soul,
That is the best for the new morning's dawn,
That is the best for the last evening's dusk,
That is the best, O man, for a new life.

MOURNING FOR THYSELF.

LET not the beauty of this world so spoil
Thy heart, that thou shalt pity thy dear dead
For this, that it shall be enjoyed no more
By them, no more beheld! though it be only
The morning red, or but the evening star
So clear, so beautiful, that makes thee weep
With its gold beam — *without them any more;*
Yea, though it were the faces soft and sweet
Of children now in tears. Do not esteem
Thyself so highly, as almost to pity
The dead for this: that they no more have *thee!*
Love will, 'tis true, make happy: that indeed
Is her employment and her joy. And that
Thou grudgest not them who once loved thee. — But
Thou hast *them* not! Be that thy noble grief!
For death brings sorrow, *though it were a God*
Who died and though it were a God survived.
Pity thyself thou never wilt nor canst
When thou art dead; thou clearly knowest now
That thou art good as dead, else of thyself
Know'st nothing. Pity no unconscious thing;
The dead have verily not *lost* at all
God and the world, have lost them less by far

Than one born blind has ever lost the sun.
To miss thyself seems something less to thee
And lighter, as a modest, pious man;
But in *prophetic dream* to miss the world
That seems to thee far harder. And wouldst thou
Beforehand tear the sun away from heaven,
Get Titans to reduce the world to powder,
That none might longer live when thou wast dead?
If thou canst not root love out of thy breast,
Let truth, let wisdom solace love itself!
And let the heavy woe rest light on thee!
* Be not dismayed that all thine eyes behold
Shall still remain one day when thou art gone:
The house wherein still shines the silent sun;
The moon, as if each night she sought thee there;
The mountain, and the clouds still sailing by;
The trees that every spring bloom out anew,
That every autumn loads again with fruit.
Let all this pass, with calm, glad, pious heart.
For all this comes to pass for those who need it
In *their* days, as it came to pass for *thee*
In thine, as beautifully, blessedly,
As to all generations that of old
Came upon earth, to thousands all at once,
And to each individual in his place.
Lament not for the sun who still in heaven
Shall stand and shine and warm the earth and man —

*The remainder of the piece from this point was (perhaps designedly) repeated by the author in this volume after the piece entitled "Health," as a separate poem, and called a "Solace for the Sick."

Nay *feel thou rather all the children's joy*
With which he will be greeted, even as thou
Art greeted, as he greets thy children too !
Compassionate not the earth that she must stay
And give to other, unknown hands her flowers
And ripen them her harvests, nor bewail
The wood that shall for others wear new green,
The bread that still shall lie upon the board —
They too will need all these the very *day*
After thou goest, and ever, ever more !
— And thou no more need them ! But smile to think :
How pleasant it will be above thy grave . . .
How full all things will be of life and joy,
To grace thee too with monumental pomp,*
With such a silver bright celestial lamp,
That thou mayest not so miserably lie
Cast out from God, in darkness buried there.
This house of heaven is the fair home of all,
Mysterious heritage from sire to son !
This house of heaven is to all dead the fair,
The infinitely venerable tomb !
In parting, to imagine all the bliss
All beings in all days of coming time
Shall yet enjoy in this great heavenly house . . .
To feel it thousand-fold within thy heart
Through which it thrilled and flamed, and glows e'en now
So that thine eyes still trickle down with tears,

* The reader may well be reminded, by the tone of the poem here and onward, of Bryant's "Thanatopsis," which it might almost seem as if the author had taken for his theme, pursuing it into a more exalted and cheering region of faith. — T.

As flowers that drip with drops from the spent clouds —
Clearly to feel at parting all that joy
Is the beginning of eternal bliss !
Going to sleep with it, thou'rt blest forever ;
For, sure, " eternal " is the spell-bound hour,
Lost in far depths, and vanished clean away !

MARRIAGE.

WHY would it seem to the heart-broken wife,
Returning from her husband's funeral,
To wed, the evening of that very day,
Another man: adultery? . . . yet why not
Adultery when the year of mourning ends?
How can mere days change for us virtue's laws
Or nights affect our duty to the dead
Of truth and love? What worldly feeling this,
Distracting, deadening all men's heart and sense,
That makes men's usage and morality?
That no one blames the newly married one,
That the most strict old dame excuses her,
And says: "The dead man's dead and gone! — she lives."
But man and wife have not the modesty,
Are not content: to have enjoyed their heart's
Great rapture once — and only once forever,
And then thus early to have lost it, yea
Have given it up as lost forevermore . . .
Yet after all does not the old heart still live?
So will they *now in memory* at least
Still celebrate life's great high festival;
The best of earth's good things they e'er have known
Shall be to them at least a good thing still,

A solace and a comfort even in woe;
Their life shall in their hearts repeat itself!
A true heart's dream! Oft sorely expiated;
A dream impossible to be fulfilled,
That never can become full blooming truth!
It contravenes man's right divine and might,
His sun-like might, the law of love and joy! —
  Yet what necessity does not, love does not.
Love does much that necessity seems to do,
For *love is at the bottom of each act*
Of woman, and her smallest work! search thou,
And study her, and thou shalt find it so!
Yet sharply see: from love to *whom*, perchance,
She seems to act against and without love
And thereby often does a secret wrong
To others, to the unloved, with a sigh
Over her *sore fidelity* which she
Towards her *dead* husband exercises still,
In the new husband's arms, for children's sake . . .
For their sake whom he left to her in charge,
Who need a father, — a protector she.
To fear for others and to care for them,
To suffer and be sad in others' place,
The bitter cup which fate's chastising hand
Has poured out for *her dear ones*, secretly
To drain in silence . . . yea even die for them,
That can a noble, delicate woman do.

Yet that is not the heart's pure happiness,
And after happiness must man aspire;

Then hear, ye happy ones, and do my word:
A *life-long* friend and helpmeet is the wife
To man, *for many years*, and every day
Of higher and a genuine heavenly worth;
Ever more precious, worthier, holier.
No other lives, even though a younger one,
A richer, a more beautiful, or even
One more intelligent and amiable,
Who to the husband ever could be *that*
Which through these holy years *she* has *become*,
Has *been* to him! and *is* to him to-day:
The joint possessor of his very life,
His days, his every lightest pang of woe
And every joy! no *other ever could*
Be that to him again! nor yet could he
Be to another what he is to her.
The want of time would of itself prevent
Another's ever doing *that* for him,
The want of time would also prevent his
Receiving that at any other's hands!
To every husband then, an only one
His wife is for all time; to every wife
Her husband is, for all eternity.
All other men, however young and fair,
Are to the wife simply: *impossibles;*
Impossibles all other wives to him,
However loving, young and beautiful.
For *one thing* not even love itself can do:
Rejuvenate the heart, set back the hour
On the world clock and bring *life* back again!

Once only can she . . . make it beautiful
Once only can she make it . . . beautify it
And fill it with rich bliss for every soul!
Know this, ye fair, young, breathing, heavenly shapes!
And cast not down your eyes at it. — *Respect*
Yourselves! and him uniquely whom you love.

But thou, young man, and thou, young woman, hear;
None else than he who has accompanied
A wife from childhood up even to old age,
And watched her with a close and searching eye,
Could ever know what a wife truly is —
Needs — and a husband therefore owes to her.
The wife is much in ever-changing forms,
And great are her requirements all life long.
The wife is not a lightning flash of beauty!
A day of youth, or even a spring alone.
She is to man a whole earth festival;
And who has from gray old antiquity
Accompanied the wife and scrutinized
And recognized her with a searching glance, —
That is the Eternal Reason in man's soul!
And this, O young man, make thy property,
Take wisdom to thyself as one would take
Gold from a hill of gold which blessed spirits
Had with industrious hands piled up for *him;*
Till thou as nature's miracle venerate
The wife, and willest *all* that the wife *is*
And will be to thyself and to thy children
Long years, — the mother, and earth's younger sister,

The earth's, the gracious mother of us all.
So wilt thou not offend against thy wife!
So wilt thou sternly scorn the maid herself
Who *for a day* would be thy wedded wife —
As if the apple-tree should offer thee
Its blossoming branch to make a broom! The sun
Himself for night-lamp! — Couldst thou with a spark
Of reverence accept it? — couldst thou dash
Statues of gods to atoms? — Maim not then
The woman, Earth herself in heavenly form!

Immortals only can behold immortals,
And all good souls are deathless and divine.
Divinely the good soul both lives and sees.
So high, such heavenly rich reward it yields
To know ourselves: "*Whose spirit we are of!*"

CHILD AND OLD MAN.

A HALO floats around confiding youth,
Which, though its time is measured out to it
Already, never measures it, itself,
As if life were eternal. Soon the man
Reaches the summit of existence ; and
Although he well might reckon how much time
With the best prospect he had still to run,
He reckons that not yet. Thus life is missed
Only at last ; as in a bag of gold
One misses not a piece or two at first —
And does not feel the loss till near the end.
Only the last years are the ones man weighs,
And what there haply might be need to do
Distributes to their months. The aged man
Counts life by weeks and days — *and at the end*
Each has enough to spare . . . because there was
No need of doing any thing, (as he
Now by experience taught can clearly see,)
Save to be man in all the things of earth ;
But earthly things are quite innumerable
And inexhaustible, even if the bucket
Failed not by leaking at the golden well,
Even if man ended not as man at death.

THE HUMAN MOTHER.

THOU good but all too modest human mother,
Five children, so thou deemest, thou hast borne—
Five suns hast thou created! Five earths, too,
And moons no less; and many hundred springs,
And many hundred thousand roses, fruits;—
For to glad hearts alone creation is
Five mothers, one to each, five fathers, too,
Hast thou created for *love's* tenderness,
And childhood's veneration for thyself!
For childless parents, ah! assuredly
They are unloved, unreverenced; and like them
No man, no friend, no human being else
Can ever love; therefore are children sent
Who need *thee;* whom no human soul beside
Can ever deal so kindly with as thou!
Then feel thyself rewarded for thy pains,
For all the anxious nights thou hast watched through,
For all the toil and labor of thy hands,
Yea, even for thy love's distressful dreams!
Five pure and pious children's hearts will pray
For thee at morning and for thee at night;
Five heavenly spirits, similar in form
To thee and him, thy heart's beloved one, hover

Around thee, waiting for a mother's word,
Nay for a signal of thine eye, to fly
As if with angels' wings to do thy will.
And soon thy maidens in the garden grounds
Will everywhere accompany thy walks,
Soon stand beside thee at the hearth, its flame
Reddening the rosy cheeks, and first in play,
And then in earnest lend thee faithful help,
Soon will they softly step into thy place,
They will release thee from the works of life,
Yea, *quietly at last from life itself.*
When thou art sick, they'll lead thee ; when thou'rt faint,
Carry thee in their hands ; with sorrow burn
When thou art sad, and weep, weep, at thy death,
As none on earth beside could ever weep !
Thou wilt not be forgotten on the earth
Long as they live ; and in the days to come
They to their children will delight to talk
Of thee, as thou to them wast wont to talk
About thy mother, and they listened there
As to the story of a miracle,
With reverent stillness and the frequent sigh.
Every good word to them which thou hast breathed
Into the tender, open heart of youth
Shall have a resurrection, live, work good
When thou hast long thought of and found thy rest.
While thou wast living, in their soul didst thou
Bury thyself, and *they* are now thy fair
And living monument ! Faithful to the last
In their gray hairs ! And in their hour of death

Again thou drawest near to them, as once
Thou camest softly to their cradle side ;
And if they found their mother once again . . .
They would not need to seek in heaven the father.
And if all else of life thou didst repent,
Yea, even vain, swift, stormy life itself —
One thing, one only, — *this* repent not of:
That thou hast been a mother, blessedly
Created many beauteous worlds, and these
Bestowed with rapture upon blessed ones ;
For without mother is no love ; to him
Who loves, and him alone, the world is made.
Thy children were not living, but for thee !
And *thou* — *their* mother only couldst thou be !
Not only a home-born, but *only-born*
Being, is man, is every blade of grass,
An only living one ; no grass-blade lives
Twice. Live in beauty then thy singular life,
In joy and good, thou holy human mother !

LOVE FOR ALL, NO LOVE AT ALL.*

WILT thou escape the woe of earthly life,
Then look thou down upon the earth somewhat
As does the sun. The sun sees only *forms*,
Not hearts, not spirits ; nothing *singular ;*
For what is singular returns no more,
And only what is singular pains when lost.
No state of things has for the sun an end
Forever : each relation, still renewed
Year after year comes back to him again !
And not a flower has he forfeited
In spring's new splendor. Man alone is doomed
To see his rose-wreaths one day wither all !
To him the stars unchanging stand in heaven !
From *man* the days and nights successive flee !
The sun sees nations ever swarm below —
Man sees his children fade from out his house !
The clouds that drop their rain on man are gone !
Before the sun clouds sweep forever by.
And dost thou, with the individual, cast off Love ?
The lovely mask of nature shatterest thou ?
Oh no ! oh no ! The never-varying works
Are worthy of man's love ! — " the highest love, —

* " Allgemeine Liebe — Keine Liebe," — apparently a rhymed proverb. — T.

But only *all* works, of the love of all." —
Lovest thou thy wife, thy children and thy friend,
Only because they came from Deity
And are divine ; as thou admirest
Rain-drops that from the ancient, holy heaven
Descend, not as mere idle water-drops ;
And canst thou in the mortal form behold
The immortal, then thou hast the God-like eye ;
And God-like — to my thought — is man ! and thou !
Now then thou hast no more what once seemed thine,
And yet was only in appearance thine ;
Thou reachest to thy child a father's hand
As if thou needs must part from him forever —
But lo ! he clasps it in his little one !
Thou hast thy child still ! and thy child has thee !
But now thou art as rich as God, and as
Thou only lovedst passionately before
What was thine own, so thou possessest now
And lovest all things, all things that belong
To God, and that are now no less thine own ——
Nay let me not, nor let thee, longer sin !
For hadst thou really accomplished that
Thou hast succeeded then in *murdering love* . . .
And putting *man* to death, who owns and loves
But little here, but that with all his heart,
And more divinely blessèd than the sun —
Like whom thou canst thyself now nobly shine !
As radiant emblem of all soulless things !

SHAME AND REMORSE.

WITH tearful eyes thou gazest down the vale,
Not daring to uplift them to the sun,
For *in his name* thou art *ashamed for him*,
That he still shines there overhead and will
Continue to shine on so all the days —
And they have buried there a precious friend
Of thine out yonder in the vernal earth.
Nor dar'st thou even look upon the earth ;
Thou art ashamed *for her* too, for her flowers,
Her foliage, yea, her very grass itself—
Deeming thou provest thus a pious soul.
Yet how unfeelingly the sun shines on,
Lighting the sons of men adown the vale !
The mountain stands there motionless ! The towers
Stand there like weary travellers looking round ;
The clouds sail by ; the sparkling river gleams
Like silver ; airs invisible float down
From the blue sky, and race like children round,
Frightening each other with the blossom-twigs ;
The golden flowers around thee at thy feet
Open their eyes upon the new-born world
Like children ; buzzing come young bees along
And from the chalice suck their daily bread,

The sweet celestial milk, with childlike right—
As once a dead child, born a moment since,
Upon her mother's bosom drank her fill.
Wilt thou dislodge the bees from out the cups ?
Wilt trample out, like sparks, the golden flowers ?
Oh, as the mother pitied her poor child,
So, touched with natural feeling in thy heart,
Do thou take pity too on the young grass
And every stalk that has come into life !
Is not the earth then mother of the grass,
The buds, the blossoms, each poor little leaf
That straight would die without her faithful care ?
And have they not already once all died,
The thousand blossoms, and the thousand clouds,
The silver full moons and the suns themselves
That with thy dead once held glad fellowship
In her sweet days of life, her vernal hours ! . . .
All they too who once lived before her here
Ere she came in to this her human feast !
Her too the mother had for only child.
Each simple grass-blade has its separate fate
In its short summer day : the black rain-cloud
That drenches, buries it in clotted earth ;
The goat and steer that like great dragons stalk,
The burning sun himself, at last the scythe !
Each several bud has its own special fate,
Has the cold night frost, has its caterpillar,
The thunder-storm at last—the little fruit
Which drags it down to earth without a grave.
And the fruit too fulfils its silent fate

At autumn's hand, the children's and the winter's —
And all of them are gone in the new spring.
And should then, after *one*, one single spring,
The fair earth be a widow evermore?
Quite childless? Of all mothers wretchedest?
Thy tender dream wishes her not such fate,
It grants the later children all their life,
Else wouldst thou grudge it to thy dead one, who
Came not till after numberless new springs!
And was not all fulfilled for her by her
In the great mother's-house, the children's hall?
Did not she too fulfil her destiny?
The newest children and the last, do they
Not ask for equal love and faithfulness?
And which then of earth's children are the last?
Ah, none! for, even without earth, evermore
The divine mother brings new children forth
To share her new, yet never-changing life,
Bestowing upon each the self-same gifts.
What? Dost thou not then open now thine eyes
To look up to the sun? look out upon
The earth and the new children she brings forth? —
Thou smil'st, the tears upon thy lashes still?
Dry up the bitter tears, and only weep
Soft, sweet tears now, o'er such maternal love!
For such poor children! Who wish now to live
And will live, whom thou fondly seest to-day
So still and fair; and as the breath of heaven
Breathes round thee, so let a presentiment
Of the sweet life steal o'er thee, which one day

Thousands of little ones shall live and be, —
The children's children of these very flowers
Which now thou lookest for in vain on earth!
Then gladly gaze thy fill to-day on all,
On that most gracious eye, the sun o'erhead,
On this good mother earth down here below,
Round on that radiant ring of heavenly blue —
That is the human children's father's-house,
Still holding the green cradle of thy dead,
Thy father's-house and all thy children's too!
And weepest thou again? But other tears!
The tears of gratitude, the tears of joy —
Then hast thou part in all that silent love?

THE KING OF DAY.

DAY'S children are the joys and sorrows all;
Labor and care are children of the sun.
Man finds repose when once he goes to rest,
And dreams begin; the wise man and the fool
Are on a level in the arms of sleep.
The world to sleepers *is not*, it has fled,
For they lie silent, in the grave of Time
Buried alive, prey of Eternity.
Vanished away are fear and grief and hope,
Hunger and thirst: the day-dream now is done:
Of being husband, wife, servant or king;
Vanished away, fidelity and love,
Yea, even love itself! and even were love
Felicity itself, — felicity
Is lost, to sleepers, in the grave of time,
And seems lost in the very grave of earth.
Night after night, sinking to slumber, men
Learn more and more to die, to be shut out
From home, from the loved circle of their kin,
Far from the gairish kingdom of the sun,
All they e'er dreamed to be, to have, from all
That ever gladdened, ever saddened them;
Nay of their very names themselves, in dream,

Scarce to retain the faintest consciousness.
Thus passes man away one half his life
More lightly than into a burning tree . . .
Or than into the blooming queen of night.
The dream: of being a man, man only dreams
By day, as that divine sun-flower the "*King
Of day!*" Of many days! — Only by day
He loves, he sees, he hears, is good and great,
Then is he the whole man; the *half* a being,
The poor half man, is the poor demigod.
And now, is death a sleep — *then* he no more
Is even that which yet in sleep he was,
Then is he no more even as is the flower.
But has he here been *in broad day* asleep
And dreaming, and *wakes up* refreshed by death —
Then is the sun less than the moon to him,
The bright day blacker to him than the night,
And love and bliss have been a dream of his,
And those he loved fair visions of a dream,
Which at his waking up from life have fled
And which he has no longer tears to weep. —
May then a God give His divinity
To him and of his heaven the unknown life!

THE SOUL OUR "STRONG FORTRESS." *

TO flee for refuge to one's own distress
From the world's wrongs, is one way — poor but sure:
To hide one's self within his tranquil task,
The wholesome task nature assigns to each,
Is better: but the best of refuges
Against the world is into one's own love.
Ah! *there* is life! A large life, all one's own,
Beautiful, boundless as a heavenly realm.
Once only will it end, *and with ourselves*,
Not with our loved ones, for we still love on.
What care we, hidden safe within ourselves,
That day and night, spring, winter, reign without;
If midnight clouds and stars, or moon and sun
Hang over us in heaven — they only serve
To light us to our tranquil human work —
And the least lamp will answer well enough!
Whence came the earth and whitherward it drifts,
Whence came and whither tends our pilgrimage,
Disturbs us not — are we not here alive?
That nature is so monstrous, so immense,
So limitless, affrights not us safe screened
Within our bower with roses latticed round.

* Allusion to Luther's well-known "Feste Burg." — T.

Hide thyself calmly in thy human life,
In thy day's work, wouldst thou be happy, man!
Thy neighbor's child has fallen into the brook —
And all the heavens are now shut up from thee
By this one death, which strips off all their bloom;
Thou only sav'st the child, and now for joy
Thou weepest o'er its mother's joy and thanks.
Thou hear'st beside thy hearth of all the wrongs
Fear and ambition heap on human kind,
And weep'st and burn'st — when lo! a spark of fire
Leaps out upon the loom, at which thy wife
Weaves for the child a coat — thou startest up
To quench the little ember, and forgot
Is all thy wrath and the seized knife is dropped.
Mark then: *The great is small to man and makes*
Him smaller. — But note also: *What is small*
Is great and makes him greater, even good
And happy. Now then look on human kind:
The many little, pleased with little things!
And stand amazed now at the blessedness
Which even within a flow'ret's tranquil cup
A God has placed, has placed: to find it there.

THE OLD BEGGAR-MAN.

FROM sunrise unto sundown, everywhere,
Creeps through all nature a deep shuddering,
A holy horror, a mysterious wrath,
That from the bosom of the tempest moans
And mutters heavily and wearily,
That frights us in the sparkling gleam of stars,
As if they struggled all — to fall from heaven;
That from the hollow roaring sea-wave howls,
Raves in the storm-wind with impatient rage,
Groans out of deep abysses in earth's womb . . .
As if it had been long, long ages pent,
Walled up alive and buried in her black caves.
The miner hears it not — he digs for gold.
The fisher hears it not — watching his line.
The boys upon the beach — they hear it not —
They play "church-building" on the wet sea-sand;
The girls at "cloister-building," with gay shells.
The lover hears not the night-spirit's wail —
He waits to meet his darling; nothing save
The shooting star awakes him from his dreams;
The mother hears no muttering in the clouds —
She lulls her child to sleep, bends over him,
With one more kiss and one more lullaby.

None but the old bewildered beggar-man
Sees, in his meagre shadow, in his staff,
The weary spirit, which in mockery
Blows the white hair around his pallid face,
And with an impudent toss flings his old hat
Into the river, just as if, forsooth,
To-morrow he would have no need of it ;
He looks upon his old and withered hands
On which the sun now gleams with whitening light.
He stares at the old woman with surprise
Who sought escape from misery in the stream ;
He sees her lying with her hair burnt off,
Stretched out, as she was dragged upon the shore—
The little imps of boys set her on fire
Only last night in scorn and ridicule
Of her old age.—The old man gives a shriek,
Creeps home, and after three days he is dead ;
And in the night his home burns up with him ;
A weary * lightning-flash set it on fire
And saved him thus a coffin and a grave ;
The black burnt bones themselves looked tired out.
As the old grave-digger so carefully
Buried them in a pot in sacred earth,
Depositing therein the kreutzer too,
Which he had owed him since last Saturday.

* That is, *spent*.

THE HERDSMAN'S FIRE.

WHY need'st thou much ? Life is a little thing,
And but a little time that little lasts.*
With trouble *stirred*, 'tis bitter ; and when lost
It seems to us a treasure heavenly great,
Great as our love is to the darling ones
Whom we have lost. To each it is his all ;
So with our loved ones all dies and is gone,
And even our love becomes a feverish load.
Then that which should sustain and still sustain,
Becomes our death ; even as the herdsman's fire
Left burning on when they drove home at night,
Scorches the flowers around the burning hearth.
'Tis always best, to go home with the sun,
Who graced the day for us, and rest like him.
Why need'st thou much ? Life's but a little thing,
And but a little while that little lasts.

* "Man needs but little here below." — T.

ORIGINALITY.

NOT to one thing alone do all things point,
All peoples to one people, of the race
All individuals to a single man!
Old time is not a preparation all,
The new all fruit; all hyacinths are not
A preparation for the rose; they were
And will be hyacinths eternally!
The oak comes not of preparation made
By all the thousand pine-trees; they all live
Together so upon the holy earth;
The rock does not prepare the cloud; the cloud
Does not prepare the beautiful blue rook;
The violet that so early blooms in spring
Prepares not for the aster in the fall.
Only the violet came first, and later
The aster. Later than the Jew indeed,
The German blooms; yet neither Jew nor Greek
Prepared him. *The new Roman does not make*
The old Greek never to have been at all;
He lived himself a true, original man.
So holy is each race! and every man
In every race; an individual man.
And no one is another's master. Such

Is the divinity, the liberty
Of all the creatures, even of the flowers, —
The freedom of the little violet:
Without another's beck or bid, to be
A violet by its own primeval, pure,
And chastely kept celestial energy.
So only their own sense of native worth
Allows each people, every man, to live!
And all, who were not of a slavish spirit,
Have lived so, self-creating their *fair* works,
Doing their *good* ones out of their own soul,
Never once troubled by their nearest neighbor,
More than the swan is by the eagle, or
The swallow by the temple where she builds.
And who will live, a true and genuine man,
He learns from the old stone, from the new grass,
He learns from violet and from rose to live
And love *and to be worthy of himself!*
How for his sake the whole earth teems and blooms,
How for his sake the whole full sun shines down,
How his own clear eye lights up all within,
The full soul and the full heart, full of all
The wealth, none *none ever brought to him, and none*
Can rob him of, but his own slavish spirit.

GOD'S HUMAN LIFE.

TO be a king's cup-bearer, or to hand
The beggar at thy gate a slice of bread,
There can no doubt arise, which in the sight
Of God and man is the more honorable,
And which is the more honorable to *man*.
Thou scarce wilt hand the beaker to the prince,
Remembering: God looks at thee earnestly;
Thou scarce wilt hand the beggar-man the bread,
When between him and thee the king steps in.
So between honoring and receiving honor
The human folk still hover, but not *man*,
The good, the wise, the God-like man he who
Never forbids, never denies *himself*,
And never *others*, what is right and good;
Who never, in a single point, allows
Himself, or *others*, what is bad and base.
Liberty: to be good — that take, O men!
To maim that freedom he must be ashamed,
Who is proud and lofty, courtly, insolent;
That freedom gives you dignity, and dignity
Gives honor, and that gives you all good things.
Free moral action is the only freedom!
The heavenly mother of *all* liberty;

And seek ye not another liberty ;
Ye will not find another, worth the search ;
Yet for the noblest this is full enough,
Enough, too, for the poorest man of all,
For outer welfare and for inner joy,
For every work in life ; 'tis life itself,
The only worthy life a man can live.
Nothing can be denied to the free man,
Nor is, to him who feels the dignity
Of being man ; *never* to one denied,
And naught can to a people be denied,
Who count it honor : to bear God within,
God in the heart, the soul, God in the home,
Into each little act — as thus : to smile
Upon a child, to give one's wife his hand,
Who gladly lives with him this holy life,
With a free heart, the human life of God !

GOD'S PATIENCE.

GOD was not *bound* to be, for, as the First,
He could not by another be constrained:
God did not *will* to be, for then He must
Have been already ere He came to be.
God is. And as He is, so must He be,
And as God is He must remain forever:
None is there who could rob him of His life,
And He cannot annihilate Himself,
In an unheard-of, giant suicide.
So shall then the least mote of dust still flash,
Time without end, in the last gleaming sun.
So spake He once aforetime from wise lips:
"Count therefore the long-suffering of our God
As your salvation."* And if one should ask,
Which one of all the attributes of God
Is most exalted, indispensable,
Pressingly needful to Himself and all
Who live from Him, and full of deepest joy, —
The universe would answer with one voice:
"Patience! The holy patience of our God!"
By it alone He bears, endures the world,
The world with all its sorrows and its death,

* 2 Peter iii. 15.

With all its errors, all its destinies,
With all its bitter agonies and dyings . . .
By patience most profound, yea bottomless,
Surpassing the mere lamb's, that even though dumb
Before the butcher, still will stamp its foot.
Not even the smallest promise e'er was made
A being, and so none is ever broken;
None ever yet has promised aught to God,
So none can break a promise to Him. All
That He Himself is, He Himself can keep,
His own law He can keep; *as that* He lives;
But to be *that* was His necessity
Which, with existence, He assumed forever.
To ask now: "Why is all this so?" is not
A blasphemy; it simply is in vain.
And if there were a head as large and wide
As the whole, whole wide heaven itself, a mind
Of power to pierce through all the universe,
That *mind* could never comprehend its own
Existence, for it has no origin,
No reason and no object but to be.
Therefore it is incomprehensible,
Eternal! 'Tis accountable to none
And justifiable by none. And now
As the First Power exists not by its *will*,
So has not death existence by the will
Of any being, nor has life's decay
And dying; for all this none is to blame,
No one: and He, all innocence, endures
The guiltless, innocent state of things, Himself:

All the more lightly! gladly! finding in it
A *sweet refreshment!* and above it clean
Exalted! yet a man can never give
With heart and *will* a clear *consent* to this,
But only acquiesce in it, endure it,
By virtue of God's goodness in his soul.
And no coercion lies in this decree,
And no great heart is e'er weighed down with guilt:
Not by its fault the human race expires,
Not by her fault the husband's dear wife dies;
He can forgive her then the bitter death;
Without its fault the mother's infant dies,
So in his coffin she consoles the darling
For having given her such heart-bitterness!
Not by his fault the poor wife's husband dies,
And she, she praises him, presses his hand,
Mourns and laments him; but herself still more.
Such is the goodness of the human heart.
And easier grows the solace; for all being —
God — has no aim, nor aught that comes from Him
Endowed with life, — man has no aim — *save only*
A free, a beautiful, a pious life.
This rescues from dishonor all the world,
This is the one faith that still clings to it
In misery and death, in love and life.
Innocent must man be to suffer all —
Innocent, purely to taste a single joy.
Then lay no charge of guilt upon thy soul,
Against thyself or any creature else;
So shalt thou live serenely as a child,

So shalt thou die at last more peacefully
Than even a child — shalt softly fall asleep.
God must endure Himself and the world too:
God must endure Himself, — but for us men
That means: we must endure ourselves and life.
Thus does God bear with us, and thus do we
With God. Upon a despicable thing,
Upon a thing despised can no man stake
His body and his life, his *love*, his soul.
Patience — it is the grace that reconciles
God with Himself, all beings with themselves
And one another. Bear, O man, all things,
All men; thy patience makes thee more divine.
Only be free to ward off from thyself
The *effects*, the acts that follow from *their* ways.
So thou endurest God. So too ward off
The acts of this world and their consequences,
In thy God-given liberty; and this
Thou canst accomplish easily, *pure soul!*

This word is not from Satan! for it teaches
Contentedness: contentedness, the highest,
The deepest, holiest tranquillity,
Peace in the pious soul, and joy in peace.
No hater chooses this. God only does;
This is the one, the only, will he has
And needs, to make for him that inner heaven
Which *is* peace, and a life secure in love.

GOD'S GOODNESS.

NOT without cause is God called the "*good God.*"
My faith is in a great, good, generous heart,
Which never dies, nor breaks, nor yet despairs,
From sympathy with all creation's woes —
And in an eye which weeps no seas of tears
At sight of all the dying, all the graves,
But like the sun looks steadfastly from heaven,
Mounts into every bud and kindles life —
And in a spirit who calmly lets the world
Around him pass through changes ever new,
Himself being the good spirit that fills all
And gives his peace and happiness to each,
Who can and should be also good like God,
Since verily the good God lives through him!
For *this* has man discovered, lives and dies
On this conviction: that God's spirit is
The spirit of man, that God belongs to man,
As truly as man does to God, and both
Are one in life, in worth, in length of days, —
What use to me, to thee, our *being one!*
Oneness insures not bliss, not even joy;
Freedom alone gives birth to patience. Patience
Alone gives birth to goodness; goodness breathes

God's benediction over all the world.
Thus freedom is God's very godliness,
By it He tolerates His tender soul;
With freedom only man lives blessedly.
Goodness is the free soul's activity,
For naught constrains, naught ever conquers it.
Millions of beings live a reckless life,
Owning allegiance to no law, they live
Indifferent, following but the law of lust;
Whether they lose their true life here, or whether
They suffer evil, proudly unconcerned,
Deluded by their strength and headstrong will.
Goodness can have no higher sense than *this*
And no more beautiful significance :
Complete contentment with God's nature ; for
Without the will of God His nature is ;
It is not, then, surrender to the will
To be; but to the will which says : *be good,*
Patient, and so then pure and innocent.
And never let that old doubt trouble thee :
How God is to be reconciled with man,
Whether and how He can be satisfied
Through His long being, as He looks on all,
Contented with the world and with Himself,
Nay to win joy out of *His life therein,*
And blessedness, whereas so many find
Nothing but sorrow in it, and weep, and curse,
And breathe the wish : " If only the whole world
Would perish ! None would be the loser by it !
For he who is not, is deprived of naught ;

Just as the dead, when dead, miss not themselves.
God would lose nothing, if He should not be,
Had never been, should wholly disappear . . .
Should cease . . . He would miss nothing, being naught;
For he who is not, surely loses naught;
Just as the dead, when dead, miss not themselves."
And they in non-existence, find a joy—
The great abyss, the eternal, staring void,
Wherein no star, not even a spark, gleams forth,
No breath stirs in the great dead nothingness.
They are the poorest, the most miserable:
The *guilty*, on whose heads affliction lays
A heavier burden than on pure good men.
And *them*, too, heavenly patience solaces,
God's patience: patience to endure the world
With a *free* will, with a free piety;
And such a piety bears joyfully
With God; it bears itself, itself alone:
Sweetest of burdens, stillest, easiest!
To reconcile one's self to the universe
Is greater than with a poor son of man,
Of woman born, and with his petty faults.
The wild plum is not guilty of its tree,
The goat's beard, of the goat; the horn bears not
Blame for the steer, nor yet the ear for the ass.
The dead are not responsible for death,
The sick and well are not to blame for life.
To be a child, a poor good human child,
Heartily reconciled with all the world,
A human being, with deep pity moved

To help each fellow-creature on through life
Even to death and to the very grave:
That is the goodness of the good, of God!
That is the heart of God in all men's breasts!
That is His heart in the warm sunshine's glow,
His heart, His good heart still in rain and dew,
Still His good heart in the cool, silent earth
Which gives all patient souls a grave for bed.

So man must needs then be content with God,
God must Himself needs be content with man;
And this content, that old primeval word
Expresses, handed down from heathen men:
RELIGION. This contentment is true joy,
It is felicity! Eternal life!
That life which the Eternal Goodness lives!
To make one's self a slave, put on a yoke,
To let one's self *be yoked*, such bondage scares,
With spectral terrors, gladness from the heart—
Free and spontaneous must death be and life,
Free and spontaneous, bliss itself; then are they
What they are wholly to free souls alone.

THE THREE HEAVENS.

THREE heavens distinctly recognize, nay four:
One is the heaven within thy soul, O man,
The peace with all the world, the love and joy
Which nothing outward can henceforth disturb.
That was the heaven of even the ancient Greeks,
The lofty, stern and self-determined men,
Who bravely set the freedom of their souls,
High, clear aloft o'er life and all its goods;
Who, what they could not master, at arm's length
Kept from themselves: fate, death, and others' works, —
Kings in the free realm of the God-like soul.
But that same heaven — it is the very hell
Of stupid, bad, and superstitious men. —
The second heaven is the whole universe
Full of invisible, eternal powers,
The treasure-house of beings and of life,
The store-house and the busy laboratory,
With seeds and germs of all things, even of men;
The clothing-hall of all the yet unformed,
Who, by the spirits that as rulers move
In the sun's kingdom, summoned forth at length,
By joy's sweet drawing, shaped and circumstanced
By all the busy powers encircling them,

Themselves live clearly in the spirit's stead,
Till they shall have to vanish, as *they* did,
Into the formless, fathomless, sea of heaven,
And be again that which they were before. —
The third heaven is the o'erhanging firmament,
The beauteous azure with its rainbow arch,
With its pearl dewdrops and its silvery mists,
With flush of morning and of evening red,
With sunshine, moonlight, and with falling stars,
With rosy lightning-gleams and fiery snakes,
The loud heart-agitating thunder's crash,
The speech of clouds answered by shouting rocks,*
With its soft showers that bless the fields and meads,
With its warm snow, the gracious covering
Of graves and of the year's outstanding crops.
It seemed to them of old the brazen vault
Bending near down to them above their heads,
Whence the angelic legions were to come,
And whence the Father with slight pains could come
Down to His human children here on earth.
That heaven was laid in ruins long ago,
And what was left us, is the pure, fair blue. —
The fourth heaven is the world of dreams, wherein
All shall come true and real, and be held
To every word, that ever human heart
Has wished or hoped — nay ever even needed ;
For the poor child has not yet learned and known

* So Byron : —

" Every mountain now hath found a tongue,
And Jura answers from her misty shroud
Back to the joyous Alps who call to her aloud." — T.

Which way to look, has not yet learned that all
Shall be in richer, brighter form fulfilled
Which childishly he thought to win by tears,
And to extort by blind and stubborn will.
And this last heaven will grow to glorious truth
In man himself, by wisdom, insight clear
And free and noble life, even here on earth,
Which needs no dreams, delusions, falsehoods, more ;
Which shall bestow all the three other heavens
On man for an eternal heritage,
But before all the one within his soul !

THE HOLY BODY AND THE HOLY LIFE.

A MOLLAH wise and skilled in scripture lore,
Asked me in Brusa once, by his wife's grave,
Smiling at one, to him an Infidel:
Is that a solace, is it meant to be:
"In heaven they neither marry nor are married"?
Can this be called a solace, or a hope:
"In heaven no more does one belong to another"?
Is this a hope, a pleasant piece of news:
"In heaven unknown are *husband*, *wife* and *child*,"
As even here "my mother and my brethren!"
That hope dissolves even here the *marriage*-bond!
That joy rejects e'en here the *mother's* claim!
Of *brethren* it knows nothing. So the word
Is *not* said for the *comfort* or the *hope*
Nor for the joy of wretched men on earth!
'Twas only set for life's immortalizers,
As lamp to light them to the *fount* of life!
Perhaps to test if they believed it. No,
The worst of all is, 'tis the truth. The truth
Meant to console us here *about that heaven* . . .
In heaven one day to cheer us, but not here
On earth — where it breaks up all happiness,
And ends all love, forever stifles love,

Love, that alone melts men together here
In gladness, and alone brings bliss to man.
Whoever now has no desire to reach
That utterly love-bare and heart-blank heaven,
May stay here and be blessed — let him not die,
Or let him never rise — else he must make
One in *that* heaven. But *we* console ourselves
By taking to ourselves four wives on earth ;
That seems as much as for four human lives
With you, and yet is really less than *one*
Right happy ; still 'tis something *even forever* . . .
Were we not going to find our Houri there,
Who is ensured us — yes ; but not to you !
So you have marriage then only on earth,
And we have marriage too only on earth ;
And here alone are wife and child, and father
And mother, and a life so true, so fair
I dread to think of being glad to die —
I want no Houri there *to be my wife*,
The greatest bliss is only upon earth,
This real earth of ours, this real heaven,
Where sweet love is reality, true love,
Sweet smiles, sweet lips, sweet language of the heart,
And the sweet face, the heavenly, beauteous eye ! . . .
Where is a child in heaven ? O where : my child ?
My child, that runs to meet me wild with joy,
And climbs delighted on his father's knee !
I am content with earth, fully content
With life, with man, content with woman — Oh,
Not holy is the soul alone ; *the body*,

That too is holy if the whole man is;
Just as the temple with the name of God,
So he, with God, who wears Himself our form,
That here with eye and ear and every sense,
He may take in all beauty, blissfully
Rejoice in loving and in being loved,
Which only then is no vain thing to him,
When he himself enjoys it, living it. —
Thou who hast happily a wife and children,
Weigh well the precious words of faithful love,
Of heavenly satisfaction and content;
Shut thyself from all heavens within thy house,
Shut out from thee all distant things, and live
There with thy loved ones as a blessed soul!
There prize thy wife and children and thyself! —
So spake he softly, and wept bitterly.

HEALTH.

THE corner-stone of life is health. It is
The root from which grows up the Tree of Life,
Whence Love in beauty blooms, and all the joys.
Man's body is his kingdom, sweeter far
To him, than any king's. And if dear life
Has some . . . though limited and doubtful worth;
Then health has clear and unambiguous worth;
It gives a man the power no more to feel
The presence of his body or his soul,
Even as the fruit-tree does not feel its boughs,
Nor the rose-bush its roses or its thorns; —
To bear, forget existence; — live in joy,
As being pure existence of itself; —
To keep back and ward off for long, long days,
Sickness: that terrible enemy of life,
To guard against humanity's worst plague:
Untimely death, that mars the peace of hearts,
Poisons with endless sorrow the whole house, —
For "life-long" means to man *eternally*.
And if life is a hidden happiness
In some unknown abyss of the far future,
Or if the most inevitable of ills —
Untimely death is still the highest woe,

The *cloud-burst* of afflictions which had else
Rained softly down ; the falling of the house
Which else had sheltered the poor travellers long.
'Tis the *up-flying* of our ship of life
In burning fragments hurled into the air ;
It is the blowing up of the whole heaven,
Where death becomes a demon, joy is turned
To poison. Health is the fair mariner
Who guides with joy and skill our bark of life
To the steep cataract in the stream of death,
Nay, sails with us over the precipice
And goes down *softly* with us in the mist. —
The husband must be strong to meet life's toil,
Whether he drive the plough or drive the plane,
Strong and well able to protect his kin ;
And strength, even without work, is a constant joy,
Yea soundly, splendidly the strong man sleeps,
And all delights enjoys a thousand-fold.
The husband must be long-lived for his wife,
To live with her on to a glad old age,
To rear the children, and in hoary hairs
To sit there for the grandchildren to see
A God-like image of the elder world.
The wife too must have strength for household work,
The women's battle — where as a reward
A child is laid upon the victor's arm ;
To share in all house joys, to help her daughters,
Yea, even the youngest, when the wedding comes,
To see *their* children's joy, yea, even to see
How *after her* earth still shall bloom, who then

Shall occupy her house, who piously
Remember her, still honor her when dead.
He who was always well, grows old; the old
Sated and tired with life, alone dies not—
He only *sinks to sleep*, calm as a child.
Live wisely then, that thou may'st rightly live
Thy days out, blest and making blest thy kin,
Not by untimely death to kill their love,
No, but to fill their eyes with holy tears
And leave a benediction in their hearts
On thee and on themselves, that they may go
Home from the grave in peace, because they know
Thy peace is now made perfect. Wisely live
That so thy children may enjoy like bliss,
And thy grandchildren. Live as if thou wert
To live through all futurity; as if
Thou wert to make all happy; even God.
That is well worth the pains! if any thing
Is worth pains-taking. For in health alone
Man owns the world, the days and every joy.
The sick man starves . . . he even *suffers* life:
Suffers the very spring-time, sun and year!
The sick, the suffering, the weak must needs
Forego, to his sore grief and harm, the good
God bade him do and sets before his eyes;
Must leave the child to drown without his help!
Neglect the work that would support his sire;
The limbs unexercised are like the limbs
Of malefactors and of criminals;
Non-use is misuse. By enforced repose

How sorely suffers even the good man's soul!
Man lives for others also, and life's joy
Finds only, living for his kin. They should
Have joy in him, not sorrow, shame and grief.
Health is the foremost duty of a man,
The holiest, high o'er all in sacredness.
For without health, no life, no energy,
No courage, even *no possibility*
To do the good and right thing vigorously,
No possibility of winning heaven.
Even like the soul itself, which is the true
Sense of our life and of the universe,
So must the *body* sacredly be trained,
The body, which the fools from the next world,*
The tedious comforters — their text the grave —
Respect not, slight, yea blindly disrespect,
And treat more foolishly than any fool,
With their presumptuous, frightful blasphemy!
Let each man be his own full property!
And that he may wholly possess himself,
Then must the organ of his God-like will
And human being represent him fully,
Merely so much as to exist. And *that*
Can never come by sickness or by death!
So, by the side of all the temples, stand,
Has ever stood and will forever stand
The whole, entire lore and law of life,
For all to teach, to learn and to live out.

* Literally *the other world,* and implying the fault Coleridge called "other-worldiness."

So side by side with all the dreams still stands
The true kingdom of heaven, and over all
The wisdom that embraces soul and body. —
Naught can scorn health except the *elements;*
But all they form is mortal and grows sick
And suffers; even yonder sun himself,
The stars, within them bear their germ of death,
As every flower and every child of man.
Sound at the core is man and fitted well
To live his life out, even as the pine
And as the vine lives out its rightful time.
But the God-spirit itself is new, as child,
It, too, must learn to live. Wouldst thou maintain
A wise behavior towards all heavenly forms,
And earthly forces, thou must *know them well.*
— For that how much man needs, and needs it long! —
Then must thou be inviolably just;
Must will in all things the life-bringing right;
The heavenly sustainer of thy life
Reason alone can be and the pure soul!
They'll never let a sickness fall on thee,
They'll ward off from thee every evil thing,
They'll heal thee through themselves alone, albeit
With simples which they choose, but only they!
The power of culture is the healing power,
'Tis the divine physician dwelling in thee,
Even as the beaver dwells within his house.
And yet the destiny of man rests not
In his own hand alone. The ignorant
And blind around him help determine it,

So that in death and bitter misery
Nothing is left him but his innocence,
Guiltless to bear the errors of his race,
All its shortcomings, even its unborn faults!
For this his doom was he alone made man,
And just as he calls good for them their sad
Existence, so he does his own for him!
Not the most eminent godliness of soul
Can make the child born blind to have his sight;
The purest virtue leaves the lame to limp —
It needs that *all the rest* should know and will
And do that which shall be the health of one;
They must have willed, *have done it* ages long
In all the generations that went by
Before his birth! for every new-born child
A holy building is, an unveiled work
Of all earth's spirits ever since the flood;
Only at that great feast which they have all
Prepared for him, at *that* alone he sits.
Inherited sin — that was a dream, a wild
Delusion; the inherited *consequences*
Of sin, of folly and of superstition,
How real they! what woe they bring to man!
To every people its past life still clings,
Each wrong, each robbery — and pays *interest!*
Each noble deed too, *that* with interest!
And a pure will brings with it a pure life,
And only healthy spirits bring, one day,
A healthy human child into the world.
Struggle towards freedom, O humanity!

That no physicians may be needed, *that*
Is every good physician's noble aim ;
That they may one day cease from among men
Like priests, is their divine and generous wish.
Teachers shall soon be the all-honored name,
Teachers of what is good for human souls,
Teachers of what is good for human bodies.
And *both* have but one aim : to teach the truth,
Wisdom and knowledge of the universe.
Into this lore all teachings flow together
From every time, from every clime of earth :
Into this knowledge, every seeker's toil,
Experience, art and work, and good intent,
All finding in man's weal their rich reward.

From the physicians wrest their wisdom then,
And from the priests wrest ye their learning too,
And let them pass into each house and heart
And out again, and day as well as night,
Each one be true to all who are your own !
That which the people know not, no one knows !
That which the people cannot do, none can !
That which the people does not, is undone !

THE THREE DEATHS.

THREE deaths has every man to live through, three
Only, if even such good should be his lot :
His father's and his mother's death — for each
In nature should outlast his parents' lives —
And then, as spouse, haply a spouse's death.
For seldom does that best good fortune come,
That *without losing one another*, both
In one and the same blessed moment die.
The unloved die to no man ; to each die
Only his own : to love alone, is death
That which it is, completely, utterly !
Our kindred's death is our severest life.
Our childhood's divine images grow old,
That round our cradles like immortals stood,
And at our childish play looked on with joy ;
And innocently they too break at last
Our true, piously grateful, childish hearts,
Whose heavenly bliss *this* sweet delusion was :
" Their passing on is not passing away ! their stay
Is not a steady, silent, shifting show !
Although their words have always flown away,
Yet the beloved and venerable form,
Still always cherished with the self-same love,

That has not wings, *that* does not bear away
Mysteriously therewith, each night, *itself*
And us! each morn a new one does not rise!"
Until at last before our terrified
And weeping eyes an old and haggard man
Stands frightful with gray eyes, who bears the name
Of *father*, — and a pale old woman too,
Our mother she is called! and verily
That hard hand is the same good mother's hand!
That dim, weak eye is still the mother's eye,
For out of it smiles unmistakably,
Though with autumnal, faded countenance,
The true old love in all its youthful bloom.
Joy to these even now half-sainted forms,
When now their son, too, a new father is!
The daughter a new mother! For to rock
The grandchild on their knees, — that to the hearts
Of parents is a touching sign of death;
Grandma weeps softly at this messenger
Of heaven, and blesses him and breathes a sigh:
" Ah, well with him, who never lost a child!
That has no compensation; not on earth —
And surely not in any spirit-heaven;
That is the sorrow that *is ever fresh*,
For which no reparation man should ask,
For all irreparable to noble souls
Is grief for an eternally-matchless good.
True lovers need no solace and wish none;
Their love, as tender sorrow, is their bliss."
And softly flow her tears for the dead child

The little grandson so reminds her of,
And now her heart, with holy peace again,
Strengthened by God, goes down into the grave.
To true love, death is not to be begrudged,
But the two children, midway on in life,
By thinking of their parents' death forewarned
Of their own death and parting from their loves, —
Are thus admonished: so to regulate
Their means of joy, that they shall never fail,
And to be quick for mutual kindnesses,
That so the sun for them may not in vain
Lavish his costly oil, but that their hearts
May still beat only for their dear one's joy,
So long as man still recognizes man.
For overhead in the warm chamber sits
The father's father, ninety years of age.
There comes a thunder crash — he hears it not! —
A flash — he sees it not, knows nothing of it.
He has forgot the world, and even himself.
His good son grasps his hand to comfort him —
He starts as if a ghost came to affright him.
"It thunders!" screams the son into his ear. —
"Ay, ay, there did some such thing happen once
Long, long ago, they tell us, in old times,
But who art thou then? and what dost thou here?"
Then screams the son still louder in his ear:
"Ah, father! know'st thou then thy son no more?" —
The blind old man then fumbles for his crutch,
Beats his low bending reverent son and cries,
"Thou! thou! wouldst jeer at an old man like me!

I ever had a son? . . . Who am I then?
At last thou wilt perhaps make bold to say
I had a wife! — a wife! — pray what is that?
What was it? I, I can no longer tell
If once I dreamed of such a friendly thing!
But some one slept beside me, *he* must know!
But he perhaps will say: dreams, dreams, moonbeams! *
Make me a fire! I'm cold! to bed! to bed!"
So dreams the old man, sinks suddenly and dies,
And rubs, for only prayer, his rigid hands.

* The German proverb is: *Träume, Schäume* (Dreams, Foams.) — T.

THE THREE FESTIVALS OF LIFE.

THREE sacred, solemn works man celebrates,
The highest, holiest, oldest, everywhere
Done by all creatures upon all the stars,
Where one would ask in vain about our earth,
Where ne'er a word, never a name of it,
Has reached, as of a glittering mote of dust!
All things that live have these three works to do,
That swim beneath the waters, cleave the air,
Or live upon or in the earth. And so
The works — the eternal three — primevally
Are hallowed, only worthy, blessedest
To celebrate; and as *clear truth*, these three,
With highest honor all things solemnize,
Though silently as blossoms do on trees,
Though secretly as do the flowers of spring,
Though instantaneously as the Phœnix * does.
The three works are: Coming, renewing youth,
And going. The unique holy festivals:
Are *Birth*, *Rejuvenescence*, *Death;* which all
Around him celebrate, as a sign to man,
That all else is an idle dream of his —
Here current, there rejected; yesterday

* Literally: *Bird of the Sun.* — T.

Nothing, to-morrow nothing, vain, pernicious.
Yet — *marriage* is what all prepare them for,
From earliest childhood up; the little lark,
The fig-tree and the youthful polar bear;
Toward *that* all with glad yearning grow apace,
The little almond-tree, the little maid,
The boy, and the young roe-buck and the stork
To stand one day in the parental home
As mother by a husband's side, — for that
The mother hourly trains her little girls,
And this they learn in playing with their dolls,
Full of the bliss of still presentiment.
For that alone they briskly help their mother
In house and garden-ground, from dawn till dark,
And rock their little brother joyfully,
Conscious that they perform a holy work,
Dear to their mother; for she sees the future!
And what the boy learns, what he learns to do
Of all the thousand works of human life,
And now rehearses, oh it all refers
To one at least of these three festivals:
That all may celebrate them, haply *all.*
Thereby he earns the right, himself to keep them.
Then, when his greatest day at length arrives,
He now forgets all that he dreamed and was,
For thinking of his darling; casts his all
Into her lap, a joyous sacrifice:
His childhood and his youth; all his bright hopes
Into her blooming form flow visibly
Together, and he clasps it in his arms,

And it in turn enfolds him to its heart . . .
And soon, for love and joy and purest bliss,
Gives back to him the image of himself!
And soon he lays in her maternal arms
Her very self, made a sweet child again !
To see itself thus self-rejuvenated
Fills the whole soul with deep astonishment ;
It clothes man in his God-like dignity —
And he, the modest, blessed mortal man,
Drops grateful tears upon his wife, his child.
Thus is the festival of youth's return
The highest, blissfullest, love celebrates,
Full of sweet strength to meet life's blossom-time.
It is the twice-rich, double-festival
When man made young perpetuates himself —
And the child celebrates the holy birth,
Treasuring up the pregnant memory :
"The heavens and the earth long ages stood
Ere thou wast born. And long shall they exist
When thou art gone. Up ! live thou ! leave thy like ! "
And by the mother first brought forth to life,
Who shows him to the sun and to the moon,
The child soon treads himself the old magic floor,
And now the father's life begins again ;
Meanwhile the daughter carries on the mother's,
That so the glorious form of maidenhood . . .
That so maternal love may not die out . . .
That man may keep the holy festivals.
But sternest is the parting festival.
For that is man preparing all life-long,

But fitly only *by a happy life;*
And parting — *that* he learns from childhood up! —
Let not thy dear ones die as if in sleep;
Thou robb'st them of the preciousness of death,
Which He alone possesses, the deep sense:
How blest we were on earth here, how *beloved!*
That only would the Spirit know — for that
He came, and for this proud sense only, goes;
Just to be dead, repays not all the pains. —
— With holy joy keep in your homes these feasts,
Blest are ye, when ye keep them heartily;
They lengthen out — transfigure life for you:
You *then*, then first, are human, when you keep them,
For then you understand heaven, earth and life.

THE HOME.

THE soul is homeless in the universe,
It finds its first home in the souls it loves,
To which it gives itself eternally,
And which to it eternally are given.
Man loses in the heart beloved his heart
And very love ; he makes himself immortal
And it. Love only teaches him to live,
And love alone, too, teaches him to die,
If that *is* dead to us which still is loved.
With unfamiliar ones man will not live,
With the unloved he never is content.
So the old man is fain to quit the earth
How fair and young soe'er it still blooms on,
How bright soe'er the sun still shines in heaven ;
To him the morning's dawn brings : *gloomy day !*
And earth's new population : *solitude !*
He yearns to where his loves have gone before
Who first transformed existence into life
For him, who make for him the universe
A habitable world, the house a home.
Yes, even should he never find them more —
Yet will he leave behind this gloomy hole,
Wherein he lingers lonely, *the last man !*

Nay, where he now has *ceased to be a man!*
As all have ceased before him, in their turn,
Abstracted, lost, withdrawn into their life,
The life now swallowed in eternity,
Become for evermore immovable,
Which no, no power can evermore destroy,
Remove, annihilate, or even disturb;
As even the lightning flash no longer makes
The dead man in his coffin *wink an eye.*
So holy is the might, the eternity,
The still duration of the *thing that was.*
What is *completed*, satisfies, contents
The heart *for evermore*, and from the last
In sorrow's house extorts the *God-like smile.*
The might of noble pride inspires his soul
As he reflects: "I loved and I was loved.
For all is vanity, uncertainty,—
Or certain only one day to be lost,—
That never ends, that does not fix itself
In the majestic, calm, *eternal* state:
Eternal: though with men it sound like *dead;*
Though deemed to mean, and though it did mean: *lost!*
Lost crowns, lost sceptres and lost dignities
Give the first real proof of the old king;
The coffin of the world, the dead therein,
First truly proves the living, holy king
Of sun and earth, heaven and the universe,
The spirit of Love and the eternal life."

THE HOUSE OF LIFE.

AND why, now, art thou so in love with life?
Because a sun shines up in yonder heaven?
Because the moon comes out and shines at dusk?
— "They only light this dwelling-place of mine." —
Because thou canst at night lie down and sleep,
And golden stars glitter above thy head?
— "I only rest then from the day's hard work." —
Because spring, summer, autumn, winter, come?
Because the roses bloom? the grape, the peach?
— "That I enjoyed, too, when I was a child." —
Because thou hast a child? and that child's mother,
Thy wife? because thou hast thy parents' graves?
Because a human people lives with thee?
Because thou hast the sweet sense in thy heart,
As if a memory: what beauty once
And majesty was of old time on earth;
Because thou hast the sweet presentiment
What greater glory and what sweeter bliss
Shall one day for the first time come on earth —
For which of these now art thou glad to be?
For which one of them art thou glad to stay? —
— "It takes a heaven of stars to make up heaven,
And many a thousand flowers to make the spring,

And many a thousand joys to fill the heart . . .
All, all of that which thou hast named to me,
And all my love, my whole soul joined thereto —
Conspires to build up a heaven for me,
Whose wealth so leaves me in a blissful maze,
I have no power of choice and scarce of speech;
Ah, all that maze of beauty and of joy!
For *that* I have such deep, still love of life.
From each thing singly I could haply part:
Neither the violet, the rose, the year,
Neither the clouds, the noonday nor the night,
Not one of these should hold me on the earth;
Only *with* those I love would I go hence!
But they have all grown to a flowery chain
That binds me round with sweet and magic might.
It is the all — 'tis life — the being a man,
That binds me so to this sweet human life;
The heavenly sea that on its bosom bears
Yon sun, bears me too wholly: so I float
As buoyed by magic power, so lightly, yet
So firmly and securely; as a steel
Reposes in fair equipoise of powers.
Amidst encircling magnets. So 'tis said
The dead Mohammed in his coffin floats;
But I float living in the house of life."

THE CREDO.

THE whole truth not enough for happiness?
For peace?... Forsakes man in the hour of need?
Oh woe on you! then God forsakes him too:
Eternal fulness and eternal truth;
For God is truth, as all the wise have said.
But, O ye dolts, ye set your God aside,
Spinning a cobweb brain-work of a creed,
The vain, wild figments your blind hearts invent
Wilfully, godlessly, concerning God,
Chaff blown away by breath of common sense —
That is to be the statue, shield of faith
In which you, dreaming, image your own heads.
Ye sing, pray, persecute, live, die, and bury
In the true, only faith; what ye believe
That shall in spite of God for you be truth.
"Ye shall not make of God a graven image!"
Ye shall not image or imagine him,
Nor make your brain a chamber of imagery.*
God is called *love* indeed and called the *truth;*
Yet nowhere is God ever called: the faith.

* Ezekiel viii. 12. — "Every man in the chambers of his imagery." — T.

Whoso is true to God, renounces self.
But *truth* * is that which you erroneously
Have transformed into faith. Be true to God;
Then has your soul, to you, become the truth.
The ancient Credo has its root in *trust.*

* Πίστις; *fede* with the modern Romans, who have no word for *Faith* [in the theological sense. — T.]

THE HOLY FRATERNITY.

THE poet is the finest guide to life.
The word is the eternal spirit's flame.
Not till the clear word comes, the spirit comes ;
It is itself the spirit, the innermost
Sense and intelligence of the universe.
Prophets and hypophets * both teach indeed
That which is good, is right, but never can
Give the good action, the good soul to men.
As wakeners, as warners, they are good.
Wretched and miserable as man were,
And ruined, without what to him is *good*,
Still the *good* soul waits for the fairest thing,
The needfulest for a divinely clear,
A lovely-visioned, feeling-gifted life.
The poet makes life a clear thing and true,
Yea, everlasting, even in one short song ;
He comes and makes life beautiful to men
And sweet. A well-closed song is longer than
A thousand open years, the world itself.
It brings a rapture in the word divine,
Brings, in the holy beaker, heaven to man,

* "Hypophet: (ὑποφήτης.) An interpreter, an expounder. (R.) *Bunsen.*" [Worcester's Dictionary.]

Brings, in the golden cithern, heavenly peace.
No idle children's words the poet speaks
In all his tones, his colors and his forms —
He carries in his bosom the world's heart;
Whatever stirs and thrills with woe or bliss *
One human heart, the whole humanity,
He feels it all, he draws it deep and full
Into life's well, as a complete, whole man.
His glowing soul, like a poor child, enchained
By a world full of beauty, there he stands
And marks with mute and wondering ecstasy
Each blade of grass, each shadow of a flower,
As if, God's holy servant, he must give
Him and the blest exact report of all,
And never miss a word. And so he notes,
As heavenly listener to His world's goings-on,
The thousand wonders all, from child's-play up:
The zest of youth; the silver-haired old man;
The pale, dead mother; bride and marriage feast;
Marks what the sorrowing widow tells her child;
And funeral and farewell, death and the grave;
Yea, even inspects the flowers upon the graves,
The moon that shines on them in the still night.
To him the dead all rest as in his heart,
To him rise sadly all the flowers of spring,
As out of his own life. To him the lark
Only from out his bosom sings her song.
The poor man's tears bedew *his* eyelashes,

* See Barry Cornwall's lines on the power of song: —
"Song should breathe of scents and flowers," &c. — T.

The very rainbow springs from out his brain,
The stars dart forth as sparks from out his eyes,
The sun comes up out of his very soul ;
The beauteous maiden blooms from out his blood,
Wherein she as his mystery lay hid ;
The beautiful and raptured lovers all
They love with *his* love. For from him, from him
As Son of God are echoed word and world !
Even as pious child he took each word
Home to *himself*, as spoken to him alone!
The whole humanity is his one teacher,
And conscious of his soul's celestial worth,
He feels himself God's worthy messenger,
His world's interpreter and decorator,
Bringer of beauty to the truth of life ;
And joyously he calls all men to share
His clearness, all his treasury of wealth ;
And is rewarded, when all see, like him,
And feel the beauty and the bliss of life,
And when, without his woes, pure as a child,
His great song is to thee the highest truth,
And he completes at length the round of man
From infancy to age — one God-like song.

THE PRIMEVAL WORD.

[BIBLE; JESUS-SIRACH XLIII. 27.*]

WHOSO distinguishes not himself, at all,
His spirit, with his body and his life,
From God, but absolutely feels and lives
As indistinguishably one with Him,
That man simply *remains* that which he is,
He clearly is what he forever was.
He who requires himself and other men
To do what good soever God can do,
He has already in *all other men*,
In every child, recognized God Himself,
Who beauteously lives in beauteous forms;
He treads not down one violet's honored life! —
True to himself he lives. He robs not, steals not;
He knows: the clear, sweet eye in the child's head
Is his own, own original property;
The wee white tooth itself, the small plump arms,
The little fingers on the little hands,
The golden hair, and the tongue in the mouth,
That stammers "Father" with great pains; the love
That shines from him: these all belong

* "Wherefore in sum, He is all." [Το Πᾶν ἐστιν αὐτός — (author's version:) the all is He Himself.] — T.

To wife and children one day to be his ;
And to his mother is her joy in him
Her soul's original, own property.
But so is she the father's ; and the daughter
Already is her future husband's wife. —
He lies not. For he has so much of good
And true and beautiful and salutary
And helpful to his loved ones round about
To say ! and lovingly he knows and feels :
All men's salvation is the truth alone.
No error, no delusion, then he spares.
He runs his course serenely as the sun,
Like him he rises, with his eye surveys
The world, while lasts his day ; then he goes down
In light, himself the light, the primal light.
Who then still says : "That too ends in itself
Which thou hast done, and were it the fairest, best,
'Twas simply useless ;" says at the same time :
"He too who did it, he ends in himself,
The whole of life itself ends in itself
And he who lives it as mere hireling —"
Whoso can utter such a lofty word
Has looked far, far down through the ancient depths
He feels and knows the holy mystery :
Naught, naught is needful, not even being is ;
Yet for the sake of those who *are*, who live,
For soft endurance and sweet sense of life
Love to the dear ones is a needful thing,
And freedom, honesty and kindliness ;
That to each soul its every word and work

May well forth softly as a fount 'mid flowers —
And nothing more, itself too nothing more ;
Yet that is the most possible, the highest.

He now who fain would rob the human heart
Of this essential unity with God
In goodness, power, yea, length of life itself —
He would not only rob man of his *God*,
But would rob God — (the highest sacrilege) —
Of *men*, of all that lives, yea, of the whole
Great universe throughout eternity,
Wherein He lives ; for God is life itself.
And all that lives is He, even He Himself,
So is the attempt abortive. For the bee
Still builds her cell in holy quietness !
So is the attempt abortive. For the bird
Still sings his song in glad security !
So is the attempt abortive. For the soul
Of man loves on in its own blessedness !

THE THREE WORKS

TO come well, live well, well depart again,
All this is only *one* tripartite life.
To sow well the good seed, to tend it well,
At the right time to reap — *that* is to sow ;
To set out the good fruit-tree, watch it well,
And nurse it till its end — *that* is to plant ;
To build on solid ground, then keep the house
In order, to improve it, and at last
With care remove the old walls — *that* is to build.
To base the realm on truth and righteousness,
Then well to keep it as a house wherein
Rejoicing generations long may live,
And then when like a house it crumbles down,
To end it honorably with power and fame,
That is a people's one and *life-long* work.
For nations too, like generations, die.
A people is but man, a thousand times,
Large, long-lived : and in turn each one has died.
Each man at last dies also ; and to make
His dying light, is the physician's great
And holiest work. His *coming* on the earth,
That was his parents' work ; his living here,
That was his own. Sweet dying, a soft death,
Closes in beauty even the hardest life !

THE CLEAR MYSTERY.

STARE no more at the world, in dull amaze
That any thing exists, that God exists,
That thou art, and that all things are divine.
Not for astonishment has man been born,
If yet for reverence and for recognition.
The spirit lives not to adore forever;
It will not, needs not, be self-deified,
It craves a higher good, the very highest:
Thy life it wishes, *and its own*, in one.
And fearest thou, thou art not near Him *then*,
And dost not know Him, if thou liv'st as man?
One thing believe, — it is the sacred truth:
If e'er thy soul with rapture thrills and glows,
Though only for a flower . . . if e'er thy heart
Beats with emotion . . . when thou only speakest
A loving word in whisper to thy child . . .
When thou dost good to any fellow-man,
Even in the dark, in silent solitude —
Then art thou far within the sanctuary,
The very innermost mystery of God;
Never canst thou rise higher, or be greater;
And round thee shines the silent universe
In all its holy fire, its centre thou,

Its very heart, its soul, its light, its glow.
Whoso respects not here his faithful life,
For him there is no longer help from — death!
And if the good holds *his* in rare esteem,
. . . What more does *he* want, but eternity? —
But even a breath of love eternal is!
. . . What needs he more, save greatness? — Yet less great
The universe than a glad human heart!
A man is surely not *too good* for heaven,
Not to say for the earth, where living is done
Harder yet noblier, though in woe and death;
And the good God is not too good for earth
Where first He lives out His full blessedness;
And though thou mightest else well say: "Lo! there
Spirits bear home the dead with dirges meet;" —
"Yonder sit *spirits* at a marriage board
With a fair friendly *spirit* . . . the blooming bride;" —
"There, has in yonder house a little *spirit*
Just come — they lay him in his mother's arms;" —
Yet now on earth, as man, thou callest them,
And rightly: men! For *a deep mystery*
Is the name man, though a familiar one
To you, who live with one another here
As friend with friend, who do in earthly days
Such little works, and call each thing by name!

THE TRANSITORY.

REVILE all things in heaven and all on earth,
Revile all powers and worldly customs all,
Only revile not Transitoriness.
Else thou revil'st the dead, revilest life,
The Maker too, who called all beings forth
Out of the sea-depths of the universe;
Thou makest Him the child with hands hewn off,
A stone, a (now really) by-gone God.
Immeasurable, enormous, is indeed
The number of all beings living *now*
On all the stars in all the universe.
This mighty, swarming, myriad-peopled *now*
Is an eternity of blessed ones, —
And yet one phantom only, but one moment,
One instant flash of lightning from the cloud
Of this vast universe, that endlessly
Through the *great night of time* goes sailing by,
As an eternal tempest, fructifying,
And rains down blessed beings numberless;
This unexhausted, inexhaustible
Creation, this "eternal rain of beings,"
Is what thou blindly scornest, hatest, cursest,
When thou revilest *Transitoriness.*
But, exiled from all beauty, hast thou given
A dumb assent to *the* eternal life, . . .

Consented that the fathers should be dead,
Then hast thou murdered thy own mother, all
Thy children and thy wife, in spirit — ah !
A heavy blood-guilt lies upon thy soul . . .
If they are killed: not — merely passed away !
Thou hadst a part in murdering the whole world,
If it has passed away — not, rather, come !
Yet hast thou part in the eternal Maker,
By simply willing: that *the world* shall *come!*
That all thy loves shall have already come !
View not the present as a dying man,
Look not upon the future as a wreck,
As private judgment-day in every garden !
For that scares all good spirits away from thee,
As frighted swallows whirr around the house
Where they had built their nests, when now the flames
Of its fierce burning roar on every side ;
It lames the hand for work, cripples the foot;
Thou'rt like the snail that with misgiving eye
Has just touched poison, suddenly draws it back
Burning, crawls back into her house and dies.
The world was over on creation-day,
Life absolutely never had begun,
Had not the very stars been doomed to fade.
Man would not even have been *possible*
But for the law of transitoriness !
Thou hadst not come, had not thy fathers gone !
Thy children never could have come, if thou:
The boy ; thy wife: the maiden ; if ye both,
Ye two fair *children*, had not passed away !
The cloud had not come floating in, had not

Its purpose been to scatter rain — to die;
The sun had not arisen, had he not willed
To journey through the heavens and set, —*had not*
His purpose been to be the sun. Oh see:
What makes man *rich* is transitoriness!
That constitutes him heir of all the earth,
Heir of all generations that have been;
By it alone his eye surveys old times,
By it his mind lives as a lofty sun.
The going of things is life and coming life,
It gives man every thing that makes him man,
Each feeling of the heart, each smile, each tear!
And, after joy, still, to complete his bliss,
The holy, yearning wail for the divine!
And nothing hast thou, nothing canst thou gain,
But for the blessed *crowding out* of all things!
No hyacinth would bloom for thee without
Transfiguration of the mother-bulb!
Never a second sweet word wouldst thou hear
Fall from thy darling's lips, wouldst never hear
A song, did not the first sound die away!
Thou wouldst be lying now a cradled child,
Had not the heavenly powers transmuted thee.
Thus does man owe, yea God Himself, his life
To that blest transformation, among men
Called — perishableness — with God: *Creation.*
So must then, that one violet may bloom,
The whole world pass away, and yet again,
And so forever. For one mother's life
Among her children, all the flowers and stars
Must die. *All priests and kings would, on their knees,*

In vain implore the spring: to stay away!
In vain implore the night: not to be gone!
In vain implore the maiden not to ripen
To full young-womanhood. — The Transitory
Is then life's coming! being! life itself!
Because the sharers of life's boon with thee
All pass away and all things swiftly pass,
The clouds, the sunbeams, flowers and men, is that
A reason for respecting them no more?
Oh nothing is more sinful, blasphemous,
Than to cast scorn upon the Transitory,
Which even Omnipotence itself could thus . . .
Could only by rotation bring to life,
Just as a mother brings her children forth.
The highest value has the Transitory,
The value of the priceless, the unique,
That which no eye will ever see again!
'Twere better, thou shouldst at a poor man's feet
Fall down as to the image of a God,
Than to pass by him with the careless word:
"A hundred years — thy hunger will be gone!"
Or say to thy still friend: "Why love I thee?
In thirty years thou wilt be quite forgot!"
Is not, to thee, the fleeting beyond price, —
Thy working, striving, living are in vain,
Then God Himself creates, strives, lives in vain,
Then all His past creating has been vain;
Then is His living vain for evermore.
But see the Transitory does exist!
It lives, it loves, it is ineffably fair!

The living manifests the entire God
With all His skill and might and majesty.
And wilt thou not see God creating now?
See God in all things, see His loveliness
And love, His beauty and His tenderness, —
Then not the least of things shall die to thee,
Then shalt thou see ungrieved the Transitory,
Shalt even look on it with highest joy —
Then thou canst love it, not do otherwise,
Thou knowest *who* it is, who *now* it is,
And *will be never more*, strange human heart!
Let not the heavenly apparition be
A stranger to thee longer, *for thou art*
The self-same apparition, thou thyself.
Behold the smile a lovely mother beams
Upon her child, *as blessed as the child!*
Let a fair eye delight thee, a true word
As much as God; He had not formed it else,
He had not spoken it. Oh thus enjoy
Thy love for all the human myriads,
For all the living and for all the dead!
Thou know'st them still! Thou knowest still their works;
Keep all in thy remembrance, all their life,
So buildest thou a heavenly kingdom in thee,
Which none can e'er possess, but thou alone;
Think above all upon thy life itself,
Which none else will remember *but* thyself,
Which none shall ever live but thou; not even
The ever-new soul of the universe,
The holy Pilgrim through the endless times!

THE ROSE FOR ALL.

DESPITE all heavens, despite all Paradises,
In spite of a new world and heavenly city,
Wherein the tribes of man shall live, they say,
One day as blessed spirits ; in despite
Of *that*, nay *by* it is *this* life on earth
Surely and veritably done and gone
For man forever, evermore, at death.
The soft fair flesh, the lovely form he wore,
As child, is in the deep abyss of time
Forever swallowed : all his suns, his loves,
Before him, with him, all for evermore
Went down, went out, expired and were lost
In hoary, raven-white eternity.
Thou, too, thyself, thy wife, your children all,
As once thou sawest, embraced and kissed them here,
As once they led thee *here* with pious hand,
And lisped their pretty prattlings in thy ear,
Smiled on thee and danced round thee with delight. . .
Thou wilt thyself, and they themselves will all
Forever, ever, down the deep abyss
Of time be plunged and utterly buried there,
Thrown in with sun-dust of ten billion suns,
A heap of rubbish daily, yearly higher,

Deep under hills, yea mountains, buried up,
Of dry and withered flowers, from all the springs,
Which sweeping on, on, from still distances,
Still coming forth out of the grave of earth,
As gayly-decorated spectres here
Still for their moment hold a fleeting sway,
Till they too, as the grave-dust of the dead,
Down the abyss are swept, and sealed up fast
By Death, who sees none but life-weary ones,
Of all their beauty silently bereft,
Yet, undeluded, holds a tranquil reign.
And canst thou *his* calm mood with ease attain,
Thence an old word of truth shall come to thee :
With every human eye expires the sun
That lighted it. To every man, and him
Alone, is his own beating heart the cithern
On which the world played its old song to him,
Forever one, *once* new to every child ;
Old, just expiring, in the ear of age ;
Inaudible, extinct, dumb, to the dead.
To them the sun, the great world clock, is still ;
To them the day, the moment, is no more,
Far less to them is the whole after-*world*
Than even an Orcus ; and more shadowy.
Eternity unto the dead is not
One hour's duration. O'er all possible
Sublimest Gods are they exalted high ;
They have forever done with this child's-dream —
Thy loves miss thee no more, far less will miss
The universe forever. Let thy love

For them, on their account, have deep repose.
And that thou must henceforth forever miss
Their lovely form, the cheek, the eye, the hair,
And the sweet voice — 'tis only *thy* delusion,
Thy dream, projecting thy short human days
To a long shadow stretched across the heaven
As by the magic of the evening sun.
The dead are holier, ineffably,
Than any living man can e'er conceive,
Because the flame of his life dazzles him.
Vast as the universe appears, although
It seems immeasurable, it is as small
As any being, and of single ones
Consists, as does the poppy-head of grains ;
Endless it seems, yet always has an end,
It dies with every being, it is dead.
Thus is it pure and innocent as a child,
And lovely as a rose — I say a rose !

THE RETURN OF ALL THINGS.

THE thought: God only lives! will let thee wish
For the return of all things nevermore;
Such wish degrades Him to a puppet-player,
His holy world to a great barrel-organ;
Whereas He lives forever new, and great
In His eternal shows majestical,
In all of which His Spirit only lives.
A new existence; a new universe—
Oh never, never sure, were there *first things*,
And never therefore can there be *last things*,
And then a final rest, a death of God,
As if He were worn out and tired of life,
Old, like an old man, yearning for the grave!
And if the universe were constantly
Chewing * the dead over and over again,
If all things had been destined to return,
Then would they oft already have returned,
Then must they surely have a secret thought:
"To have come back." *But now if living men*
Have no such thought, then surely never yet
Have they come back, if e'er they should return!
True, the return of all things *seems* so blest,

* Symbolized by the sacred ox of the Jews and Egyptians.

So just, so satisfying to the heart;
It *seems* a recompense for each short life,
Which shall hereafter be an endless one;
But each *for others only* prizes it;
Scarcely would *one* live o'er again the life
He once has lived; toil through again the toil
Already toiled through, worry through again
The worry all life long he worried through;
His *whole* life must forever *pass away*
Again, as it has once already passed —
Unless *one* beauteous moment of it were
Turned into stone, and *he* should be the stone!
Who then would drink twice over the same wine?
To have the self-same feeling twice would be
Impossible, were man not man again, —
And then what would he have, but *what he had?*
'Tis the divinest thing to be forever
Unique; thou wondrous, nobly loving man,
Thou art the only husband to thy wife
Forever! Be such to her, with true love;
Thou to thy children art for evermore
Their only father! *Be* thou such to them,
The heavenly near them in a human form!
They are thy only children too, forever.
Thy wife forever is thy only wife;
Oh then respect her as the heavenly one,
Purely, for her love is the eternal love!

AGAPÉ,* NOT "LOVE."

ONLY what man can do, the wise require
That he shall thoughtfully and freely do.
What he *must* do, does eagerly of himself
From childhood up: eat, drink, sleep, walk and talk—
Only a fool prescribes for him to do.
Who ever made a law: that little girls
Should go forth in the spring to gather flowers;
That boys should play at ball twice in the year:
On the *green* earth, and when the leaves fall off?
So no one ever was the fool to say:
"The marriageable youth shall take to wife
The marriageable maid, on pain of death,
And then shall they provide for little ones!"
For all the birds would have laughed right out loud
At such a prophet, asses would for once
Have really spoken, all the beasts of the wood,
The blossoms on the trees and fishes all
Would have had speech given them to hoot at him.
And if none wisely e'er commanded that,
O men, so too has none enjoined on you
To *love*. *That*, that you have with rapturous bliss
Been doing since man's life on earth began.

* Paul's Greek word, rendered *charity*.—T.

So blind, irrational, none ever was,
But would have been the more, the more he held
Himself to be a God or even God.
Yet a reflection of the only true
And blessed love, the love of man for wife,
And wife for husband, and the love they both
Feel for *their* children and for them alone, —
The warm and kindly shadow of this love
To shed on all men, saint and sage required
Of heathen people in the olden time,
Ere Moses came ; *in* his day, and like him ;
And no one after him could e'er ask more,
And no one ever did ask more than this :
"Wish well to all ; do good to all around thee."
And fully would this word meet all men's wants,
If truly and with zeal obeyed by all ;
It furnishes a holy work to men
All everywhere through all the days of life,
It makes all friends, yea step-brothers and sisters
Of myriad mothers, yet one Father only,
The Spirit of Life ; comforts the miserable,
Gives courage to the faint, zeal to the slow,
Gives brothers to the lonely and forlorn —
'Tis the reflection of the blessed love,
That yearns to share with others all its wealth !

THE SWEETNESS OF LIFE.

PROPHETS, and even no despicable ones,
Stretched out the staff and woke the dead to life,
Trembling embraced them then and kissed their lips;
Yea, men of old woke even those who "stank,"
And with loud voice bade them from out the grave
"Come forth!" Rather than let them yet depart
To heaven, they granted them a few more days
Of the sweet life of earth, though at the price,
The terrible price of having twice to die!
I never saw the dying weep for joy
To think of dying. Only wretched men
Who in their anguish cried aloud for death,
And would have given the axe into my hand
That I might, guiltless, kindly take their life —
Them have I seen! and have heard others sigh:
"Ah! ah! how would I weep, if weep I could!
But all the tears I had to shed are gone."
Yet others have I seen lying on graves,
And when I softly asked, I learned that they
Desired not to go to those they loved,
But only have *them back* — from heaven itself!
The best of men begged that the cup of death
Might pass from them, if it were possible!

So sweet it is to the eternal spirit
As man on earth to live: love and be loved;
For nowhere has he more, or lives he better.
So the most loving and the best all wish
To dwell in endless union with their loves;
To let the whole wide world all pass away
And rest within their arms, if only 'twere
To slumber calmly with them in one grave,
Forgot by all the coming sons of men.

THE PAST.

THERE are no dead: and so there is no Past.
How could the Past have a reality,
Since only of past *things* it could be made,
And past things are things perished, are no more,
And can make nothing, therefore not a Past?
And so the stars in an eternity
Have many times over bloomed their last in heaven,
In their *great* spring-times, as the flowers on earth
Have, in their *little* spring-times here below.
Yet, budding, blooming, so they lived, and when
Past blooming, softly closed a rounded life;
Only so long as they were, was their heaven;
Earth lasts, for every flower, only so long
As *it* lasts, then they die to one another;
And if one mourned, it should be Earth alone —
No eyes have the dead flowers to weep their doom,
No tongues to murmur at their destiny:
The thousand blossom-leaves that sank to earth,
The many thousand withered roses all,
The Mayflowers and the spikes of lavender, —
There is no mighty urn, where these are all
Kept, to perfume the mansion of the gods;
The many hundred thousand rainbows all,

The lightning-snakes from all the thunder-clouds,
There's no old rubbish-chamber holds them all
Collected! Having once been born of force,
Struck out therefrom like spark from flint and steel . . .
They straightway melted back to force again,
As winter snow into spring water melts
And skyey perfume. — Life is but a show —
Joy, evanescent as a falling star;
No joy can be detained and treasured up,
Not even the taste of honey on the tongue,
The diamond-glistering of a drop of dew,
No, not a gleam of sunlight in the eye,
Still less a feeling, even a thrill of bliss!
Beauty is good but for its little hour,
That man may still be free for something new,
Open to new delight and to new life —
For there is *One*, to whom it *is* a show;
The Spirit in the still eternal Now.
The awful sense of our eternity
Comes from the transitoriness of things.
What we have once possessed is past, not lost —
Not lost, but *won!* The past eternity
It was, that gave the soul the bliss of love,
And it will still give bliss that knows no end.
None mourns the dread, unnumbered host of dead
Who lie in the old world's vast sepulchre:
There nowhere lives aught that could mourn for them;
The eyes fell from their sockets ages gone,
As from their dry shells fall the hazel-nuts;
Their hearts are ashes, and their bones are dust.

So there is no one lost to any one!
The present generation but bewails,
As the grave-digger of the perishing,
Its love alone — in pity to itself!
The Past is all one great sarcophagus
Vast as the universe — but look therein,
'Tis empty! empty all! no dead is there!
Not one — not even a dead violet,
Not of one little rose the skeleton —
The great sarcophagus, it swarms with life,
Its rustling fans thee with spring-fragrances,
And myriads of flowers bloom out of it,
And young birds flutter up in myriads
Through all the heavens and warble in the clouds;
The sun himself comes gleaming up from it,
The stars emerge from out its depths and shine! —
Just as to-day there is no future, nor
Will ever be a future, never aught
But a perpetual Present — nay, a Life —
So was there never a Past, nor ever will be
A Past, but only an Eternal Life.
If all past life, all that was lived and loved,
All that was e'er enjoyed, *was nothing — then*,
Then has the great, immense, primeval world,
The long eternity that, age on age,
Before our earth, flashed life, been nothing too,
Void! Dust and ashes! God were then a dream,
A non-essential being — a mere name! —
Nay, but God lived! And that we can ourselves
So much as dream the Past, is proof to us:

We live! and now the universe is ours!
All is for all, to every spark of mind
Each feeling now belongs, and every thought,
Every delight belongs, and every tear!
The things that pass, they can be only gained;
The Past is gained, it never can be lost;
Else through one long eternity till now
Has God Himself been useless — must be still
Useless for an eternity to come,
For all that is to come shall pass away
And be as still as the dead Death himself.

CONTEMPT OF THE WORLD.

DESPISE *the world?* — Cease that! ye pious souls,
Nor yet encourage any man thereto,
Calling it dismal and detestable!
You scorn the spirit that lives and dwells therein,
Created and conceived it, as you say.
Fling not away this life, as if, forsooth,
Not worth the living! So, to your own hands
You spoil it, so you *make* it horrible!
You scorn yourselves, wretchedly spite yourselves;
For the contemptuous has within his heart
A root of bitterness; the despising soul
Grows to be utterly despised itself,
Bitterly wretched, neighbor to the wish:
"Oh would there were no God! had never been!
Or at the very least that God would die!
That so this bloody, shameful work of his,
Full of corruption, woe and death, might vanish
To endless night, into its well-earned grave, —
With all the spirits it ever made to groan!"
Far sooner hide, as men do before kings,
As much as possible, earth's wretched ways;
Banish the poor; say, "Things go charmingly!
We are content and happy to belong

To such a land and its wise counsellors ! " —
Root out the evils that exasperate
Your secret souls ; and *set yourselves to work*
With thoughtful hearts to make yourselves content !
Not, every day, more and more malcontent !
Even in the pit, there needs must be a place
Where it is not so hot. The sick man finds
At last one posture that is tolerable,
And whimpers an approval. The abyss
No longer seems so frightful, when one toils
In earnest day and night to fill it up,
Though vainly. Welcome the necessity,
Daily returning, hard necessity,
Which brings each day a new access of toil,
And a new load of care — and all for naught.
Illusion is itself worth more than wealth.
As clean and beautiful as is *your* life,
In calm composure and tranquillity,
So clean and beautiful, yea sweet and dear
Will life itself, at last, appear to you ;
For only *as you live*, so is the world,
No better and no worse, but just so good.
Masters are you not of the stubborn world,
But masters of *your own life* certainly ;
Even of your death indisputably so.
Hear now one word from the deep human breast :
The spirit demands not even thanks from you,
For your existence or its own — if *that*
In aught oppress you. *But be ye too, spirit.*
Reflect : that which within you hates — contemns —

Must be itself a great and holy thing,
Nobler than all the starry firmament,
And all the entire universe brings forth ;
And now, that spirit you yourselves must be,
And therefore must you bear within yourselves
The *purest*, *highest*, *most desirable*,
If only as a feeling — as a thought.
As then you cannot hate your very selves,
Despise yourselves and wish annihilation —
Unless the great Supreme Himself shall be
Naught else than hateful and detestable ;
You cannot wish death to this universe,
Wherein the great Supreme Intelligence lives,
Because you also have yourselves your life
From the great Spirit of the universe.
And if you *love* a beauteous living thing,
Your love will wish for it not only life,
But all this beauteous universe beside ;
You praise this world that it *contains* for you,
This beautiful, this one beloved thing !
And if this unique treasure should be *lost*,
This beauty snatched away and swept from sight,
Yea, were it irrecoverably gone,
Forever lost to you, itself and all —
Not yet, for that, can you despise this world ;
Because it once *contained* that beauteous thing !
And if you weep and mourn, yea even despair,
You prize it more than ever more than all,
And idolize a transitory thing
As if it were the saving of your love,

Instead of seeing now for the first time,
And rapturously rejoicing in the thought,
That the salvation was your very love. —

Tell me no more how you despise the world.
He who despises, ne'er despised *himself*,
He clasps himself with adamantine chains,
With the sweet bonds of his own blessedness.

THE GLEANING OF LIFE.

WHO prizes at their worth the precious days
Of inward fellowship with those he loves!
Who bears within his heart, at every hour,
A full and perfect sense, how rich is life!
Who, 'midst his dear ones, charges every word
With all the unutterable wealth of love; —
Puts his whole soul into each smallest work?
No living man! No lover constantly!
Who is not by the moment borne away,
Who is not dazzled by the passing hour?
For whom does not the merest speck of cloud
Fling a cool shadow o'er the sun in heaven! —
And what will man, for all the glow of love,
For life's glad sunshine, set himself to do!
Shall he all day be staring at the sun?
All night long fold his hands before the stars?
Shall he hold fast in one eternal clasp
His loved ones to his heart? Or with his lips
Repeat "Oh how I love thee!" all day long?
Does not thy presence tell *them* day by day
That story? does not the unswerving eye
That watches for their weal from morn to night?
Does not thy smile say that to *them*, whene'er

Thou meetest them? Does not their silent nod
Say it to *thee*, whene'er they come, or when
Thou goest? Does not all their care for thee,
The pains they take, their toil in thy behalf,
Assure thee *first*, in speech transcending words:
"Oh how I love thee!" It is life that first
Gives to the heart assurance of our love,
Announces and divinely utters it,
As even the all-present Spirit speaks to men
Through flowers and glow of sun and balmy sleep! —
And so, in silence, imperceptibly
The holy days glide from beneath our hands;
Nights with the calm effulgence of their moons
Glimmer and fade: that we may greatly live
And love, in the great sense of the divine,
In conscious being's calm security, —
A feeling which no word could ever speak,
Only a thousand deeds could e'er express,
Yet not exhaust in many thousand days!
So comes, with lingering snail-pace creeping on,
The end of our most sweet companionship;
Our living and our striving side by side
Are ended — not the influence; endeth not
Thy loving. Yet doth end thy *being loved!*
And with it ends for thee the joy of life.
To lose the love of those we love — ah! that
Is to us mortal men the half of death!
One thing alone remains — but that is sure:
From the whole life of those thou lovedst, let
The breath of love be wafted o'er thy soul;

Feel in its touch the living breeze of heaven!
And what they severally were . . . this day
And that, this autumn and the other spring,
In the bright morning and the moonlit nights . . .
All that they ever said and did to thee,
All that they were to thee ten thousand times,
In the entrancing charms of sense and soul —
That gather with thy heart's whole energy
From their completed, culminating life;
Let it draw near and stand before thy eyes
As the now visible and total man;
The one, unique, and *verily divine;*
And as the unutterably gracious spirit
Of heaven, enshrine that presence in thy heart,
Till thou for rapture tremblest even to tears
Of awe and gratitude and holy dread!
— So shall the love wherewith thou once wast loved
Waft thee its fragrance, as the breath of flowers
Follows the seaman from a blooming coast.

LOVE AND THE WORLD.

WHAT is, believe thou *that* . . . but the world is,
Clear, palpable to all, raised far above
" I pray, believe me ! " — Soul and world belong
To one another, just as man and wife :
Men, and all things that live, their children are.
O Love, without the world, what wert thou ! far
More wretched than the world were with no Love.
What were a light in a dark waste of death,
Shining on naught but black and horrid night —
All the more dismal, were that light the sun !
What were the human eye, if men were not !
What were a human heart without a world —
All the more dismal, were't the heart of God !
And what were Love without a child to love,
Without a husband, and without a wife —
All the more dismal, were't the Love of God !
Nay, *with* the world, is man himself divine,
And soul itself without the world, a dream.
So is the world eternal as its soul ;
And if the world were a created thing —
Upon the second day of God's first being
The world had come too late, been made too late
For joy unmeasured in the infinite
Ethereal all, the house of blessedness,

The stork's nest and the laboratory of Love, —
Which cannot live without somewhat to love,
More than the sun, without a blade of grass,
An eye, to shine upon and shine into.
Were there no world, there were no clasp of hands,
No mutual glance of soul from eye to eye,
Oh heaven! no language, not a word of love,
No sigh of joy or sorrow, no embrace,
No seeing, no reunion's glad surprise,
Oh heaven! no song, no rapture of the heart
Felt by the mother at the child's first cry,
Oh heaven! no beauty! — 'Tis all over now,
And all these mourners for the world would say:
We envy not a soul its solitude,
We would not, at the price of a lost world,
Be God — as God Himself would not *so* wish
To be, is not and never was, nor yet
Will ever be through all eternity,
Alone with all His consciousness of power.
The artists all are weeping bitter tears;
None longer cares to live; no singer will,
With no breast-full of air to swell his tones —
No poet will, with none to hear his song,
No painter will, when canvas there is none,
Not even a coal to trace his beauteous forms;
And men themselves — no soul of them will live
Without the artists, ay, those sons of God,
Who beauteously transfigure all their life,
Who lay it as a child upon their breast,
As a beloved heart, a beautiful
Great heart all full of rapture — ah, their own

Heart, their own being, made divinely fair.
No maid is beauteous now — no man is brave,
No more shall this sweet life be sacrificed
To mercy, there is, no more, noble death !
There is no more a good deed to be done,
No tear-drop glistening in a grateful eye,
No child henceforth can give a crust of bread
To feed the hungry ; no industrious hand
Stirs any longer ; all delight is gone —
Nay, never has begun ! all love is fled —
Nay, never into any breast has flown ! " —
— The soul, the man, will through these thoughts at last
Come to a clear conception of the truth
Incarnate in the Eternal. To what end
Were life, and why the tribes of living ones,
If the mere *dream of spirit* were enough
Of life, if life itself did not begin
In feeling of the fulness of the world,
As the first actual, wakeful, *living* thought!
In all things thou beholdest, there the Eternal
Has its first *resurrection !* bodily !
In *any single* hand *all* hands exist,
In that *one* woman do all women live,
In that *one* rose, all roses. If the good,
If love, joy, beauty, in the conscious man
Have not their dwelling-place, if he does not
The good, if he loves not the beautiful,
Then is it nowhere — sleeps the sleep of death.
— But lo ! the world is, and it stays — it stays,
Eternal as the Spirit and as Love ;

The holy beaker of this universe
Needs lips to quaff its nectar, yea, it needs
A bosom to enrapture with its bliss.
Man's beauteous body, the world's body, is
Divinely needful, is the Spirit's wife ;
For without body soul is null — is naught,
A dead-man's-eye, a struggler in the grave.
This very earth supplies a good man more
Than heaven itself can ever yield to him ;
The joy a mother feels, whose only child
Sits upright in his coffin raised to life,
Even that, — and thousands dearer to the heart,
Heaven never had ! can never give to man !
The universe can show no miracle
Like to a beauteous mother in her shroud ;
A God himself were not more *wonderful.*
Such grace, such majesty she never wore !
Dead suns could never be so beautiful
As are her eyes ! Not all the tongues of spirits
So thrill with eloquence as her *dumb lips !*
The stir of life through all the concave heaven
Moves not to tears like the repose of her
Unbreathing bosom ; the Almighty hand
Is not so mighty as her still, dead hand !
To see our dearest longings, all our hopes,
And all our happiness lie cold and dead
There with our loved ones, nay, to have to die,
Ourselves, upon our love, — ah, that — ay that —
Transcends, heaven-high, the reach of all the Gods !
That thrill, the Holiest in heaven, Himself,
Can never feel ; for there no death can part

The living from their loved ones ; there no grave
Opens its black abyss to swallow up
The silent dead. Such miracles can come
To mortals only, honored above Gods
By sorrow's shafts — who needed all the strength
Of Gods — yet have no help but silent tears.
The fulness of the world fills full man's heart.
And reckonest thou then *this* for naught — for naught —
That they who love each other on this earth
See one another ! meet again ! Oh then
Such bliss is theirs, as when one buried blind,
Rising with unscaled eyes, for the first time
Looks out upon the glory of the heavens.
Oh what a joy, to look on living men !
To see them in the beauteous world as Gods,
In beauty, youthful prime and grace and love ;
To see them in this hurly, this old grave
Of earth, like works by holy magic wrought !
That is as much, *as if the universe*
Itself sprang into being ! That, ay that
Is the inalienable blessedness,
Which peacefully has reckoned in advance
With death, with that fixed doom : to die again ;
Which richly for the parting has prepared,
And nevermore believes in any loss.
Oh a divinely unique thing is man
Upon this earth ; as there, to-day and here,
He lives, the universe has not, till now,
So had him, heaven has never had him yet !
And earth will never have him so again.

WISDOM.

"THOU wilt not certainly call *wise* the fire,
That falls upon thy hand and burns it up?
Thou wilt not call the water wise, that falls
Wolf-like upon the fire and quenches it:
The wind — but wilt thou haply call *that* wise,
Which drives the clouds and piles the waters up,
That sweep *one* lucky mariner to port,
And dig that *other* wretched one a grave?
Wilt thou call wise the war of elements,
Where every force, following its nature's law,
Assails the others, conquers now, now yields,
And now concludes with it a bond of peace,
When it brings forth a *third*, a son to itself,
Who fights again, in turn, with other sons,
Fiercely assails them, conquers now, now yields,
And now concludes with them a bond of peace, —
When it brings forth a daughter, child of all.
All these according to their natures, each,
Bestir *themselves*. They are themselves, none else;
Are aboriginal. No one's thought or will
Has given them being, bowed them to the yoke
Of any work, of any other task
Than they pursue. An immemorial thing

Is force, all force. *Before* it nothing was,
No thought was there, nor even yet a will!
For will proceeds from force — the lightning flash
Of force, and force is not a dream of will.
Whence now to wisdom could there come a *force?*
Foreknowledge it would be, ere aught existed
To know, the hollow spectre of itself.
But Wisdom is: the ordering to an end
Of a material ready to its hand.
So from the forces flashes like a light
Wisdom before man's eyes: in its own way,
Wisdom to order and to guide his life.
It is not the beginning of the world,
Wisdom's the end for which the world is made,
It is the spirit of life, and life itself.
And as mankind have seated Paradise
At the world's entrance, so have they transposed
Wisdom far back into a chaos, which
Never existed. For *before all* things
Was *no* thing, not a thought, nor even a dream!
Wisdom is in the *world:* to know the world
And by it faithfully to guide our life,
So that the fool may not be crushed by Force.
The only folly is to *disobey*,
The labor-wasting, hard and hopeless fight
With every force and its established nature,
To which, *unwillingly* or *willingly*,
All things must bow; the willing blessedly,
The stubborn and rebellious, bruised and crushed —
A doom befitting the self-blinded fool

Who will not see: *Spirit is the breath of Force,*
That He is both the spirit and mind of Force,
The light that flashes from the thunder-cloud." —
— *So counsel they holy obedience,*
The spirits, who do not misplace the SPIRIT
Back of the world, but wholly *in* the world.
And thou — strive not for what is wholly vain
And useless. Thou art not a single inch
The greater, more immortal by a day,
Scarce nobler — *whether as the spirit's work*
Or as the spirit of the Spirit itself;
Still thy descent — thy nature — is divine.
Then exercise unwavering obedience
To the great Force that sweeps through all the world,
Which must at last make all like to itself,
Blest like itself — who willingly fulfil
Its own sweet law. "Divinely live!" Thus thou
Createst wisdom, and thyself a man.

BEAUTY.

BEAUTY, soft splendor and the pomp of hues
Flow silently around the life of man,
As round the bather flows a silver sea ;
And even the terrible and monstrous thing
Within this heaven of beauty finds its place.
'Tis made a wonder by its *wondrous place!*
And *lovely* things ineffably more fair!
So cosily the Spirit made his world,
His place of sojourn in the house of earth.
Not merely for an answering love Love yearned,
Not from blind beggars does she ask for alms!
Nor as blind beggar will take alms herself—
In her unmeasured bliss Love still would be
Loved and admired by the beautiful,
Will in the Beautiful admire herself!
The heavenly nectar of the gods she fain
Would drink from heavenly vessels, and would feed
The fire upon her hearth with ambergris,
From fairer, sweeter than rose-chalices
Would drink the strange-familiar magic tones ;
From precious stones more brilliant than Turquoises,
Would see the strange-familiar fire gleam out.
And that she may not, on this opaque earth,

Wander in disappointment, joylessly,
Her jewel — even the magic light of heaven —
She brings with her — *within her* — to the earth,
Which by the power and splendor of its *own*
Intrinsic beauty, gives to every form,
The human form, the form of every flower,
To shine transfigured in her sight and wear
A golden lustre, and for each creates,
Once in this niggard life, a heaven on earth,
When, in his blooming-time, entranced with bliss ! —
And though the magic light then fade away,
The form once touched is sacred evermore.
So on a golden eventide embarks
A bridegroom with his young and blooming bride,
For a long sail ; and though dark night comes down
On bark and sea and on the beauteous bride,
Still murmur on through the dark space of night
The gentle accents of the invisible one,
And still he loves, adores her as before,
Nay more and more, in the sweet dusk of night ! —
Love will not, even in the dark, expire . . .
Nor sink into the pit and charnel-house,
By night beleaguered at the very door,
With a cold shudder shrinking from the host
Of shadowy horrors that assail the soul
From out the stark, black distance looming forth —
Once more her magic light flames up for her,
And with a golden glow illumes the pit,
And makes it beautiful with lustrous gems,
Like an enchanted grotto on whose walls

The flaming splendors of the evening sun
Shed an unutterable loveliness.
So long for each her light sheds friendly glow,
Like to an ever-burning lamp's mild gleam,
On all the day of life. In spring it flashes
Ten thousand variegated sparks ; in autumn,
A hundred thousand. He who drives his plough
At early morn beholds it overhead
Move through the heavens, a blazing ball of fire ;
Yea, he who draws up water from the well,
Sees it glance up from mirrored heavens below,
And from the flowers that deck the fountain's marge ;
And when the weary traveller in the woods
Stretches his limbs upon the grass, the pines
Bloom like a thousand roses o'er his head
And through the twigs the heavenly glory breaks, —
What beauty, splendor soft and pomp of hues,
Flow silently around the life of man,
As round a bather flow the silver-waves !
Each period of the world still blooms on earth,
Blooms in the young man and the old alike ;
They all alike still through each period
Keep journeying on, but with the speed of gods
They move through life, and tarry long in none,
As races once did through long centuries.
Still ever born in the old Paradise,
All children sweetly live as live the flowers,
And those that die therein have never known
The bitter taste of guilt or grief or death.
But they who young, as pilgrims, wander forth

Into earth's realm, feel themselves exiles there,
And each one day weeps for his youth again ;
An inexpressible, old primeval bliss
Seems to him gone forever ! — and yet, lo !
One day for the first time 'twill come to him.
He looks upon the blooming maid, and lo !
The young world of the elders, in its first
Unwithered beauty, blooms around him there !
The sweet face is a miracle, and so
The noble brow ; two eyes that beam with soul
To him are sister-suns, yea more than stars ;
Two rosy lips bring tears into his eyes ;
Brushed by her arm, touched by a finger-tip,
He trembles ; and to see the snow-white neck
And the chaste bosom thrills his being through ;
The entire blooming figure, from the crown
Even to the toe, none other than a God
Could e'er have fashioned it so beautiful. . . .
Nay she herself is all Divinity,
Clear and complete, incarnated, revealed,
Brought near in bodily presence, yea arrived
From farthest heavenly spaces, and now here !
From all the depths of distant ages, here !
And even her foot-print on the violet-turf
Is holy, and his lips will kiss the flowers
On which she walked. Glorious, ecstatic life,
A wealth and preciousness ineffable,
That is the joy of beings and of God . . .
One soul inspires the majestic whole . . .
And in that soul there glows the fire of love . . .

And love enshrines a living purity.
So too he sees! For from the chrysalis
Of the *ancients* hath sprung forth a noble spirit,
A new and God-like man has risen up
Who can be that himself, shall live that life,
Which they had hardly worshipped in their Gods.

THE PEOPLE.

THAT much berated tribe — "the common folk" —
How hearty is their life, and how divine
Their sense of being! None can praise enough
Their equanimity and dignity;
Full are they of the very highest worth,
Such as the human race, in its whole range,
Can ne'er out-bid. Were it not devilish now,
If these poor heavenly children should at last
Be doomed to forfeiture of life's best goods;
If in their spirit they were not the strong,
In heart the truest and the tenderest;
Should miss the wealth the future has in store,
The highest human knowledge, human power:
To be a man! Then there could be no men,
Not one so much as tolerable man,
Living life nobly — not, enduring it!
For every morn makes yesterday a night,
And knowledge is a never closed abyss.
Yet with the day the people's life must run,
Must struggle on to meet the eventide,
The harvest and the autumn, step by step
Still marching to the sun's fixed ordinance,
For they wait not to hear the morning's news,

Nor for the gift the coming day may bring!
They look not forward to a future day
When they will eat their slow-earned stores ; they live
From hand to mouth ; and in their children's mouths
Put the last solitary bit of bread ;
Give the last effort of the weary hand
With gladness to the very nearest work
A wife's or even a lambkin's need may ask;
And in their little house administer
In just as God-like style, as if it were
God's house and they the stewards of all wealth! —
The heart of man is, in all ages, one.
And never through its life-time does it ask
More mind, love, living energy ; it seeks
Only to manifest itself. It says :
" Thou art as noble as the first man was ;
Thou'rt worth as much as the last man shall be.
Each mortal is the first and the last man,
In his own style, his life, and look on life —
Thou also art the first and the last man
To thine own self! Thou to thy children art
First and last father. And thy wife no less
First and last mother to her children, too.
Ye are their first — last parents, both of you. —
So holy are ye, each a sacred self."

Cambridge: Press of John Wilson and Son.

www.ingramcontent.com/pod-product-compliance
Lightning Source LLC
LaVergne TN
LVHW020121110826
845151LV00001B/237

* 9 7 8 1 4 2 5 5 4 1 6 4 4 *